D0081255

THE POLITICAL ECONOMY OF SOCIAL CREDIT AND GUILD SOCIALISM

Guild socialism has frequently been regarded as a cul-de-sac in social and economic thought. However, this work breaks new ground in demonstrating its continued relevance. Focusing on the Douglas Social Credit movement, it examines the origin of the key ideas, gives an overview of the main theories and their contemporary reception.

Douglas is credited with being the author of a simple, ingenious but erroneous proposal to end depression in the inter-war years. The Social Credit Government which held power in Alberta during the middle decades of the century is equally remembered in association with Douglas. Although the Canadian party arose from an interpretation of the texts attributed to him, its policies had little in common with the original texts. Historical documentation of the social credit phenomenon has focused almost exclusively on the Canadian experience.

This work approaches the phenomenon from a different perspective. It explores the guild socialist origins of the texts, condenses the economic and social theory of the original texts into a concise exposition and documents the subsequent history. Thoroughly researched, the work provides original material of relevance to the field of political economy. This early approach to non-equilibrium economics reveals the extent of the incompatibility between capitalist growth economics and social environmental sustainability.

Frances Hutchinson has published academic papers on social credit, environmental sustainability and feminist economics. She is a member of the European Association for Evolutionary Political Economy and is attached to Plymouth Business School and the University of Bradford. She is author of *Environmental Business Management* (1997). **Brian Burkitt** is a Senior Lecturer in Economics at the University of Bradford. He is author of *Trade Unions and Wages* (1995), *Trade Unions and the Economy* (1979), *Radical Political Economy* (1984) and *There is an Alternative: Britain and its Relationship with the EU* (1996). He has written over 150 articles in academic journals.

ROUTLEDGE STUDIES IN THE HISTORY OF ECONOMICS

THE POLITICAL ECONOMY OF SOCIAL CREDIT AND GUILD SOCIALISM

Frances Hutchinson and Brian Burkitt

London and New York

First published 1997
by Routledge
11 New Fetter Lane, London EC4P 4EE

Simultaneously published in the USA and Canada
by Routledge
29 West 35th Street, New York, NY 10001

Typeset in Garamond by
Poole Typesetting (Wessex) Limited
Bournemouth, Dorset

Printed and bound in Great Britain by
MacKays of Chatham PLC, Chatham, Kent

British Library Cataloguing in Publication Data
A catalogue record for this book is available from the British Library

Library of Congress Cataloging in Publication Data
Hutchinson, Frances, 1941–
The political economy of social credit and guild socialism / Frances Hutchinson
and Brian Burkitt.
p. cm.
Includes bibliographical references and index.
1. Social credit–History. 2. Guild socialism–History.
3. Douglas, C. H. (Clifford Hugh), 1879–1952. 4. Sustainable development.
I. Burkitt, Brian. II. Title.
HG355H87 1997
335′.15–dc21
97–6276
CIP

ISBN 0–415–14709–3

To the memory of
Thomas Tinkler

CONTENTS

CONTENTS

Part II

Part III

CONTENTS

ACKNOWLEDGEMENTS

Thanks to Keith Hutchinson and John and Marli Huddleston for their patient assistance during the writing of this book. Thanks also to Mary Mellor, the late Donald Neale, Eric de Mare, Kevin Donnelly, Bill Jordan, Arthur Brown, the late James Meade, the late Audrey Fforde, Jim Generoso, Karen Spencer, Ken Palmerton, Pauline Ford, Grace Evans, Jane Hammond, Bob Jones, Pat Conaty, John Pullen, John King, Eddie Schack and James Shackleton for their help and support. Grateful thanks to Donald and Jane Martin for permission to quote from Douglas's works. Copies of the works quoted in this book can be obtained from Donald A. Martin, Bloomfield Books, 26 Meadow Lane, Sudbury, Suffolk, CO10 6TD.

INTRODUCTION

The writings of Major C.H. Douglas gave rise to the social credit movement, popular throughout the inter-war years. Douglas's earliest books, *Economic Democracy* and *Credit-Power and Democracy*, first appeared in serial form in the socialist journal the *New Age* in the period immediately following World War I. Close examination of the early 'Douglas/*New Age*' texts along-side the literature of guild socialism reveals that the editor of the *New Age*, A.R. Orage, provided Douglas with a great deal more than editorial support in the formulation of the original texts. Without Orage's guild socialist contribution Douglas's technical observation of the accounting mechanisms which underlie the role of finance in the formulation of policy on produc-tion and distribution would have provided unpromising material for a popular debate which was to be sustained over two decades throughout the English-speaking world. Orage's synthesis of contemporary heterodox economic thought contributed the vital prerequisites for a revolutionary analysis of capitalist economic orthodoxy based upon the centrality of time and finance. The resultant Douglas/*New Age* texts form the basis of an economics of socialism in line with Smith's (1962) definition as an absence of economic conflict.

In his historical review of guild socialism, Glass defines socialism as 'a movement whose principal purpose has been the emancipation of the new industrial working class that arose in Europe in the nineteenth century' (Glass 1966: 1). Both British reformist socialists and pre-1914 Continental Marxists have looked to achieve socialism through the ownership and control of industry by the community via the instrument of the state. Marxists and reformists have sought to gain control over the means of production through the instrument of territorially based (State) political power. By contrast, guild socialists sought direct control by the workers of the instruments of wealth production, including the arts, professions and community organisations. Through the union of all workers (managerial, manual and clerical) in each productive institution, organised on devolutionary lines, local communities would take control of all aspects of decision-making in the production of wealth (Glass 1966). The Douglas/*New Age* texts which arose out of guild

1

socialism provide the potential to control, rather than be controlled by, finance. By 'decommodifying' the worker and separating income from work the 'new economics' enables the economic actor to take account of values which lie outside the market mechanism. In view of the persistent failure of neoclassical economics to incorporate environmental values and forms of work traditionally undertaken by women, the Douglas/*New Age* texts offer a framework for a sustainable economics of socialism.

Part I reviews the origins and content of the Douglas/*New Age* texts. Originating in guild socialism, the social credit movement achieved world popularity in the inter-war years. Chapter 1 explores the biographical evidence for acceptance of the Douglas/*New Age* texts as a collaborative venture between Orage and Douglas. Although the texts were published in Douglas's name, the title to sole authorship is inaccurate and misleading. The texts are obscure, and at times incomprehensible, save in the light of the analysis of Chapter 1. Although there have been many attempts at interpretation of 'Douglasism', most notably Macpherson (1953), these have taken as their initial point of reference the abundant texts produced by Douglas and his supporters throughout the 1930s. These later texts would originally have been read in conjunction with the earlier collaborative works, without which their portent is obscure. Chapter 1 commences with brief biographies of the leading characters, Douglas and Orage. It proceeds with an exploration of the origins of guild socialism in the medievalism of Ruskin and Morris, political pluralism, syndicalism, Fabianism, and Belloc's concept of the 'servile state'. The monetary reform aspects of Douglasism are anticipated by distributism, Gesell and underconsumptionism.

A re-presentation of the original guild socialist economics as set out during the Douglas/Orage collaboration of 1918–22 is provided in Chapters 2 and 3. The texts comprise the four *English Review* articles, *Economic Democracy, Credit-Power and Democracy, The Control and Distribution of Production* and *Social Credit* (Douglas 1918, 1919a, 1919b, 1920, 1922b, 1924a), all of which were serialised and/or reprinted, whole or in part, in the *New Age*. Additional papers and pamphlets include *These Present Discontents and the Labour Party and Social Credit*, the *Socialist Review* article and *The Breakdown of the Employment System* (Douglas 1922a, 1922c, 1923). The texts published in 1923 and 1924 are included in this category, as, unlike some of Douglas's later work, they continued to develop guild socialist themes. In Part I the main themes are collated from these sources.

Chapters 2 and 3 follow from an annotated and cross-referenced study of the original texts. The re-presentation of the themes of the original guild socialist economics is undertaken in the light of guild socialist and related economic theories of the period. Interpretation was further assisted by insights gained from the critiques of economists, including Hawtrey and Douglas (1933), Hawtrey (1937), Cole (1927, 1933, 1944), Mehta (1983),

King (1988) and (obliquely) Meade (1938, 1989, 1993). Although Meade and Cole were conscious of the connections between guild socialism and 'Douglasism', they failed to recognise the potential of the alternative political economy represented in the Douglas/*New Age* texts. The historical chain of events of the depression years and the acceptance by the Labour Party of neoclassical orthodoxy diverted attention from a body of theory capable of producing a socially equitable and ecologically sustainable economy. Chapter 2 covers the basic economic concepts, including the A + B theorem and, arising from it, the just price concept. Chapter 3 explores the underlying social philosophy derived from guild socialism.

Contemporary reactions to the texts are summarised in Part II. Particular attention is paid to the extent to which interpretations of economists and politicians related to the original Douglas/*New Age* texts. In the main, the 'Douglasism' of the 1930s purported to be, and was interpreted as being, little more than an attempt to free the economy from its cycles of boom and depression. This conventional approach to economic questions is contrasted with evidence that the popularity of the social credit movement can be attributed, in part at least, to an emerging quest for an economics of sufficiency based upon ecologically sound socialist economics. Chapter 4 examines evidence of extensive review of the texts by orthodox economists, including Harrod, Keynes, Ramsey, Foster and Catchings, Hawtrey, Robertson, Meade and Crowther. Additionally, the body of work was examined by bankers in Canada, the Macmillan Committee in London and the *Economic Journal*. The long history of the relationship between the Labour Party and social credit in the inter-war years is reviewed in Chapter 5. The reactions of individual radical economists are reviewed in Chapter 6, including the Fabians and G.D.H. Cole, Maurice Dobb, J.A. Hobson and John Strachey. The compartmentalisation of reactions in Chapters 4–6 is necessarily contrived, since movements and personalities on the left were closely interlinked.

Part III documents the history of the social credit movement in the light of the previous chapters. This concluding section relates the material to current ecological, feminist and socialist thought, as well as to developments in mainstream politics and economics in the inter-war period. The surprising extent of popular support for an alternative approach to economics, not only in the United Kingdom but also on a worldwide basis, emerges in this section. Chapters 7 and 8 review the history of the social credit movement from an ecological guild socialist perspective. Chapter 7 documents the differing but complementary branches of the movement in the 1920s, following the end of the close collaboration between Douglas and Orage. Chapter 8 looks in detail at the growth of the movement in the 1930s, including the Social Credit Secretariat, the Chandos group and Hargrave's Green Shirts. Social credit periodicals and publications are reviewed, revealing evidence of the appeal of the movement to women, artists, farmers, the

Part I

1

THE DOUGLAS/*NEW AGE* TEXTS IN HISTORICAL CONTEXT

The social credit movement of the 1930s was the product of collaboration between Alfred Richard Orage and Major Clifford Hugh Douglas. In the years immediately following World War I Orage, the guild socialist editor of the *New Age*, opened the columns of his paper to Douglas, the engineer turned monetary reformer, and forged an economics of guild socialism. Following the end of the collaboration between Douglas and Orage in 1922, 'Douglasism' and the social credit movement came to be identified with monetary reform. The guild socialist origins of social credit were overlooked in the quest for a solution to economic stagnation. This chapter explores the background to the writing of the original Douglas/*New Age* texts, published between 1918 and 1924. Brief biographies of Douglas and Orage are followed by a review of the contemporary theories of guild socialism and monetary reform.

BIOGRAPHICAL SETTING

An early study of the social credit movement contrasted the personalities of the two central protagonists. Writing over a decade after the death of Orage, McCarthy drew upon material from Helen Corke and Philip Mairet, noting that: 'There is something of the machine about Douglas, a coldness, an aloofness, a constant inability to get off his pedestal and examine the oilers and greasers who are lubricating his wheels and shafts' (McCarthy 1947: 17). His books reveal a 'benevolent condescension', a contempt for humanity in general, be they financiers, socialists or citizens. However, 'What Douglas lacked, Orage had in plenty . . . Cole, Reckitt, William Mellor and Ivor Brown found him both an inspiration and a kindly patron' (McCarthy 1947: 18). McCarthy observed that 'many of the old views of the *New Age* appear in Social Credit writings'. References to 'Guildism', attacks on labour leaders and semi-religious appeals are articulated in the language of Orage. 'To say that Douglas was influenced by Orage is not to criticise him. No one could know Orage and remain uninfluenced' (McCarthy 1947: 19). McCarthy's brief account of the two central characters is unusual in the history of the movement. Followers of 'Douglas Social Credit' have been economical in their references to Orage, while a substantial proportion of Orage's biographers and contemporaries regretted his association with the Major.

The guild socialist Orage was central in the development of social credit theory. For this reason the biographical notes on Orage precede those on Douglas. Throughout the text the early writings published under the name of Douglas are referred to as 'the Douglas/*New Age* texts'. Until 1924 the term 'social credit' was not used by either of the authors to describe their work in a generic sense. After that date Douglas made scant reference to the guild socialist origins of his early collaboration with Orage.

Alfred Richard Orage, 1873–1934

As the first socialist weekly in London the *New Age* recorded 'the tactical history of a crucial phase in the relations between socialists and the newly created Labour Party' (Martin 1967: 5). The paper was bought in 1907 by Orage and Holbrook Jackson with the financial support of George Bernard Shaw and a merchant banker. It was edited by Orage from that date. As an 'Independent Review of Politics, Literature and Art' the *New Age* was dissociated from 'any specific formulation of economics or party' (*New Age* 1907, quoted in Martin 1967: 24). From the start of Orage's editorship the *New Age* existed in an uneasy relationship with the rising star of Fabian socialism. '*The New Age*, particularly just before and in the early part of the first world war,' wrote Margaret Cole in a letter to the *New Statesman*, 'was *the* left-wing paper' (quoted in Martin 1967: 5, emphasis original).

Orage combined political issues with literature and the arts. His ability to detect talent in the early works of young writers was noted by Martin. 'The first published works of the following authors appeared in *The New Age*: F.S. Flint, T.E. Hulme, Katherine Mansfield, John Middleton Murry, Storm Jameson, Herbert Read, Ivor Brown, Llewellyn Powys, Ruth Pitter and Edwin Muir' (Martin 1967: 58). These and other talented young writers, including G.D.H. Cole, Maurice Reckitt and Ezra Pound, benefited from Orage's patronage and guidance: several subsequently produced social credit publications. At this time notable contributors on economic analysis included J.A. Hobson and Arthur Kitson. Orage was successful in attracting contributors across the spectrum of left-wing views and consequently presided over a pivotal debate.

The guild socialism which swept through the British trade union movement between 1915 and the failure of the General Strike in 1926 (Durbin 1985: 21) was the product of earlier discussions between Orage, his lifelong friend A.J. Penty and S.G. Hobson. Guild socialism was expounded by G.D.H. Cole and Maurice Reckitt (Orage 1926: 402). Support for this radical departure from orthodox Fabianism in the columns of the *New Age* left the

Fabian socialists without a weekly paper, and the *New Statesman* was founded in 1913 to replace the *New Age* as the weekly paper of 'orthodox' socialists. Clifford Sharpe, a former director of the *New Age* and a regular contributor, became political editor of the *New Statesman*. 'One of their best writers is almost good enough for *The New Age*,' wrote H.G. Wells in the *New Witness*. 'Ideas! There is not so much as a tenth of an *Orage* in the whole enterprise' (quoted in Martin 1967: 122, emphasis original).

According to his biographer, Orage 'disliked nothing more than movements and meetings' and preferred to appeal 'to the brains of people already doing effective work' (Mairet 1936: 70). His championing of National Guilds led Cole, Reckitt and others to form the National Guilds League in 1915, which subsequently received the support of R.H. Tawney (Mairet 1936: 69; Martin 1967: 210). In 1917 Orage published *An Alphabet of Economics*, which anticipated Douglas's critique of capitalist economy and society 'to a remarkable extent, and was' (according to Macpherson) 'considerably more penetrating' (Macpherson 1962: 122). By 1918 he was convinced that the whole idea of National Guilds was 'wanting in some vital part'. The problem lay in 'the relation of the whole scheme to the existing, or any prospective system of money' (Orage 1926: 402). As Reckitt and Bechhofer explained: 'unless guildsmen are to abandon themselves, and society, to the desperate expedients of Bolshevism, they must reinforce their industrial policy with an economic policy equally characteristic of the Guild idea' (Reckitt and Bechhofer 1918: 257). Orage had studied Marx, and was familiar with the writings of J.A. Hobson and of Arthur Kitson, already well known 'as a financial critic' (Mairet 1936: 74) and as a contributor to the *Financial Times* (Martin 1967: 123), both of whom were contributors to the *New Age*. Penty and Orage continued to discuss guild economics on a regular weekly basis but Penty's ideas on price fixing (the 'just price') failed to illuminate the question of money itself. At this point Douglas was introduced to Orage and invited to join in the weekly discussions between Penty and Orage (Mairet 1936: 74–5).

By Orage's own account he collaborated with Douglas in the writing of Douglas's first book, *Economic Democracy* (first published in the *New Age* in 1919 (Orage 1926), and in the Draft Scheme for the Mining Industry (1920), which was responsible for bringing the 'new economics' to the attention of trade unionists throughout the United Kingdom. Communications between Douglas and the Labour Party at the time of *The Labour Party Report on the Douglas/'New Age' Scheme* accept Douglas and Orage as joint authors (Douglas 1922a: appendix).

A further indication of the nature of the relationship between Douglas's theories and Orage appears in the text of the pamphlet *These Present Discontents and the Labour Party and Social Credit* (Douglas 1922a). The authorship of the entire pamphlet is attributed to Douglas. However, *The Labour Party and Social Credit* (pp. 16–36) and the appendices are written in the style of Orage. They do not contain one sentence as long-winded or incomprehensible as:

> Even the hard-shelled Tory, if he be anything at all of a realist, must admit that, reasonably or otherwise, his opponents are making the working of that pre-war world to which his eyes turn back with longing, and to the restoration of which his eyes are bent, an arduous and uncomfortable undertaking; while the audacious seekers after the New World so confidently promised as the logical consequence of a victorious peace, seem united on one subject only – the determination to make the old one as uncomfortable as possible for everybody.
>
> (Douglas 1922a: 3)

Pages 3–16 are written in this unmistakable style. Further evidence that Douglas and Orage collaborated closely right up to the eve of Orage's departure from England and from the editorship of the *New Age* later in 1922 appears in the same document. Douglas's reputed skill as an orator is difficult to detect from his early writings.

Major Clifford Hugh Douglas, 1879–1952

There is no biography of Douglas. His passion for secrecy about his private life prevented Philip Mairet, Orage's biographer, from including any biographical details in an introduction to *The Douglas Manual* which he edited in 1934 (Finlay 1972: 88). Marjorie Douglas, Douglas's only daughter by his first wife, honoured her father's final wishes that no biography should be written. In the absence of a biography, precise details of the years between Douglas's birth in Stockport on 20 January 1879 and his meeting with Orage in 1918 remain the subject of mystery and speculation (Finlay 1972: 85–100) which need not concern this study. What little can be said with any certainty is that, like Orage, he came from humble origins. By 1904 he was a member of the Institute of Electrical Engineers. He went up to Cambridge in 1910 at the unusually late age of 31 to study science but left after four terms without taking a degree. The title of Major was acquired whilst he was at the Royal Aircraft Factory in Farnborough from 1916 to 1918.

Three biographical elements of relevance to the current study are: (1) Douglas's own account of the factors which led to the formulation of his theories of the relationship between finance and industry; (2) the personality traits which inhibited effective dissemination of social credit theory and policies; (3) Douglas's personal financial circumstances.

Douglas's own version of the origins of his social credit theories was given in an address to the Canadian Club in Ottawa in 1923 when he was in Canada to give evidence to the Select Committee on Banking and Finance in the Canadian House of Commons (Douglas 1934a). He explained that, about fifteen years previously, he had been in India, in charge of the Westinghouse interests in the East. One of those interests concerned the survey of a large district with a view to installing hydro-electric equipment. The prospects were good. On his return to Calcutta, however, it became clear there was no money to proceed with the project. At that time labour was plentiful in India and the manufacturers in Great Britain were short of orders. Furthermore, prices for machinery in 1905, 1906 and 1907 were very low indeed. Douglas had to accept this situation, but noted the fact as curious (Douglas 1934a).

Douglas recalled having been taken into the confidence of the Comptroller-General of India in Calcutta on the matter of 'credit'. He was told of the trouble he experienced with the Treasury officials at home in England, and with their departments in India, in regard to the extraordinary operations they undertook melting down rupees in order to deal with the exchange. This was done with regard to 'what they called the quantity theory of money'. The Comptroller-General concluded that 'money and currency and the silver rupees, etc., have almost nothing to do with this situation. It almost entirely depends on credit.' Silver and currency form only a very small part of financial operations. Douglas noted this for future reference.

Some years later, before the outbreak of World War I, Douglas states he was employed by 'the British Government at home to design and ultimately to construct a railway which runs underneath London from Paddington to Whitechapel, for the Post Office'. Despite the absence of physical or engineering problems and a plentiful supply of labour, the project could not be completed. Finance lay at the root of the problem. However, as soon as the war commenced, money was available for practically anything.

After 'an interval' Douglas 'was sent down to Farnborough, to the Royal Aircraft Factory, in connection with a certain amount of muddle into which that institution had got'. Although money was not the issue, Douglas concluded that the only way to ascertain how work was being allocated 'was to go very carefully into the costing which took place'. The existing costing system produced 'admirable information about what happened three years and two months before, but that was not of any use to me'. He needed 'news, not history'. This supports the theory that Douglas's 'A + B theorem' sought to explain the dynamic characteristics of capitalist finance. Douglas went on to visit an eminent acquaintance of his, Sir Guy Calthrop, of the London and North Western Railway, who recommended the use of a 'tabulating machine' of the type newly employed in the traffic statistics department of the railways.

According to Douglas, they made use of those very early computers for their costings at Farnborough. Information was punched on to cards, and the cards were put into the machine, which processed them. Douglas used to dream of 'rivers of cards'. One day it occurred to him that by the end of the week total wages and salaries were not equal to the value of the goods which had been produced during that week. The two prices did not tally. Although this would obviously be the case, the fact of its happening in every factory across the land *at the same period of time* was, to Douglas, highly significant. It follows that it is true of every factory every week. Therefore the amount of purchasing power distributed in the form of wages and salaries during any week will not be sufficient to buy the product, at its price that week, unless extra money is being injected into the system each week (Douglas 1934a).

This lengthy account supports the view that Douglas's theories arose from his original observations and not from familiarity with the work of established monetary economists. Neither in the rest of his speech nor elsewhere does Douglas acknowledge his debt to Orage in similar manner to these references to the Comptroller-General in India or Sir Guy Calthrop of the LNWR. Indeed, the entire speech concentrates exclusively on the technical and financial origins, and omits all reference to the social and philosophical origins of social credit. A glance at Douglas's library in 1918 would have been highly revealing. Had he read Comte, as Finlay suggests (1972: 116)? Had he read Veblen, Hobson or Marx, as his early writings occasionally infer? Whence did he derive the idea of the cultural heritage? Did the social philosophy and political economy of the early Douglas writings originate solely from lengthy discussions with his mentor and collaborator, Orage? The speech to the Canadian Club establishes Douglas's familiarity with early computing techniques, a useful tool if his recommendations on financial planning in general, and the just price in particular, were to be implemented. Of the social conscience revealed in the texts there is no sign whatever.

'According to Pound, "Orage taught Douglas how to write"' (Martin 1967: 271). Yet, despite Orage's guidance, Douglas's prose style has been described as 'anfractuous' (Martin 1967: 270) and 'unadroit. Even when he is most intelligible his argument is reticular and hard to understand' (Mehta 1983: 126). 'It is necessary to approach Douglas's writing with rather more sympathy than normal,' claimed Finlay. 'For all his scientific attitudes, his was essentially an intuitive mind, which sensed but could never quite capture the truth' (1972: 96). It is difficult to disagree with Finlay on this, or on his view of Douglas's character. 'Douglas was essentially a solitary man, and it seems to have been a solitariness which was rooted in a sense of inferiority' (Finlay 1972: 93). In Finlay's opinion, formed from interviews and personal contact with colleagues and acquaintances of Douglas, he inspired strong positive or negative reactions. He was not personally equipped to promote his theoretical ideas in co-operation with others, nor to fulfil the role of leader of a social movement, as he later attempted. These personality factors served to obstruct rather than enhance constructive consideration of a potential alternative to the orthodox capitalist financial system.

12

By the time of the inception of social credit (1918) Douglas was sufficiently wealthy to retire from engineering. At this point, had he sought personal prestige in public life, an easier option would have been to pursue a conventional political career. Nor was his advocacy of social credit based on the pursuit of self-interest. He was already a wealthy man, and, had social credit been adopted, by his own estimation he stood to lose financially (Finlay 1972: 94–5).

Nothing was further from Douglas's original intentions than the formation of a social movement, political party or personal career as a writer or propagandist. 'I had the idea that I had got hold of some specific technical information and I had only to get it accepted,' commented Douglas some years later on the period 1917–18. 'I had the idea that I was like a clever little boy and that I had only to run to father and he would be very pleased about it' (Douglas 1939). This accords with Marjorie Douglas's recollection of learning the names of leading personalities of the time as she and her stepmother met Douglas from the train after visiting prominent people listed in *Who's Who*. Time after time he returned disheartened as each prominent economist, banker and Treasury expert failed to be impressed by his proposals.

The meeting with Orage proved the turning point in Douglas's fortunes. The two were introduced by Holbrook Jackson, Orage's friend and former colleague who had published Douglas's first unintelligible articles in the *Organiser* in 1917. Orage immediately detected the relevance of Douglas's approach to his own search for an alternative economic and monetary theory to support his guild socialist ideas. His reference to Douglas, at that time, as 'a queer fellow with a money bee in his bonnet' (Kenney 1939: 286) suggests that Douglas had yet to set his theories within the context of a social philosophy. As Douglas joined Penty and Orage at their weekly 'councils' Penty, like many of Orage's colleagues, resented Douglas's 'technical' approach, which led Orage away from the medievalist aspects of guild socialism. In short, Douglas did not have a guild socialist background, yet guild socialist terminology occurs throughout the Douglas/*New Age* texts published between 1918 and 1924. By the late 1920s and throughout the 1930s Douglas's writing was focused on reform of the 'inefficient' monetary system, with attacks on wage slavery and social injustice assuming a lower profile.

GENERAL DEFINITION OF GUILD SOCIALISM

The desire for the emancipation of the new industrial working class has been shared by socialists of all creeds and persuasions. For the majority of socialists, whether of the British reformist variety or of the pre-1914 Continental Marxist type, socialism was sought through collectivism in the form of state ownership and control of industry. For most, access to economic power could best be achieved through the avenue of a political party which would deliver state power on a territorial basis. For a minority, organisation on an industrial basis offered the most appropriate route to the acquisition of control over the means of production (Glass 1966: 1–2).

From the outset, the guild socialists rejected ownership of the means of production as a panacea. Abolition of the wage system, whereby a person's labour could be bought at a standard rate, remained the distinctive characteristic of the guild brand of socialism. Self-government in industry, coupled with a reduction in the power of the centralised state, remained key features of the underlying philosophy of the vast majority of guild socialists (Reckitt and Bechhofer 1918: xii).

> The essentials of the Guild idea are the recovery of initiative by the ordinary worker, his release from bondage to the base purposes of profit, and his achievement of complete and responsible industrial democracy.
>
> (Reckitt and Bechhofer 1918: xvi)

Concluding the introduction to the first edition of *The Meaning of National Guilds*, this statement was endorsed by A.J. Penty, author of the first work on guild socialism, and Rowland Kenney, the first editor of the *Daily Herald* and lifelong advocate of guild socialism and social credit. In essence, guild socialists opposed wage slavery. They sought an end to the commodification of labour, whether under the capitalist or the collectivist state. Hence they sought economic democracy as a means to a classless society, rather than industrial democracy for the working class alone (Reckitt and Bechhofer 1918: 256). A core concept of guild socialism was the promotion of 'all corporate work to the level of vocation', uniting in real fraternity all whose industrial destinies are intermingled (Reckitt 1941: 114). From the outset, guild socialists demanded nothing from industrial capitalism. Rather, they explored the potential for the construction of a viable alternative.

ORIGINS OF GUILD SOCIALISM

The debt to William Morris and John Ruskin is apparent from the many references to them throughout the work of guild socialist writers. To some extent the influence of the co-operative ideas of Robert Owen can also be detected. However, the five main strands can best be summarised as Penty's medievalism, political pluralism, syndicalism, Hilaire Belloc's conceptualisation of the 'servile state' and a Fabian belief in reformism as a means to social justice.

Penty and *The Restoration of the Gild System*

In 1906 the architect A.J. Penty published *The Restoration of the Gild System*. A former Fabian, Penty followed Ruskin and Morris in condemning the division of labour and the machine age. He advocated a return to hand craftsmanship through the restoration of the medieval gild (*sic*) system. The squalor and spiritual malaise of industrialism had created a general desire for an escalating supply of the commodities capable of being supplied through mechanisation and the denial of the value of the skills of hand, eye and brain. State control of industry, if achieved through the collectivist policies of the Fabians and the Labour Party, would do nothing to alleviate the situation.

A key concept introduced by Penty was the Ruskinian belief that the trade unions, as they had developed through the nineteenth century, had adopted some of the functions of the gilds, offering regulation of pay and working conditions, together with support for members in sickness and adversity. As masters and men united on an industry-wide basis, trade unions would be transformed into gilds. They could then convert into hand-craft-based gilds, following the lead of the arts and crafts movement.

Penty viewed the small workshop based upon hand production for the local market as the most appropriate alternative to a productive system motivated by greed and exploitation and resulting in mass production. He pedalled his 'hopelessly impractical' (Glass 1966: 18) dream to his sympathetic, though sceptical, colleagues (Reckitt 1941: 115–17). Nevertheless, in essence Penty had outlined guild (to use the more common spelling) theory and its fundamental questioning of the redistribution of wealth as an end in itself. Higher wages and improved working conditions for the working class would merely increase their share of the products of capitalism. It would do nothing, in Penty's view, to end the evils of industrialism.

Political pluralism

Guild socialism was strongly influenced by the parallel development of political pluralism as outlined, for example, by J.N. Figgis in his *Churches in the Modern State* (Glass 1966: 22–3; Reckitt 1941: 113). Pluralist political theory rejects the notion that the state is, or should be, the sole source of power and focus of authority. In a medieval society, for example, the monarchy and the Church were co-equal rulers, each having authority over its own sphere. In such a society the craft guilds and the feudal landlord were governed by similar bonds of obligation to and from the citizen. Pluralists argued that even in the twentieth-century state *de facto* centres of alternative political allegiance exist, not only in the Church but also in trade unions, industrial associations and municipalities. In this pluralist state, Church and trade unions antedate political monism (Glass 1966: 22–3).

Syndicalism

The guild socialists viewed the trade unions as the authentic voice of the working class and the true expression of labour's opposition to profit-motivated capitalism. Syndicalism, one of the basic sources of guild socialism, is defined by Cole as 'revolutionary Trade Unionism' (1913: 351). French syndicalism, as it evolved in the first six years of the twentieth century, envisaged the industrial overturn of society, using strikes, particularly the General Strike, to destroy capitalism. Direct sabotage of capitalism would lead to co-operative worker control in industry. Syndicalism differed from socialism on two counts. Syndicalists did not seek alliances with socialist political parties, regarding the ballot box as an irrelevance. Further, French syndicalism was based upon direct worker ownership and control of the factory and the workplace. Centralised and international workers' movements based upon the nation state, as in conventional socialist and Marxist movements, were viewed with suspicion by the syndicalists. Reformists, they argued, were prepared to use trade unions as a means to defend the interests of workers under capitalism. Syndicalists argued that industrial organisation in the form of self-governing workshops would bring an end to the capitalist state. Subsequently these ideas were adopted in modified forms in the United States and the United Kingdom (Carpenter 1973: 22).

The core element of the guild idea focused upon the trade unions. From French syndicalism it championed the producer. From American syndicalism it promoted organisation on an industry basis. Additionally, it drew from Marxism the attack on capitalist enslavement of the mass of the working class (Reckitt and Bechhofer 1918: xiv). Articles on syndicalism appeared in the *New Age* between 1906 and 1912.

Belloc and *The Servile State*

Hilaire Belloc's conceptualisation of the 'servile state' first appeared in the *New Age* and was published as *The Servile State* in 1912. Belloc contrasted the political freedom of the worker with his or her 'industrial servitude', which negated political freedom. The capitalist had become tenant-in-chief of the state, degrading work into toil and creating the degradation of the 'wage-slave morality'. To the capitalist the potential ability of the trade unions to create a free society was a grave danger. Economic order would end, argues the capitalist, if profiteering was eliminated. The 'privateer' is socially and economically indispensable to all forms of progress and stability in society. Without his enterprise, civilisation would come to a standstill (Reckitt and Bechhofer 1918: 19).

The capitalist argues that he uses his powers, including his capital and mental activity, to keep production expanding. He should therefore be regarded as a public benefactor. He is responsible to the state for those citizens entrusted to his care, to use them as material for the business which he is public-spirited enough to carry on. The good employer accepts responsibility for ensuring that the state has no cause to call him to account for the health and well-being of his workers. In return the capitalist expects the state to assist him, not those who oppose him. If the state fails him in this it will strengthen the forces which oppose the capitalist, and hinder him in discharging his task of increasing national output and fulfilling his mission of keeping a portion of the working class usefully employed (Reckitt and Bechhofer 1918: 20).

In the servile state the state guarantees the stability essential to the smooth functioning of capitalism by regulating the lives of workers with the sanction of law. As it evolved the law would come to recognise two classes of people. One sanctioned as possessed of the means of production: the other as wage slaves, employed and secure in the necessities of life but legally bound to work for the owning class. In Belloc's view, a socialism which merely sought the abolition of destitution and economic insecurity would be content with a servile state. State ownership and control of the means of production alone would necessitate precisely the same form of regulation of the lives of workers (Glass 1966: 21–2). Hence the opposition of Belloc, Orage and other guild socialists to the National Insurance Bill of 1911. The terminology of the 'servile state' and wage slavery was used widely throughout guild socialist literature.

Fabians

A number of leading guild socialists, including Cole, Orage and Reckitt, spent some time in the Fabian Society. Fabians rejected Marxism in favour of a gradualist, revisionist approach. Motivated by witness of the injustices of capitalist production, which tolerated low wages, unemployment, poverty, insecurity, and appalling working and living conditions, the Fabians sought accommodation with the orthodox approach to economic management. Founded in 1884 by a small group of middle-class visionaries, the Fabian Society sought the gradual elimination of capitalism through the implementation of economic and social reforms. Expansion of the role of government and state ownership was to be based on empirical evidence. The Fabians embarked on a programme of statistical research which set them apart from other socialist groups. They had, according to Orage in 1896,

> a positive genius for the commonplace. The spirit of Captain Cuttle is in every Fabian tradition, and 'when found, make note of' applies to everything the mysterious society publishes . . . I am convinced that when the rest of the world shall have taken Mark Twain's advice and 'shuffled off this mortal coil', there will still be the Fabian Society to prepare neat and accurate tables of averages and percentages for the judgement day.
>
> (Quoted in Martin 1967: 21,
> from the *Labour Leader*, February 1896)

The Fabians used the marginalist economics of the 1870s to develop their own theory of rent as an explanation of exploitation. This was the substance of Fabian economic theory, which ignored finance and accepted labour as the sole ethical means of access to an income (Durbin 1985). Fabian determination to work within the framework of orthodoxy was encapsulated in the decision to found the London School of Economics 'with funds over which they [the Webbs] had exclusive control' (Burkitt 1984: 111). Its purpose was to familiarise socialist policy-makers with the theories of economic orthodoxy. The Fabian scientific approach was in keeping with the character of the British working class as expressed through the trade union movement, which sought the gradual advance of workers within the capitalist system rather than the overthrow of their oppressors. In the late nineteenth and early twentieth centuries trade unions toyed with the idea of aligning politically with the Liberal Party, before the parliamentary Labour Party was firmly established on Fabian principles. Indeed, Beatrice Webb co-operated with the Liberals in the formulation of the National Insurance Act of 1911.

Labour politics emerged from a Fabian blend of socialist idealism with economic orthodoxy. However, in the early years of the twentieth century socialism was not yet

> either the popular or unpopular vogue it has since become; but it was much more of a cult, with affiliations in directions now quite disowned – in theosophy, arts and crafts, vegetarianism, the 'simple life' . . . Morris had shed a medieval glamour over it with his stained glass News from Nowhere . . . Keir Hardie had clothed it in a cloth cap and a red tie.

> (Orage 1926: 376)

Although the Marxian analysis of capitalism informed socialism in general, the emergence of a Labour Party based on a single class of the wage-earner was bitterly resented by many socialists as leading to the perpetuation of capitalist–labour relations, and hence of capitalism itself.

GUILD SOCIALISTS

Guild socialist theories were developed by two interlinked but distinct groups. Differences of policy and strategy can be discerned between Orage and the contributors to the *New Age*, on the one hand, and Cole and the National Guilds League on the other. Although Cole contributed to the *New Age*, and S.G. Hobson, a prominent colleague of Orage, was a key member of the National Guilds League, there were tensions between the two (Reckitt and Bechhofer 1918: xiv). Both sought to work through the trade unions to free the producer from capitalism. Both warned of the potential for the state to become the handmaid of the powerful employer or large corporation. However, while the *New Age* envisaged a classless society, Cole and the National Guilds League sought to champion the working class and their conditions of labour.

The '*New Age*' guild socialists envisaged the end of economic conflict as a prerequisite for the emergence of socialism. Since each guild held the machinery and materials of the industry in trust, on behalf of the community as a whole, they would not compete to accumulate wealth as under capitalism. Cole's guild socialism, with its rules and democratically determined regulations, retained a more conventional world view.

Orage and the *New Age*

In a series of articles in the *New Age* in 1912–13 Penty, in collaboration with Orage, drew together the themes of guild socialism. These were published in book form as *The National Guilds: an Inquiry into the Wage System*. Edited by Orage, the book was translated into many languages and ran to three English editions between 1914 and 1920 (Glass 1966: 29).

In *The National Guilds* Hobson and Orage attacked the commodification of labour as the greatest evil of the capitalist system, incapable of solution by such orthodox socialist measures as security of employment, higher wages, better working conditions or unemployment benefit. By accepting wages the workers sold their common inheritance, their right to the industrial fabric of the economy. In doing so they lost all right to govern their conditions of work or to control the distribution of the product of their labour.

Guild socialists drew a distinction between wages, which buy labour power, and payment for service. Using an analogy which has its limitations, they argued that people in the armed services receive 'pay', whether they are training, on stand-by, fighting or in hospital. They offer their service, and are not expected to produce a profit for an employer. By contrast, the miner, or other waged worker, is also a human being with pride and aspirations. However, in this case the wage system treats labour as 'fodder', keeping the labourer alive and serviced so that the commodity 'labour power' can be bought. The industrial employer is not concerned with the labourer as a human being, possessing functions, aims and aspirations beyond the employment situation. The guild socialists envisaged a system of National Guilds in which the watchword 'service' replaced 'profit' and a scramble for a greater share of it (Kenney 1939: 200–1).

The National Guilds were conceived of as vertically integrated trade unions. Ownership of each industry would be vested in the state but administered by the individual guilds, which would be decentralised on the subsidiarity basis to the lowest practical local level. Unlike traditional trade unions, however, the guilds would consist of all workers in an industry, from managers to unskilled workers, clerical and manual. Payment would be on a service basis, rather than as remuneration for piecework or number of hours worked. The National Guild idea was a pioneering attempt to break away from the conception that wealth was created purely within the manufacturing sector of industry. Hence the guilds would include not only traditional industries like textiles, mining, fishing and building, but also agriculture, domestic service, the civil service. On the basis of statistics for 1911, for example, Hobson listed:

Class	Number
1 Civil service – general and municipal	253,865
2 Defence (excluding those abroad)	203,993
3 Professional and subordinate services	733,582
4 Domestic service	2,199,517
5 Commercial occupations	712,465
6 Transit	1,497,629
7 Agriculture	2,262,629
8 Fishing	61,925
9 Mines and quarries (in and about)	943,880
10 Metals, machines, implements, etc.	1,475,410
11 Precious metals, jewels, watches, games	168,344
12 Building and construction	1,335,820
13 Wood, furniture, fittings and decorations	307,632
14 Brick, cement, pottery and glass	189,856
15 Chemicals	149,675
16 Leather, skins, hair, feathers	117,866
17 Paper, printing, books, stationery	334,261
18 Textiles	1,462,001
19 Clothing	1,395,795
20 Food, tobacco, drink and lodging	1,301,076
21 Gas, water and sanitary	78,686
22 General and undefined	1,075,414

(Hobson 1919: 159)

Professions, including law, medicine and education, were viewed as already 'guilds in embryo' (Hobson 1914: 159–63). To these would be added the 'profession of ideas, as distinct from the actual production and distribution of concrete wealth'. Professions included those of 'priests and preachers, artists, craftsmen, journalists and authors'. Other guilds would manage the work of inventors and of those 'devoted to the initiation of new ideas and inventions not yet accepted by their appropriate Guilds', of pure scientists and all devoted to original research, and any groups in which the 'wage system may persist' (Hobson 1914: 163).

Later, in 1920, Hobson elaborated upon the definition of 'producer' and the relationship between 'producer' and consumer. To do so he dismissed the notion that a distinction could be drawn between producer and non-producer. The basic tenet of the guild idea was the rejection of the 'commodity theory of labour', necessitating acceptance of the control of industry by the producer. Hobson extended the community of workers to include not only the miner or textile worker (manufacturing) but also the railway worker, the journalist (services) and 'housekeeping women' (normally excluded as economic agents). By this definition all consumers are also producers. Because the community of all producers correlates with the community of all consumers, exploitation of the latter by the former becomes a contradiction in terms. The traditional distinction between workers producing wealth in the form of tangible goods for which there is an effective demand and those producing services required by society as a whole is not particularly helpful. Leaving aside the question of 'non-workers, whether investors or tramps', the economy remains dependent upon a range of socially necessary services. The 'social demand' or need for those services is not necessarily reflected in terms of effective demand. The opportunity for exploitation of producers of goods and providers of services would not survive under a guild system. Furthermore, priests, journalists, artists and authors would be freed from dependence upon the patronage of the rich and could serve the interests of all (Hobson 1920: 4–5).

In *The National Guilds and the State* Hobson drew a distinction between the national guilds and the guild socialism from which they emerged. Guild socialism can be regarded as a body of theory formulated by middle-class intellectuals, with the national guilds acting as their propaganda machine. The guilds were incapable of forming an effective movement to end capitalism. The objective was to educate and influence the community of wage-earners. Only the trade unions, with an informed and motivated membership, could lead to the creation of a productive system capable of ending exploitation (Hobson 1920: vi).

Hobson and Orage contrasted the situation of the wage slave under capitalism with the worker in the medieval guilds. The wage slave had no alternative to remaining an economic commodity. The apprentice and journeyman, on the other hand, could become masters in their craft or trade. Shoddy work was a crime and labour was honourable, developing the mental, moral and spiritual faculties of the worker (Kenney 1939: 201). Concern with the mental, moral and spiritual aspects of work remained the distinguishing feature of guild socialism. The rejection of the idea that intrinsically unsatisfying work could result in production of any value save in money terms was a difficult one to understand, even for certain guild socialists. As a result, guild socialism appeared to be a hopelessly idealistic attempt to return to a stylised past utopia. Careful perusal of the original texts reveals, however, that guild socialist writers had appraised the philosophies of capitalism and labourist socialism, finding both to be unsustainable in social and environmental terms.

Capitalism, they noted, is defended on the grounds that it alone provides the economic motivation without which the worker would not work at all. Adherents to this line of argument are incapable of understanding that the removal from industry of opportunity for the 'exercise of human free-will and self-expression' can only destroy motivation and degrade work into unsatisfying toil.

> For it is a spiritual conception, and the philosophy of Capitalism is materialist from beginning to end. It bases itself on the maxim that 'the greatest benefactor of humankind is the man who makes two blades of grass grow where one grew before', caring nothing for the soil from which it springs, nor the texture of the grass when it appears.
>
> (Reckitt and Bechhofer 1918: 20)

The guild socialism of Orage, Hobson, Reckitt and Bechhofer provided a comprehensive critique of a production system driven purely by the profit motive and the desire for monetary reward. Their practical proposals were, however, dependent upon an idealised conception of the trade unions as champions of an emancipated working class. It fell to the young Cole and his friend William Mellor to engage in a more practical dialogue with organised labour.

G.D.H. Cole

Like William Morris, guild socialists asked:

> What is it you want from the labour movement? Higher wages? More regular employment? Shorter working hours? Better education for your children, old age pensions, libraries, parks and the rest? . . . but WHAT ELSE DO YOU WANT? If you cannot answer the question straight-forwardly, I must say you are wandering on a road the outcome of which you cannot tell . . . If you can answer it and say, 'Yes, that is all we want,' then I say, here is the real advice to give you: don't meddle with socialism.
>
> (Morris, quoted in Seabrook 1996: 29)

Although fired by Morris's idealism, Cole accepted the machine age as lightening the load of the manual worker. Cole sought to iron out the flaws in the industrial system which, although inhuman, was here to stay. In 1913, at the age of 24, he published *The World of Labour*, still regarded as a key text on syndicalism and industrial unionism in Britain (Carpenter 1973: 23). Although Cole had not, at this stage, fully assimilated the guild socialist ideas of Orage and Hobson, as expressed in the pages of the *New Age*, he was tending towards a similar rejection of the bureaucratic paternalistic socialism of the Webbs' version of the 'servile state' (Carpenter 1973: 22). Publication of *The World of Labour* attracted to Cole the nucleus of the National Guilds League.

Nevertheless, Cole's world view remained closer to that of the Webbs and the other Fabians than did that of the other prominent guild socialist writers. Although he shared their belief in the trade unions as the avenue to the emancipation of the working class he did not share the guild socialist rejection of political action as the primary means to achieve a classless society free of exploitation. Equally, his quest for co-operation between manual and 'brain' workers through democratic control of the managerial sector of the work force indicates belief in the continuation of the division of labour which was rejected by the other guild socialists (Cole 1913: xx–xxi; Reckitt and Bechhofer 1918: xv). Cole led the guild socialist assault on the Fabian Society. When that failed, he dominated the Labour Research Department (LRD), formerly the Fabian Research Department. Guild socialists predominated in the LRD, bringing their ideas into the main body of the labour movement through summer schools, study circles and the Workers' Educational Association (Reckitt 1941: 131–3; Carpenter 1973: 30–4).

Cole shared the guild socialists' repudiation of power-sharing in industry. In Cole's view the co-option of trade unionists to the boards of management of large industrial conglomerates was merely a capitalist device to pacify labour (Cole 1913: xiv–xv). He dismissed as a 'new feudalism' the 'state-aided capitalism' deemed necessary to maintain production during the war years (Cole 1913: xxiv). Nevertheless, his world view led him to believe that economic power would continue to require political restraint. Unchecked, the 'producer power' of the trade unions in transition to guilds could hold the consumer and society as a whole to ransom.

While acknowledging Cole as the person who 'to a pre-eminent degree made guild socialism' Reckitt nevertheless drew a distinction between Cole and the other guild socialists (Reckitt 1941: 124). Quoting from *Social Theory*, he and Bechhofer noted the danger of seeking to eradicate community by replacing each function with a series of committees. A fabricated economic order based more upon imagination than upon fact would result in an endless series of joint committees. The individual was likely to succumb to boredom and apathy, leaving the direction of affairs in the hands of 'a few busy bodies with a taste for interfering in the lives of others'. An over-elaborate system of political machinery, such as that proposed by Cole, would result in less, not more, democracy. 'Boredom and freedom are incompatible' (Reckitt and Bechhofer 1918: 239–40).

Cole remained convinced that guild ideas would threaten productivity and living standards unless guild activities were supervised by a series of joint congresses or communes. In his view, the workers would continue to need discipline to accept the necessity for mobility of labour, shift work and other unpopular measures necessary to achieve economic efficiency (Glass 1966: 59–60).

Furthermore, as Reckitt shrewdly observed, 'it was in social and not in economic theory that his talents lay' (Reckitt 1941: 122). Cole's later 'unceasing stream of more or less synthetic books' failed to build upon the excellence of *The World of Labour, Social Theory* and *The Life of Cobbett* (Reckitt 1941: 124). He recognised the connections between syndicalism, political pluralism and the co-operative movement. However, the young classical scholar did not, at that crucial stage, appreciate the significance of the embryonic but distinctive economics of guild socialism which emerged from the Douglas/Orage collaboration. Cole's rejection of 'Douglasism' as a flawed idea, incompatible with orthodox economic theory, was the single most significant determining factor in the subsequent history not only of social credit but also of guild socialism.

By dismissing the possibility that the capitalist financial system was a vital element in the power relationship between capitalism and the wage slave, Cole appeared to have made guild socialism a more practical proposition. In reality, Cole's profuse output merely brought guild socialist insights into the service of capitalism through the 'labourist' reforms of the Labour Party. His blueprint for a democratically controlled co-operative society was less feasible than the seemingly unpractical proposals for a review of the relationship between financial mechanisms and the motivation of the processes of production, distribution and exchange set out in the Douglas/*New Age* texts. As Glass notes, it was the financial unpracticality of the National Building Guild which resulted in the failure of the guild experiment (Glass 1966: 55). Although socialism and capitalist finance were proved to be incompatible in practice, Cole failed to recognise the significance of Douglas's monetary theories.

MONETARY THEORIES

The Douglas/*New Age* texts provide a unique combination of theoretical arguments for social justice with practical proposals for the necessary reform of capitalism. Although the texts appeared to be independent of guild socialism, they were developed within that context. Indeed, the 1920 edition of Reckitt and Bechhofer's *The Meaning of National Guilds* contains an eighteen-page review of 'finance, credit and guild policy' as developed by the '*New Age* writers – and in particular Major C.H. Douglas and the writer of the weekly Notes [Orage]' (Reckitt and Bechhofer 1918: 254). Taken out of the guild socialist context, Douglas's monetary reform is little more than a minor addition to the medley of heretical economic theories. Indeed, it is less coherent than the work of many writers contributing to, or influencing contributors to, the *New Age* before 1918.

The popularity of the Douglas/*New Age* texts and the social credit movement to which they gave rise has been attributed to the attraction of monetary reform theories in times of economic recession (see e.g. Gaitskell 1933: 347). Indeed, critics focused almost exclusively upon the maligned and misinterpreted 'A + B theorem' (see Chapter 2). Set within the context of capitalist finance, with which they are assumed to be consistent (Gaitskell 1933: 367–9), the 'A + B' observations appear nonsensical. Shorn of its guild socialism context, Douglasism can be dismissed alongside the work of other monetary reformers as a misguided remedy for the economic ills of capitalism.

The majority of monetary reformers fall into the category of individualists, seizing upon some aspect of orthodox finance as a means of correcting the supposed inefficiencies of capitalism. Some, though by no means all, present their proposals in the context of a quest for social justice. Nevertheless, none of those which antedate the Douglas/*New Age* texts contains so thorough a critique of the capitalist system when the texts are read in the context of guild socialist theory. Furthermore, several elements of Douglas/*New Age* monetary theory can be traced to the work of earlier writers on monetary reform. As editor of the *New Age* Orage published, and was therefore familiar with, the work of contemporary monetary reformers.

Distributists

Distributism was one of the roots of guild socialism and forms a significant part in the evolution of the Douglas/Orage writings. A number of distributists, including Mairet and Reckitt, became leading social crediters. Sagar (*c.* 1940) explained distributism in the following terms. The individual needs access to land, and also to a store of capital, in order to live. Equally necessary is a system of control. Each society requires laws to govern access to land and capital, since a free-for-all cannot be sustained. There are three options. First, ownership and control of land and capital may be vested in the hands of a small group who can compel the dispossessed to labour. An example is slavery, a form of social arrangement which was logically consistent in that persons dispossessed of economic power were not offered the fiction of political power. Second, no individual may have any control. Land and capital are owned by the state, which directs the individual to work. The individual is like an ant in an anthill, save that 'the state' or 'the community' cannot make decisions; certain individuals make decisions from positions of power. Third, the law may give families ownership of land and capital. The *theory* of capitalism falls short in practice because of the existence of unequal distribution.

Distributists seek an end to the *concentration* of ownership, whether private or public. They consider state ownership illusory as a means to avoid slavery and oppression. Later distributists were lukewarm about social credit proposals to restore freedom via 'a new system of double entry' to provide a universal income without restoring universal individual property ownership. At the time of writing, however, Sagar recognised that distributist proposals were little more than an idealistic pipe dream. The sham fight between 'those blood-brothers, Capitalism and Socialism' is

25

ending but the proletariat is likely to 'vote itself into slavery in its sleep'. Sagar foresaw an era of scarcity which would not be 'conjured away by changing the name of Industrial Capitalism to Industrial Socialism' (Sagar c. 1940). Under both regimes property was concentrated into increasingly large units, remote from human control. Belloc, author of *The Servile State*, was a leading distributist.

Silvio Gesell

Although Gesell's *The Natural Economic Order* was not translated into English until 1929, his ideas on 'free land' and 'free money' were widely circulated in Germany, Austria and Switzerland from the time of his earliest work in 1891, and were later to be taken up by the American Irving Fisher (Gaitskell 1933: 385–401). Gesell's proposals for the gradual repossession of land by the state on behalf of the community through the issue of 'free money' by the state show a striking resemblance to the Douglas/Orage proposal for the repossession of industrial capital by the trade unions through the Draft Mining Scheme (see Chapter 3). Like Belloc, Gesell rejected ownership of the industrial means of production as the primary means to achieve social justice.

Underconsumptionists

The term 'underconsumptionist' is applied to those who believe that production depends upon consumption, so that slumps and stagnation are caused by blocks to consumption. Underconsumptionist theories extend back at least as far as Malthus (Burkitt 1984).

Blocks to consumption may take two basic forms. The first is associated with the control of 'credit' issue by the state. In the 1880s early underconsumptionists, including O.E. Weslau and A.E. Hake, attacked the Bank Act of 1844, which effectively restricted note issue to one central bank on the basis of gold backing. Centralisation of credit issue ended the old localism based on the creditworthiness of individuals known in a community and replaced it with a bank lending policy in which borrowing was restricted to the already rich. The effect was to deny funds to small-scale, innovative enterprises and to exacerbate the tendency to conglomeration and large-scale production (Finlay 1972). Writing in this vein, Arthur Kitson concluded that 'credit should be based on the productive capacity of the whole of society' (Kitson 1894). To this end, the medium of exchange should be free from government control or the control of powerful individuals.

Kitson developed the second theme of underconsumptionism by attacking the theory that trade and industry must necessarily be financed from savings, i.e. from abstinence and the surplus of the idle rich. Consumption, and not abstinence, was the means to stimulate production and create wealth. Later, reviewing the prosperity generated by the 'Great War', Kitson was of the opinion that peace should bring 'National Wealth in place of National Debt' (Kitson 1920). The association of underconsumptionism with Douglas in the post-1924 period, particularly during the early 1930s, led to a general presupposition that 'Douglasism' was little more than an attempt to explain cyclical economic depression. The impression was compounded by Douglas's responses to questions in this general subject area. Consequently 'Douglasism' appeared superfluous once Keynes had published his *General Theory*. The present authors therefore distinguish between the theories developed before 1924 and the subsequent economic writings of Douglas and other 'social crediters'.

From differing socialist perspectives J.A. Hobson and P. Kropotkin anticipated the major themes of social credit. Both observed the tendency to overproduction in conjunction with a deficiency in working-class purchasing power. To Hobson, underconsumption in the home market resulted from excessive savings by the wealthy and was the cause of capital exports leading to international rivalry, imperialism and ultimately to war (Hobson 1900, 1902). Kropotkin recognised that the potential for technology to facilitate the provision of life's necessities with the 'least possible waste of human energy' was frustrated by the capitalist economic system. Most strikingly, however, he criticised emerging 'labourism', the political emphasis of Labour politicians on the right to *work*, as preceding the right to well-being (Kropotkin 1906). Surplus value existed because men, women and children were forced of dire necessity to sell their labour for a fraction of its productive value. From such a perspective, the right to work was a strange demand for socialists.

J.A. Hobson, the leading individualist proponent of underconsumption, was a regular contributor to the *New Age*. His *Work and Wealth: a Human Valuation* presents the case for a normative economic theory. Equally consistent with guild socialism is his argument that 'utility may well be derived from productive activity, that is, from work' while consumption may involve disutility (Richmond 1978: 292). His underconsumptionist theory that a general state of overproduction was the result of increased accumulation of capital resulting from an 'undue exercise of saving' (Richmond 1978: 284) was at variance with the monetary reform aspects of the Douglas/*New Age* texts. The superficial similarities between the theories of Hobson and Douglas in the 1930s may have contributed to the 'standard misinterpretation' of A + B, outlined by Mehta (1983) and explored in Chapter 2.

CONCLUSION

Although Gaitskell devoted well over twice as many pages to refuting the heresies of Douglas as he did to any other monetary reformer, he identified

Douglas as a purely monetary theorist and ignored the guild socialist aspects of his arguments. By the 1930s the guild socialist elements in Douglas's writings had diminished in force, yet they remained an attractive feature in the original texts, which were widely circulated at the time. Without the social justice aspects of *Economic Democracy, Credit-Power and Democracy, The Control and Distribution of Production*, and *Social Credit*, Douglas's monetary reform would not have given rise to a world-wide movement. Like the theories of Gesell, Soddy (also a social crediter) and Eisler, Douglasism would have interested few beyond a handful of scholars on the fringes of academia.

The originality of the Douglas/*New Age* proposals lay in their criticism of the insistence by capitalist and state socialist alike on an artificial, unbreakable bond between personal income and employment. The decommodification of labour was proposed as an alternative to 'labourism' and the means-tested, employment-related welfare state which was in process of evolving through the 1909 Poor Law Commission minority report and the National Insurance Act of 1911 and which culminated in the Beveridge Report of 1942 and its subsequent enactment. Beatrice Webb, a leading Fabian, advised the Liberals on these measures. (For a useful summary of the evolution of Fabian influence see Pimlott 1984). The Douglas/*New Age* proposals, with their emphasis on the freedom to work on socially necessary projects in the arts and engineering, espouse a more comprehensive view of human nature than that which enforces the necessity to accept paid employment on any terms as an essential prerequisite for a non-means-tested subsistence income. The texts tackle the question 'Where is the money to come from?' by answering the more fundamental questions of the origins of money and the purpose of its creation.

Later assumptions that national dividend proposals were an attempt to introduce 'funny money' in order to stimulate trade and increase the production and consumption of material goods are more revealing of prevailing orthodoxy than of the original inspiration behind social credit and its guild socialist origins. The texts possessed the potential to develop a financial system for a guild socialist political economy. Rejecting economic orthodoxy, they acknowledged that an economy run purely for 'financial aggrandisement' would inevitably result in social injustice and environmental degradation.

> The existing social system, based upon wage slavery and controlled by profiteers, cannot at this time of day sell an article at less expense than it costs to make. Our methods of exchange have grown grotesque; their wastefulness is a national sin; their burden is becoming intolerable.
>
> (Orage 1914: 91)

Orage recognised that guild socialism could be grafted on to neither the existing political system nor the existing financial system, since the two worked hand in hand. The guild socialism which Orage envisaged was in line with William Morris's vision. According to Cole, in his 1934 introduction to Morris's selected works, Morris

> believed that the ordinary things men made ought to be so made as to be a 'joy to the maker and to the user,' and that where most men spent their working days joylessly making ugly things, the death of civilisation was at hand.
>
> (Morris 1944: xvii)

The Douglas/*New Age* texts bore the potential for Morris's dream to become a reality.

2

DOUGLAS/*NEW AGE* ECONOMICS

THE TEXTS

In combination, Douglas's empirical observations of cost accounting in leading enterprises of his time and Orage's central position within guild socialism produced a powerful critique of the two major economic philosophies of capitalism and of the 'orthodox' varieties of socialism. All the major themes covered in the texts were developed, if only in embryonic form, in *Economic Democracy*. They were subsequently 'simplified', often to the point of obscurity, in later books, pamphlets, articles and speeches by Douglas and other proponents of social credit. Even in *Economic Democracy*, acknowledged to have been co-authored by Orage (Orage 1926: 435; Hattersley 1922), themes are incoherently juxtaposed, flowing from one to another not merely within the same paragraph but even within the convoluted sentences. 'Major Douglas' writings are not models of either clarity or concision' (*New Statesman* 1922: 553). Certain passages are unintelligible, whilst others acquire meaning only in conjunction with material in previous chapters or texts. In view of the complete absence of editing by the original author(s), the variety of simplistic and often misleading interpretations, sympathetic or otherwise, is scarcely remarkable. More remarkable is the furore of debate the texts generated, and the subsequent strength of the social credit movement which arose from them. Most surprising of all is the extent of grudging acknowledgement that Douglas's work aroused in contemporary intellectuals (discussed in Part II).

Mairet's *The Douglas Manual* (1934), an attempt to collate Douglas's writings under subject headings, is hardly more illuminating than the original texts or Douglas's 'post-Orage' writings. Although Finlay (1972) presents a partial (and sympathetic) summary of elements of Douglas's thought, the present account is the first systematic review of the original texts from outside the social credit movement.

BASIC PRINCIPLES

In S*ocial Credit Principles* (1924b) Douglas set out the basic philosophy behind 'social credit', the name most generally applied to the body of writings which originated from the Douglas/Orage collaboration. Economic organisation exists to meet demand with efficiency and minimum adverse impact upon other aspects of society and the environment. Three principles underlie the proposed reform of the financial system:

1 The cash credits available to the citizens of any country should, within a given period, be collectively equal to aggregate cash prices for consumable goods available for sale in that country. On the purchase of goods for consumption, these cash credits should be cancelled.
2 The credits required to finance production should not be supplied from savings. Investment should be financed from new credits relating to new production.
3 The distribution of cash credits (incomes) to individuals should be progressively less dependent upon employment. In other words, the dividend should gradually displace the wage and salary as the basic source of income (Douglas 1924b: 6).

Attempts to review individual social credit proposals in the light of orthodoxy are counterproductive: each theme exists within the framework of an alternative economic theory and social philosophy. Thus the control of credit issue and the provision of a universal benefit in the form of a National Dividend constitute part of a comprehensive scheme for an economic alternative to both private capitalism and 'socialism' more aptly described as state capitalism.

In the view of Henry Smith (1962), socialism is the economic equivalent of political freedom, equality and fellowship. Its defining criterion is the reduction to a minimum of conflict due to economic causes. It cannot occur where the motive power of the economy is dependent upon workers as consumers being stimulated to want higher standards of living so much that they feel compelled to work hard to achieve them. Public ownership cannot be taken as the defining criterion of socialism because it will not *necessarily* result in an absence of economic conflict. Economic conflict is likely to be eliminated only in a world where 'the marginal disutility of labour and the marginal efficiency of capital were both very low indeed' (Smith 1962: 208). It is argued here that the Douglas/*New Age* economics provides the basis of a socialist economics consistent with Smith's definition. That it failed to emerge to full adulthood was due to the economic, social and political factors related in Parts II and III.

On studying the texts Reckitt, a leading social crediter, became convinced that:

the creation of credit by the banks constituted the usurpation of a national function which was not only unjustifiable in itself, but had disastrous results; that the present hypotheses concerning what was assumed to be debt to the banks involved the accounting of unreal elements of cost into prices; and that as a result the community was not in a position to buy or exchange what it was able to produce – these contentions of the Douglas analysis seemed (and still seem) to me irresistible. The Douglas proposals follow from that analysis. The community must resume control over the conditions on which is issued what is essentially its own credit; it must establish a true basis for prices which will enable goods to be sold below financial cost; and instead of striving artificially to tie income to employment, it must distribute a proportion of the unearned increment of association in the form of a universal dividend.

(Reckitt 1941: 169)

Put simply, the motive power for the decommodification of labour, and hence for the introduction of an economics of socialism, is a relatively minor reform of finance.

The following pages summarise the main themes developed by Douglas and Orage between 1918 and 1922, described here as 'Douglas/*New Age* economics', which subsequently formed the basis of social credit theory. As in the case of the *Social Credit Principles* quoted above, use has been made of later texts where they provide a convenient summary of themes developed in the earlier publications. Although published after 1922, the book *Social Credit* (1924a) and the pamphlet *The Breakdown of the Employment System* (1923) provide some concise expositions of the original themes.

TIME AND MONEY: AN EXPLANATORY NOTE

In neoclassical theory time and money do not exist. Hence the revolutionary analysis of the Douglas/*New Age* economics appeared incompatible with economic orthodoxy based upon the assumptions underlying general competitive equilibrium. Within the bounds of orthodoxy the economic model can be 'fine-tuned' by Keynesian-style demand-side adjustments or monetarist supply-side modifications. It cannot, however, accommodate the realities of markets which do not clear, changing technology, a profit rate which is not always and everywhere equal and a financial system which is not functionally neutral. Until recently, a set of disguised postulates, essential to the simultaneous method, underpinned economic theorising: markets were thought to clear at each stage; technology was unchanging; the profit rate was equal; and money was a pure numeraire (Freeman 1995). Rejection of these postulates enables the Douglas analysis to be viewed as a comprehensive body of economics based upon non-equilibrium theory. As such it has relevance to the social and ecological problems of post-industrialisation.

Douglas observed that the economy is regulated by a system of finance designed for the pre-industrial era. Understanding of the role of finance in economic activity could lead to adaptation of the economy in order to provide the consumer with a sufficiency of economic welfare at the cost of minimum disutility of labour and environmental destruction. A financial system which can operate only by restricting consumption and creating a superfluity of production is limited in its usefulness. Under a rational system 'the limitations placed upon the distribution of goods shall be either the physical limitations of the productive system . . . [which technology has rendered virtually non-existent] . . . or the limitations imposed by psychological and physical satiety' (Douglas 1932: 21). At the heart of the matter is the general failure to recognise the nature of the relationship between production, distribution and finance.

Single-stage production

Douglas stressed that production does not create money. In order to bring into focus the relationship between production and exchange, it is possible to imagine a producer in a system of single-stage production. Having access to land (which has not been bought) and a second-hand spade (discarded), and having saved seed potato and horse manure (discarded), it is possible for a producer/farmer to plant, tend and harvest a potato crop at no financial cost. The crop can be put in a discarded sack and sold to a neighbour for £5. Has the producer created £5? Or any money at all? The transaction may have increased the purchasing power of money.

Nevertheless, at the point of exchange no value is created. However sophisticated the system, production of all commodities follows the same pattern as the potato example. All production requires inputs from the natural world, including land, fertilisers, minerals and other natural materials which the economy cannot create. All production requires human inputs. These fall into two categories. First, an inherited body of knowledge, as in the ability to save seed, cope with pests and drought and so on. Second, a 'producer', who may be employed or self-employed, but who comes to the task already physically developed from infancy to maturity and still requires social care. Neither form of 'human input' is produced through exchange on the market. The transformation of natural materials by the producer creates wealth. Wealth creation can take place outside the exchange economy.

Single-stage production and exchange

We can imagine two or more products, e.g. potatoes and leather shoes, being produced from the non-monetised economy through single-stage production and being exchanged through the medium of money. Where all products are of this type, money can facilitate a barter-style exchange system in which markets clear and money is a pure numeraire. In the idealised local market described by Braudel (1979: 228–30) supply and demand equal price, and perfect knowledge of the market can be assumed. Money operates according to standard definitions. It is a commodity in itself, in fixed supply. It cannot generate production but merely calls goods on to the market for exchange.

Up to this point the assumptions upon which micro-economic neoclassical theory are based hold true: the market clears at each act of circulation and money is a pure numeraire. Crucially, in single-stage production a large proportion of subsistence requirements can be seen to be produced outside the formal economy. Hence in newly monetised economies 'cheap' labour occurs because subsistence requirements continue to be provided from outside the cash economy.

Multiple-stage production and finance

Neoclassical general equilibrium theory is founded upon the assumption that the conditions described in the above section continue to apply in multiple-stage production, where labour becomes a commodity, 'the market' is national and international, and finance governs the initiation of production. The A + B theorem, which forms a key section of this chapter, demonstrates the dynamic relationship between incomes dispersed in the early period of multiple-stage production, accumulated costs and the money supply.

MONEY AND CREDIT

Money is the initiating element for any economic activity to take place in an industrial exchange economy. If the factors of production (land, labour and capital) are to be combined in a productive process, money is an essential prerequisite. If primary, intermediate or finished products are to be exchanged on the market, the presence or absence of money is the determining factor. Without money there is no production for exchange, so that no 'social labour' will occur. Production and exchange for money define capitalism. An analysis of money and its mode of creation is therefore essential to any examination of the operations of the economic system.

The uses of money

The texts explore the phenomenon of money in detail, noting that money is most properly described as a mechanism which has been designed for specific purposes. It has no intrinsic properties, only those which people choose to give it. Hence a comment such as 'There is no money in the country with which to do such and so' is meaningless, unless it is an indication that the goods and services required to perform the task in question do not exist and cannot be produced. In that event it would be useless to create the money equivalent of the non-existent resources. On the other hand, it is misleading to argue that the country has 'no money' for social betterment, or for any other purpose, when it possesses the skill, the labour and the material and plant to create that betterment. The financial system in the form of the banks or the Treasury can, if they so wish, create the necessary money in five minutes. Indeed, they are creating money for 'necessary' tasks every day, and have done so for centuries (Douglas 1922a: 1–2).

Money can be described as a 'ticket system', whereby money 'tickets' grant the right to participate in the economy. They function like railway tickets. The demand for a railway ticket offers the management of a railway a clear indication of the transport required. This makes it possible for a programme of transport to be drawn up, enabling the traveller to make appropriate plans. The ticket office is not the place where the measurement of productive capacity should take place. The proper role of the ticket office, or its financial equivalent, the banking system, is to enable the product or service to be distributed in accordance with the wishes of the consumer. Further, it is the function of the ticket office or bank to relay the indication of consumer preferences to those responsible for operating industry. The texts maintain that it is not the business of the banking system to determine what is produced, any more than it is the business of the railway ticket office to decide on travellers' right to travel, their destination or the conditions under which they travel (Douglas 1924a: 62–3). To orthodox economists steeped in general competitive equilibrium theory the dynamic relationship between money creation and policy formation in production and distribution was incomprehensible.

In examining the nature of money it is necessary to explore the relationship between money and production. The production of goods does not create money. Nor does money create value, or even measure value in any meaningful sense. If A. grows a ton of potatoes and exchanges those potatoes for five currency notes of £1 each held at the moment by A.'s neighbour, B., all that has happened is that A. possesses £5 that B. had before. A.'s ton of potatoes has not increased the number of pounds (money), although it may increase the purchasing power of each existing pound. If we postulate that this £5 is the only £5 in existence, and that money is the only effective demand for goods, no one will be able to exchange goods until A. relinquishes at least part of the original £5 (Douglas 1924a: 130–1).

The money value of the potatoes depends upon the quantity of money in existence at the particular point of time. Their value in relation to other goods is not affected by the quantity of money, by fluctuations in that quantity, or by the money value assigned to potatoes in comparison with other goods. However, in a multiple-stage industrial economy the ability of a farm to produce potatoes, or of a firm to produce industrial goods, is affected by the quantity of money available for the purchase of machinery, raw materials and labour. The expansion of money stimulates production, whilst its restriction inhibits production. The texts are clear that it is simplistic to imagine that production can be increased or checked merely by changing the amount of money in existence. The problems are to define exactly what money is, to know how it is created and to know how precisely its production is used to regulate economic activity.

The making of money

Money may take the form of cash or financial credit which is convertible into cash. The texts note that Walker defined money as 'any medium which has reached such a degree of acceptability that no matter what it is made of, and no matter why people want it, no one will refuse it in exchange for his product' (quoted in Douglas 1919b: 47). The means by which this vital commodity comes into existence is incredibly haphazard. The gold standard appeared to offer a degree of stability, but fluctuations in the amount of gold in existence may arbitrarily affect money values, as occurred, for instance, in 1890.

The texts refer to Arthur Kitson's observation that the credit structure was historically based upon gold, the existence of which bears no relation to human requirements for goods and services. In the past, gold production, quite illogically, exerted a disproportionate effect on the mechanism of prices and credit. The United Kingdom came off the gold standard in 1914, and only partially returned in 1925, after the texts were written. Although Britain finally abandoned the gold standard in 1931, Meade (1938) still counted it as a possible option in foreign trade. However, as the texts noted, even under the gold standard the public could destroy the credit structure based on gold by calling the bankers' bluff and demanding their paper credits be redeemed in gold at face value (Douglas 1920: 104). Furthermore, the commercial purposes for which paper credits (loans) could be issued on the strength of gold reserves were determined by the banks.

The amount of money in a community depends on the policy of the banking system. However, the use of gold, a commodity of relatively high intrinsic value, as a global monetary standard, replacing other forms of token money, blurred the distinction between the function of money as a medium of exchange and its secondary function as a store of wealth. As O'Duffy later explained, it is easy to slip into the belief that money is real wealth, even the only real wealth. In reality money will not feed or clothe anyone. 'A community of people wrecked on a fertile island would not starve for lack of gold' (O'Duffy 1934: 7). If all the gold in the world were to disappear overnight, farms and factories would still exist, and be capable of producing the necessities of life. However, for multiple-stage production and distribution to occur it would be necessary to invent some other medium of exchange. This indeed has happened. Writing in the 1930s, O'Duffy followed Douglas in demonstrating that paper money, including cheques, is acceptable not because people believe it can be redeemed in the form of gold but because they have faith that it will be redeemed in the form of goods. Belief is what gives paper money its value. 'The function of money is to facilitate *the exchange of wealth*; and it derives its value purely from the willingness of the people to accept it' (O'Duffy 1934: 7, emphasis added). The differentiation between money and wealth is fundamental to the Douglas/*New Age* analysis.

In popular belief, banking is understood to be no more than a private pawnbroking transaction between borrower and lender: lenders place their savings in a bank, and borrowers take that same money to invest in new machinery, labour and materials. In reality the banker is in a 'unique position. He is probably the only known instance of the possibility of lending something without parting with anything, and making a profit on the transaction' (Douglas 1923). The bank lends new money: bank loans create deposits. Since bank loans/deposits constitute money, the quantity of money and the uses to which it can be put are dependent upon these transactions (Douglas 1922c: 143). Every credit transaction affects the interests of every person in the credit area concerned, either through its effect upon prices or through the diversion of the energies available for production purposes (Douglas 1922c: 144). An overdraft, arranged perhaps on the basis of the title deeds of a factory, facilitates production. However, the overdraft is new money exactly as if the banker had coined goods for sale (Douglas 1920: 31–2). Practically all the money loaned by banks is fresh purchasing power.

Hence the granting of credit by a financial institution is more realistically viewed as the creation of a mortgage on future production than as the allocation of the past savings of industry. As bankers explained, in a booklet provided for the Canadian House of Commons Committee on Banking and Commerce in 1923, to which Douglas gave evidence:

> Nearly all loans are made by credits entered on the books of a bank or by cheques or by drafts or by acceptances; these pass into the general clearings of the community of which only the resulting balances are settled in money. Hence the mere plentifulness of money is only remotely connected with the supply of loanable funds.
>
> (House of Commons, Canada 1923: 425)

The multiple expansion process lies at the heart of the modern monetary system. The term 'deposits' is highly misleading, implying something deposited for safe keeping, like jewels in a safe deposit. Bank deposits are not like that. The deposits of commercial banks are to them liabilities, although they are assets of their holders. The banks' assets are their reserves, i.e. currency plus deposits with other banks, and their loans and investments, such as bonds and other securities. Since the inception of banking, the growth of deposits in this way has increased the total sum of money, far beyond that available to be held in reserves. As later explained in an encyclopaedia:

A bank that received, say, $100 in gold might add $25 to its reserves and lend out $75. But the recipient of the $75 loan would himself spend it. Some of those who received gold in this way would hold it as gold but others would deposit it in this bank or in other banks. If, for example, two-thirds was redeposited, some bank or banks would find $50 added to deposits and to reserves and would repeat the process, adding $12½ to its reserves and lending out $37½. When this multiple expansion process worked itself out fully, total deposits would have increased by $200, bank reserves by $50, and $50 of the initial $100 deposited would have been retained as 'currency outside banks'.

(*Encyclopaedia Britannica* 1979: 352)

This is the principle upon which the banking system as a whole, rather than one individual bank, creates money. The process of money creation is inextricably bound up with the operation of the overall economy.

Money as an institution

Money is the initiating element for any activity to take place in an industrial exchange economy. Following Marx, the activity may be termed 'production', the appropriation of nature within the social relations of the workplace, or the activity may be termed 'circulation', the appropriation of the product within the social relations between people inside and outside the labour process. In either case, money is the essential prerequisite if the factors of production are to be combined in a productive process. If primary, intermediary or finished products are to be exchanged on the market, the presence or absence of money is the determining factor. Without money there is no production for exchange; no 'social labour', as Marx calls it, will take place. Freeman (1995: 56) has pointed out that 'the exchange of commodities for money is what capitalism *is*' (emphasis original). While the Douglas/*New Age* texts, and Marx before them, remained fully conscious of the critical role of money in the functioning of the economy, economic orthodoxy dropped the concept of money as anything but a pure numeraire in the construction of general equilibrium analysis. A lot flows from this apparently small point. 'Money,' according to Marx, 'is not a thing, it is a social relation . . . a production relation like any other economic relation' (Marx 1941: 68). In other words, money is an institution serving particular social needs.

To recap, money is constantly being created by the banking system for specific purposes. As it is created, the quantity of money in existence, its velocity of circulation and its relationship with the quantity of goods and services on offer in the economy at any one time can be monitored. Within certain limits it can be controlled to serve particular ends. Problems occur when the banking system operates according to its own agenda, with the requirements of the consumer a secondary consideration.

Banks and the control of credit issue

From the above, it becomes apparent that all countries with an industrial economy contain 'an institution whose business it is to issue money. This institution is called a bank. Unlike the social reform business, the banking business is immensely powerful, talks very little, acts quickly, knows what it wants, chooses its employees wisely in its own interests' (Douglas 1922b: 46). The quantity of money is dependent upon the power of the banker's pen. Banks create new money which ranks equally with legal tender as a means of exchange (Douglas 1923). Although credit is more properly regarded as common property, it is administered by the banker primarily for the purpose of private profit (Douglas 1919b: 118). The ability of the banks to create money in the form of credit for private advantage enables the whole system of production and distribution to function.

According to orthodox theory, money, equivalent to the price of every article which is produced, exists in the pocket, or in the bank, of somebody somewhere in the world. In other words, it is assumed that the collective sum of the wages, salaries and dividends distributed in respect of the articles for sale at any given moment, which represents collective price, is available as purchasing power at the same moment. Some persons may have more money in their pocket or bank than they wish to spend on consumable goods. They may choose not to spend it, but instead to save it. By abstaining from consuming, they form a fund which enables capital goods, such as tools, plant and factories, to be paid for, and therefore to be produced. This process of payment ensures that capital goods become the property of those individuals who have 'saved' (Douglas 1924a: 83–4).

In reality, people who save and invest money do not save goods. They merely transfer their claim from the original commodities in existence to those produced and sold in a future period. Furthermore, they expect an increased share of them as a reward for investment. Crucially, the money which they use to spend or invest is constantly created and destroyed by the banking system for its own financial advantage (Douglas 1924a: 84–5).

Technically, since the Banking Act of 1844 the British banking system has based its operations on the ultimate liability to pay gold. In practice the community has come to accept cheques and bills according to its estimate of the bank credit of the individual or corporation issuing the document.

People are not concerned about the ability of the bank to meet the document with gold, and hence bank credit consists of no more than figures in a ledger. Consequently the question arises as to the criteria used by a bank to increase credit by the creation of loans to a particular applicant seeking that facility. The answer is straightforward: the bank looks at an individual's likely capacity to pay money. Credit is extended solely to the extent that bankers are satisfied that this condition will be met (Douglas 1922b: 52–3). Effectively capitalism could be renamed 'creditism', i.e. the dominance of financial credit over real credit. The texts depict finance as exerting a dominant policy formation role in the system of production, distribution and exchange.

'Real' and 'financial' credit

Exploration of the relationship between finance and material production and consumption is central to the understanding of all aspects of the Douglas/*New Age* texts. Under orthodox tenets, financial viability determines choices even when needs go unmet while resources lie idle. A prerequisite of any economic activity to occur is the belief, amounting to a religious conviction, that the outcome perceived is the likely result. The faith or 'credit' which provides the motive power for the economy is divided into two categories: 'financial credit' and 'real credit'. 'Financial credit', the estimated capacity of the ability to pay money, is the driving force behind the creation of loan credit. Financial credit controls production policy and is generated by the banking system (Douglas 1922b: 35). In other words, purchasing power is created on financial criteria. Producers of goods can borrow to initiate production if they are also potential producers of money. In his explanatory notes on the Draft Mining Scheme, which appear in the appendix to *Credit-Power and Democracy*, Orage distinguishes between 'real' and 'financial' credit:

> If we say that Real Credit concerns the supply of goods while Financial Credit concerns the supply of money, the distinction may be a little clearer. Real Credit is not measured by the actual supply of goods, but by their *potential* supply. The measure of Real Credit is, in fact, the correct estimate of ability to produce and deliver goods as and when and where required . . . by the potential consumer.
> (Douglas 1920: 156–7, original emphasis)

Real credit is the 'effective reserve of energy belonging to the community'. Its administration has fallen to the banking system and financial institutions generally. Consequently the 'creative energy of mankind' becomes subject to artificial restrictions which bear no relationship to the realities of everyday existence (Douglas 1919b: 118). The potential real wealth of society is communal in origin, and should therefore be subject to the control of the entire community. Financial credit is administered by the banking system 'primarily for the purpose of private profit' (Douglas 1919b: 118). It is more accurate to view financial credit as communal property, rather than a focus for vested interests, the financial institutions.

The texts note that banking originated as a private venture, observing that at the time of writing the Bank of England remained a private institution. Nevertheless, the guild socialists did not consider that a politically controlled central bank would be truly independent of private banking interests. Just as state capitalism, i.e. a socialist government under the existing economic conditions, would produce wage slavery as effectively as private capitalism, so too would state banking continue the *status quo* in terms of financial control over industrial policy. Hence Orage's derision at the Labour Party, on its rejection of the 'Douglas/*New Age* Scheme' in 1922, opting for a policy of nationalising the central bank (Douglas 1922a).

The distinction between 'real' and 'financial' credit is a central theme. 'Real credit' is the 'dynamic capacity' of the community to deliver goods and services as and when required. 'Financial credit' appears to be no more than a device through which this capacity is utilised. In fact financial credit measures the rate at which an individual or organisation can produce money. The link between money and commodities may at times be tenuous (Douglas 1922b: 2). In this analysis, the word 'demanded' is equivalent to 'required', as distinct from the economic term denoting 'called on to the market'. The distinction draws attention to the ability to draw profit from scarcity, whether real or artificially induced through advertising or other means.

The properties of money are central to the operation of the economy. If people are asked why they produce certain goods, they will reply that they need to 'make' money. In a lecture to the National Guilds League in September 1919, Douglas anticipated Maslow (1970) in noting that individuals want money for two reasons. In the first place they need money to obtain goods and services essential for subsistence. In the second place, however, they seek money 'to give expression, often perverted, to the creative instinct through power' (Douglas 1922b: 53–4). The initiation of production is determined by control of the issuing of credit. Thereafter, articles can be forced on a 'misguided public' by 'advertisement and monopoly'. The public exercise no 'valid, flexible, active control' over the initiation, development and modification of production (Douglas 1920: 91–2).

The economy as at present constituted would cease to operate if the financial mechanisms did not constantly provide a source of purchasing power, i.e. new money, in the form of bank loans and credit instruments. The money does not arise out of wages, salaries or dividends paid out for past production. The creation of 'financial credit' ensures that 'industry becomes mortgaged to the banking system' (Douglas 1924a: 95).

Appreciation of the role of finance in initiating economic activity was noted in *The National Guilds*, edited by Orage (1914) and originally printed as a series of articles by S.G. Hobson in the *New Age* in 1912–13. A 'great financial network covers the world', operating on an informal but highly centralised basis. 'To this power principalities bow; it rules the rulers of kingdoms' (Orage 1914: 173). Here Hobson and Orage note the difficulty of operating the guild idea within the capitalist financial system. The problem was 'to meet effective demand [i.e. real need] unhampered by the dominance of finance . . . Guild administration associated with private capitalism would be a contradiction in terms' (Orage 1914: 178). The whole banking system would have to be reformed, since banks were 'purely capitalistic organisations, buying and selling money for profit' (Orage 1914: 178). Having abolished interest and the wage system, the guilds would have to struggle against falling into dependence upon the gold standard or any other capitalist monetary system for the purposes of international trade. At this point, Hobson and Orage went no further than suggesting that the (industry-based) guilds would have to become their own bankers, working through a national clearing house (Orage 1914: 178–84). Douglas provided a crucial insight with his 'A + B theorem'.

'Real' and 'financial' terminology

The distinction between 'real' and 'financial' wealth, like the distinction between 'real' and 'financial' capital, was, and remains, a difficult one to assimilate. In terms of neoclassical orthodoxy there is no such distinction. 'Capital' means physical stock, measured in money terms and transferable in the form of financial tokens. Similarly 'wealth' is the power to call upon physical goods and services, although it may take the form of token promises to pay. The Douglas/*New Age* texts can be read by mentally dropping the word 'real', and interpreting all references to 'capital' and 'wealth' in orthodox terms. The result is to render the Douglas/*New Age* economics unintelligible.

The ability to draw a distinction between 'real' and 'financial' is crucial to an understanding of the texts. Real capital is the potential to make the commodities required by the community. Financial capital is the potential to make a financial return. The latter may occur through the production of waste in the form, for example, of disposable packaging or junk mail. Equally, it may occur through pure speculation. 'Financial' indicates 'a paper title to'. Whether the paper title is to 'wealth' or to 'capital', it bears no *necessary* relation to the potential to meet the physical, social or spiritual requirements of the community. The distinction between 'real' and 'financial' can be seen in the concept of alternative economic indicators as explored in the 1990s (Anderson 1991). Car crashes may increase financial wealth through the generation of insurance claims, demand for new cars, hospital care and so forth. However, it appears rational only in terms of neoclassical orthodoxy to reckon the emotional, physical and environmental damage resulting from a road accident as an increase in 'wealth'. The incapacity of neoclassical orthodoxy to distinguish between 'real' and 'financial' wealth has profound implications for policy formation in the spheres of production, distribution and exchange.

THE A + B THEOREM

Douglas noted that existing financial arrangements necessitate a steady, escalating expansion of financial credit, i.e. debt. They require constantly growing production, which can find effective demand only through exports and the issue of more credit. Since price is a linear function of cost, distribution is limited and controlled by those with large credits (Douglas 1922b: 58).

The situation was first analysed in *Economic Democracy*. Here Douglas and Orage observed that any organisation engaged in production has two functions: it operates within the economy to produce goods or services but it also possesses a financial aspect. It acts 'as a device for the distribution of purchasing power to individuals through the media of wages, salaries, and dividends' (Douglas 1920: 22) while simultaneously it determines prices, what may be termed 'financial values'. A firm's payments fall into two groups: (A) payments made to individuals in the form of wages, salaries and dividends, and (B) payments made to other organisations in respect of purchases of raw materials and other costs (see Fig. 1). In effect, purchasing power flows to individuals through the 'A' payments. However, all payments, present (in the form of 'A' payments) and past (in the form of 'B' payments), must be incorporated to determine the price at which the final goods are offered for sale. Therefore commodities appear on the market at prices which reflect both 'A' and 'B' payments, although some of the items for which 'B' payments have been made in the past do not appear on the current consumer market, being intermediate goods (machinery, energy, past labour and so forth). Hence 'since A will not purchase A + B, a proportion of the product at least equivalent to B must be distributed by a form of purchasing power which is not comprised in the descriptions grouped under A' (Douglas 1920: 21–4). The necessary additional purchasing power is supplied by a constant flow of loans, bank overdrafts or export credit. Clearly this is a straightforward statement of fact. Money is constantly created to finance future production so that goods manufactured in a previous period can be exchanged at present prices. Past costs are incurred at past prices determined by past market conditions. There is no necessary connection between past costs and present prices.

Goods which appear on the market have been produced on borrowed money. The money used to buy them goes to extinguish the debt. That

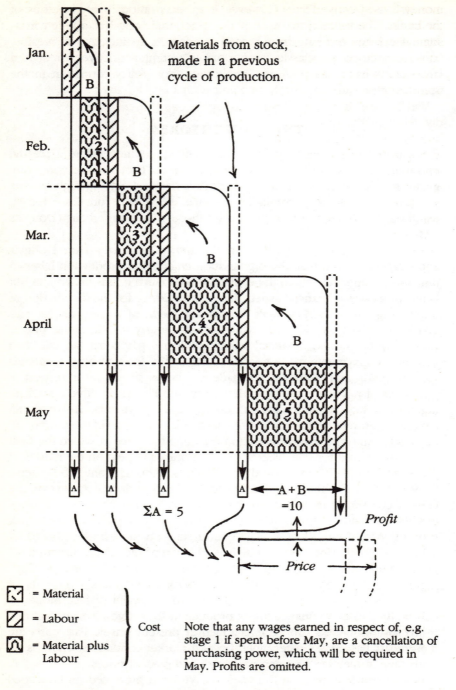

Materials from stock, made in a previous cycle of production.

Jan.

Feb.

Mar.

April

May

ΣA = 5

A + B = 10

Price

Profit

[X] = Material

[/] = Labour

[M] = Material plus Labour

} Cost

Note that any wages earned in respect of, e.g. stage 1 if spent before May, are a cancellation of purchasing power, which will be required in May. Profits are omitted.

Figure 1 The A + B theorem. *Source* Douglas (1931b: 31).

money is itself derived from credits which were previously borrowed from the banks. The value of that money must therefore appear in selling prices somewhere, to be recovered in due course from the consumer so that the banks can be repaid their advances. As one credit is cancelled, another larger credit has to be created in order to circulate the additional production (Douglas 1920: 21–4).

Without the 'B' payments (which may be spent on wages, salaries and dividends in the production of intermediate products) people could not buy the existing volume of consumable goods. They must therefore remain in a state of permanent servility to the manufacturers and the financiers who hold ultimate control. Note that Douglas appears to include plant and machinery as 'intermediate products'. The following amplification of the 'A + B theorem' develops Mehta's (1983) exposition, which derives largely from Douglas's response to J.A. Hobson (Douglas 1922c).

The 'A + B theorem' sets out to explore the way in which purchasing power is created and distributed in a dynamic economy. Purchasing power is distributed in respect of capital production and ultimate consumer products. Virtually all purchasing power is retrieved in the prices of consumer products. In effect, this leaves the community in the position of having bought both the plants and the product, but having got delivery, i.e. control, only of the product (Douglas 1920: 34–5). Control of 'the plant' remains with the creators of financial credit, who thereby determine economic activity, since purchasing power distributed in respect of future production is increasingly drawn from financial credit created by the banks. The ability of banks to create credit is crucial to the continuation of economic activity and the maintenance of economic equilibrium.

The creation of bank credit for the purpose of investment is both demand-increasing and capacity-creating. Note that:

> the wages, salaries and dividends distributed during a given period do not, and cannot, buy the production of that period; that production can only be bought, i.e. distributed under present conditions by a draft, and an increasing draft, on the purchasing power in respect of future production, and this latter is mainly and increasingly derived from financial credit created by the banks.
>
> (Douglas 1922c: 140–1)

The economy is essentially dynamic.

> It is not physically possible for the incomes of the current week to buy the production of the current week because the products of that week are not yet available for purchase on the market (see Fig. 1). On average, it may be up to six months before they do come on to the market. Present incomes are buying the production of a fairly long past period. This is done by drawing on the purchasing power which

goes to make up the future costs of an unknown quantity and variety of goods which will be delivered at some time in the future.

(Douglas 1922c: 140)

Douglas amplifies this statement by explaining that 'the rate at which money can be spent this week does not depend at all on the goods which can be, and are, supplied this week'. Any increase in the money paid out in this period, for whatever purposes, is in effect inflationary. It results in a widening of effective demand, which acts both to stimulate production and to raise prices. 'There is nothing in the arrangement which guarantees that a larger amount of consumable goods per head can be bought in the future as a result of a larger amount of money distributed this week' (Douglas 1922c: 125).

In other words, 'B' payments are a form of new purchasing power which stimulates demand and hence prices in the present period without simultaneously increasing supply in that same period. However, current investment increases the supply of consumer goods in the future period. Hence 'B' payments of the right amount must be undertaken in the future: if the production of the present period is to be distributed, a debt based upon the purchasing power in respect of future production must be created. Significantly, it must be an increasing debt on future purchasing power if markets are to clear, maintaining equilibrium in the economy.

In a barter economy with little division of labour, single-stage production and exchange based on a double coincidence of wants, demand and supply are readily matched, so that general overproduction is impossible. In an industrialised economy, however, a mismatch is possible unless remedial action is taken. Douglas focused upon the dynamics of financial flows caused by the ever increasing time lag created by new technologies between the original financing of a productive process and the appearance of the finished commodity on the market.

Foster and Catchings (1925: 308–11) pursued a similar line of argument. Assuming a single corporation, that consumers spend all their income within the year they receive it and that sales dispose of the output of the previous year, the situation will be:

Output (units of goods)	1,000,000
Sales (units)	1,000,000
Receipts ($)	1,000,000
Wages ($)	900,000
Dividends ($)	100,000

Index of prices = 100

The above rests on the assumption that the supply of money remains constant. The existence of a bank can be posited. If the bank lends the corporation $90,000, $90,000 is added to the total volume of money in circulation. Assuming that the corporation uses the money to increase its production in the current year by 100,000 units, and, to do so, pays out all its new money in wages, the statement for that year would be:

Output (units of goods)	1,100,000
Sales (units)	1,000,000
Receipts ($)	1,090,000
Wages ($)	990,000
Dividends($)	100,000

Index of prices = 109

Note that sales are in respect of the output of the previous year. The increased output of the current year is yet to arrive on the market. Prices rise because demand (wages) increased while supply remained constant.

Foster and Catchings point out, however, that 'in the following year, prices cannot be sustained at the new level of 109 unless there is not only another increase in the volume of money, but *a larger increase* than in the previous year' (emphasis in original). This is demonstrated by a third balance sheet:

Output (units of goods)	1,200,000
Sales (units)	1,100,000
Receipts ($)	1,180,000
Wages ($)	1,080,000
Dividends ($)	100,000

Index of prices = 107

As production expands over a period the volume of money is increased, resulting in a higher price level which can be sustained only if the volume of money rises at an accelerating rate. Under capitalism prices cannot fall below cost plus a minimum rate of profit, since profit provides the inducement to produce (Douglas 1922c: 141). The above scenario would be radically altered if the corporation was merely content to recoup the extra $90,000 outlay and break even.

Investment increases the capacity to produce over the long run: it expands the community's 'real credit'. However, Douglas noted that, under capitalist finance, technological innovation must lead to rising prices (instead of falling prices, as might logically be anticipated), or unemployment and a consequent failure of distribution (Douglas 1922c: 141). In the dynamic economy here described a rise in money supply in the present period is essential to generate investment in future production. The creation of a 'just price' mechanism to regulate prices through relating productivity to consumption would bring finance into line with the volume of material resources (i.e. land, labour and productive capital). Inventions designed to increase supply and decrease prices would cease to provide an incentive to wasteful production as an alternative to a failure in distribution (Douglas 1919b: 110; 1924a: 97–105).

IMPLICATIONS OF THE A + B THEOREM

The implications of the 'A + B theorem' are repeated throughout the texts: money is constantly created and destroyed by the financial system for the specific purpose of making money in the future. The speech to the National Guilds League, first published in the *New Age* in 1919 and reprinted in *The Control and Distribution of Production* (Douglas 1922b), makes it clear that the 'A + B theorem' is not seeking to suggest a deficiency in purchasing power. Sufficient purchasing power exists in the system. The problem lies with the impact of seemingly neutral accounting mechanisms upon policy formation. By issuing financial credit, banks create a claim upon future production. They base their operations on faith. The banking system generates purchasing power by issuing overdrafts to capitalists. Individual capitalists require no more consuming power than anyone else. They need food, clothes and lodging in adequate proportions. Their surplus purchasing power is therefore invested largely in machinery and raw materials. As a result, production is stimulated. The increased output called from the community is 'that which is required by the industrial machine'. Although money is distributed by this process, there is no reason to suppose that the production which results is required by humanity. The net result is that the cost of living is constantly rising, while the production of useless as well as useful items is stimulated on an increasing scale (Douglas 1922b: 56–7). Passages of this type indicate that the Douglas/*New Age* texts originally promoted an economics of sufficiency, having faith in the ability of an industrial economy to meet need and abolish 'wage slave' labour.

The texts draw a distinction between 'financial costs' and 'real costs'. They note that financial costs do not necessarily relate to real costs. The investor finances capital goods in order to receive an increased amount of money in the future. This money must be recouped from the public in the form of prices which include all aspects of costs. As a result, 'there are more goods in the world at each successive interval of time, because of the financial saving, and its application to fresh production'. In the meantime 'the interest, depreciation and obsolescence on this financial saving has to be carried forward into the prices of production during a succeeding period' (Douglas 1924a: 85). In other words, the negative value of depreciation, obsolescence and scrapped material is included in the costs which determine the prices at which goods can be distributed (Douglas 1919b: 150–1). Here again, the terminology is close enough to convention to be misleading. 'Depreciation' as used in the texts includes past labour, energy and raw materials expended throughout the course of production from 'cradle to grave', not merely capital depreciation.

Capitalism operates a mythical financial accounting system, manufacturing a constant increase in financial wealth that is only tenuously connected with the needs of society and the physical reality in which it exists.

> You seize any unconsidered trifle of matter which may be lying about
> . . . and you make it into something else . . . You assert by a process
> of arithmetic legerdemain known as cost accounting that the value of
> the original matter which we may call 'a' is now a+(b+c)+(d+e), 'b'
> being labour, 'c' being overhead charges, 'd' selling charges and 'e'
> profit, and that the 'wealth' of the country is increased by this oper-
> ation in respect of a sum equal to (b+c+d+e). With the aid of your
> banking system you now create credits . . .
>
> (Douglas 1922b: 45–6)

These 'credits' are supposed to reflect the increased 'wealth', minus any loss or depreciation. However, during the productive process power is dissipated, tools depreciate, and food, clothing and shelter are consumed by the work force. In reality, the result is *a* minus any portion of *a* lost in conversion. The community pays out *b*, *c*, *d*, *e* and so on, as the price of the increased adaptability of *a* to its 'needs', real or superfluous. The resulting gain, if any, to the community from this constant increase in 'production' is measurable only in terms of the peculiar cost-accounting financial system which drives the productive mechanism (Douglas 1922b: 45–6).

The effect is to frustrate the potential for liberation from toil which technological developments offer. If the production of essential goods and services is to be 'shifted from the backs of men to the backs of machines' it will be necessary to replace the 'outworn financial system', which was designed to meet the needs of the pre-machine age (Douglas 1920: 20). As new and lengthier operations are added to the productive process the rate at which 'B' payments are incurred is greater than the rate at which 'A' payments are made unless 'production, production, and yet more production' takes place, no matter what the nature of that production may be or its usefulness in satisfying human needs (Douglas 1922b: 45).

At present, goods and services are distributed through the productive system. However many commodities exist, they can be consumed only if people do more waged labour and produce more. There is no *necessary* link between an increase in 'B' payments and hence costs, and an increase in 'A' payments in the form of wages and salaries. Improvements in productive processes may simultaneously result in an increased output of goods and a decreased ability to purchase those goods from available wages and salaries. Although 'B' payments have clearly 'at some previous time been represented by payments of wages, salaries and dividends . . . it is irrelevant. The whole economic system is in ceaseless motion – purchasing power is constantly flowing back from individuals into the credit system from whence it came' (Douglas 1920: 25–6).

'B' payments can be seen as the 'financial representation of the lever of capital'. They are constantly increasing relative to 'A' payments. This means that in order to keep 'A' and the goods purchased with 'A' at a constant value, A + B must expand with every improvement of technological processes. Simultaneously the increased production must be of a type paid for by 'B' payments. At the time Douglas was writing, credit could not be extended for consumer goods. It had to take the form either of factory buildings and machinery for the production of which bank overdrafts could be obtained, or of production for export (Douglas 1920: 25–6).

The 'A + B theorem' breaks with neoclassical convention in observing that markets do not clear during each act of circulation, and that money does not act purely as a numeraire. In describing a dynamic economy in which real, i.e. disequilibrium, prices operate, Douglas equates more closely to reality than does neoclassical theory.

The just price

The original concept of a 'just price' arises from medieval times when 'arts and crafts made industry almost a sacrament, and faulty execution a social and even a legal offence'. At that time the just price mediated exchange. The idea of buying in the cheapest and selling in the dearest market was classed as usury, punishable by heavy penalties. Since the industrial revolution, technological progress offers the opportunity to create an improved economy without losing the valuable features of the past. The concept of the 'just price' reflects this situation by creating a fulcrum to establish equality between output and aggregate purchasing power at an administered 'fair' level of prices (Douglas 1919b: 100–1).

In orthodox theory supply and demand mediate between seller and buyer in such a way as to secure mutual satisfaction between the two as equilibrium is established. However, price is not, in the real world, established solely through the forces of supply and demand. 'Only the upper limit of price is thus governed, the lower limit, which under free competition would be the ruling limit, being fixed by cost plus the minimum of profit' (Douglas 1919b: 67–8). A glut of goods, deriving from economies of scale, will not bring prices down, since all costs, including deterioration and depreciation, must go into succeeding costs to determine price. The accumulation of past spending over an indefinite period determines cost. The cash price, on the other hand, requires 'a purchasing power effective at the moment of purchase' (Douglas 1919b: 68).

Costs incurred over past periods in the production cycle must be recovered if the manufacturer is to stay in business. However, the money associated with those costs has already been dispersed in the previous cycle. Depending on the conditions of the time, it may be necessary to sell above the price dictated by the interaction of supply and demand in order to recover costs. In these circumstances the extra goods will be consumed only if extra money (credit) is created in respect of future production. The just price would regulate the issue and the withdrawal of this extra element, leaving supply and demand to operate as orthodoxy suggests they do, i.e. free from the compulsive economic growth element (Douglas 1919b: 55).

The Douglas/*New Age* texts argue that the economy is not an end in itself. It is the means of satisfying the requirements of human beings and enabling them to proceed with other aspects of their lives – social, political, artistic. They note that in the manufacturing process certain items that form an element in final cost are rendered useless during production. Such 'semi-manufactures' may include, for example, electric power used for lighting in the cotton mill. By contrast, electric power used to meet direct human need is a final product.

A 'semi-manufacture' is an item to be reckoned in the assessment of 'real credit', i.e. the potential capacity to produce ultimate products (the sole object of manufacture). It represents 'an increase in credit-capital, but not of wealth' (Douglas 1919b: 126). On this assumption it is possible to envisage a clearing house to monitor the transfer of real credit between firms in the stages of manufacture in an economy based on production for use rather than exchange.

Assume a clearing house and three firms. Jones and Co. (JC) tan leather, Brown and Co. (BC) make boots and Robinson (R) sells boots. The undertakings are run on the basis of commission or profit on all labour and salary costs. The system operates as follows: JC receive raw hides to the value of £100 which require semi-manufactures to the value of £500 plus expenditure of £500 in wages and salaries to turn the hides into leather. JC turn the invoices for the hides and semi-manufactures over to the clearing house, which issues a cheque for £600 with which JC settle their accounts. The clearing house writes *up* its capital account by this sum (as for all sums it issues). JC therefore have out-of-pocket expenses (for wages, etc.) of £500. If 10 per cent profit is allowed, the cost + profit is £550. A sum of £600 is owed to the clearing house.

BC order hides from JC plus supplies from elsewhere to make boots, and submit these invoices to the clearing house, which issues a cheque to BC. BC pay JC, who retain £550 and clear their account with the clearing house by repaying the £600. BC expend a further £500 in salaries and wages and make 10 per cent profit on this. R orders the boots, and pays with a cheque from the clearing house for £2,000 which goes to BC, who pay off their debt of £1,650 and retain the remainder. R's out-of-pocket costs and commission are £300.

The purchasing power released externally in these transactions takes the form of wages, salaries and commission. As yet no goods have been released to consumers against this purchasing power (which will have been spent on existing goods), only the surplus remaining to be spent on R's stock. At this point a 'retail clearing invoice' is introduced which describes the goods and the amount paid by the purchaser for articles of ultimate consumption. The clearing house process distributes the means of purchase so that it becomes possible to fix the final price without reference to the individual interests of BC, JC or R. Cost has been charged to capital account (Douglas 1919b: 127–30).

Assume the monthly sum involved in delivering the boots to the users is £2,500. This is the total cost of the retail invoices turned in to the clearing house each month. Services to the token value of £2,500 have been rendered and remunerated over an indefinite period in the past, while the product of those services is distributed in the current month. It is necessary to set this token measure against a general value. The general value is equal to the depreciation or consumption of all goods which can be bought with the token sum. If the latter is 40 per cent, 60 per cent of the total work of the community remains available for use in a subsequent period. In this instance, the selling price of a pair of boots would be equal to 40 per cent of £2,500 divided by the number of pairs of boots distributed (*not* produced), i.e. two-fifths of commercial cost.

Therefore, in respect of the £2,500 retail invoices turned in by R (including his own labour and commission), R would be credited with 60 per cent of that sum against the cheque originally sent to him. He recovers the remaining 40 per cent from the sale of the boots and reimburses the clearing house. The clearing house writes *down* its own credits by that amount, which leaves the credit-capital of the community (the financial estimate of its capacity to deliver goods) written up by 60 per cent of £2,500, an accounting reflection of the productive situation.

All semi-manufactures are a form of capital asset. Whether they are tools which wear out over a period of years or units of energy which are dissipated in a few minutes driving an implement, they must be written down from time to time. Hence all semi-manufactures are treated as additions to communal account, subject to writing-down as they are consumed. It may be necessary to devise separate accounts for the installation of new technology and buildings for which 'writing down' (i.e. depreciation) is calculated over longer periods (Douglas 1919b: 125–32).

Implications of the just price

Just price maintains a relationship between money issued and the goods against which it is issued. For the relationship to be maintained, prices must be related to costs. The value of the unit in which costs and prices are computed must be consistently related to the changing ratio between production and consumption. At the time Douglas was writing this was not satisfactorily attained by any of the devices designed to stabilise money, because a stabilised unit of money involves the adjustment of past values on a scale which is 'fantastically impracticable'. However, it is possible to vary the purchasing power of such units without varying the accounting figures which apply to plant, machines and other real property (Douglas 1924a: 191–2).

An accurate unit of account derives from the ratio:

$$\frac{\text{consumption}}{\text{production}}$$

which is, in effect, a commodity standard as distinct from a gold standard or a labour theory of value. Hence:

$$\text{price (\pounds)} \ = \ \text{cost (\pounds)} \ \times \ \frac{p + d}{c + tp}$$

where p = cost of ultimate products consumed, d = depreciation of real capital in $\pounds$, c = credit created (in $\pounds$) and tp = cost of total production ($\pounds$) (Douglas 1919b: 192; 1920: 130–1).

In this example 'price' indicates 'just price'. Consequently values can be adjusted automatically in accordance with day-to-day observations of the relationship between supply and demand. In effect, according to Douglas (1924a: 192), the price factor becomes a question of measuring, for a selected period, the

$$\frac{\text{mean consumption rate}}{\text{mean production rate}}$$

The overall result is to create a direct relationship between effective demand and prices, as distinct from the relationship between cost and prices. The units issued to the individuals who comprise society must be such that the individuals receive in exchange all consumer goods and services which the economy can ultimately deliver. The capacity of society (in the form of plant, culture and organisation) to deliver commodities, the real credit of society, can be measured, and a consistent relationship can be maintained between the production of ultimate (consumer) goods and the expansion of capacity through the production of capital goods. Output can be moulded to the needs of consumers, so that the credits in the hands of the public are sufficient to buy the total possible output of society.

Practicality of the just price

The texts note that the practical difficulties of implementing such a pricing scheme are easily overestimated. The 'just price' proposals are, in essence, little different from the transactions in everyday operations of business. At present these operations are infinitely varied not only between different organisations but also within different departments of the same firm. By comparison the introduction of a uniform price factor would be a matter of elementary simplicity (Douglas 1924a: 193).

On a national scale, the necessary information already exists for removing the price-fixing process from the artificial operations of capitalist finance. All institutions in the economy (banks, the Treasury, the Inland Revenue, government departments, factories, farms and trade unions) produce statistical information. Douglas used early 'tabulating machines' to process the accounts at Farnborough aircraft factory in 1916–18 and was well placed to predict the ease with which complex accounting procedures could be undertaken in the future. Contemporary administration of personal income tax, VAT and benefit systems demonstrates that a 'just price' mechanism could not be ruled out purely on grounds of administrative impracticability. As Douglas later pointed out, given the political will, a variety of models could be devised to produce the desired effects, e.g. the payment of credit in the form of Treasury drafts issued via the banking system (Douglas 1931a: 106–7). Whichever system was adopted, the common feature would be the close association between credit creation and price fixing. The two are inseparably linked. To create (new) credit without the price-fixing element would be inflationary (Douglas 1923: 11–12).

Habits of thought are powerful. The suggestion that the just price of an article may be a mere percentage of its cost could, and did, induce incredulity. Nevertheless, as Orage and Douglas repeatedly pointed out, the present system results in incredible waste of materials and effort. 'Every economic force is driving the [world] community irresistibly towards war.' Perhaps, therefore, 'it is worthwhile to consider whether the accepted principles of price-making are so sacred that a world must be brought to ashes rather than that they should be analysed and revised' (quoted in Mairet 1934: 93).

NATIONAL DIVIDEND

The social credit movement's support for the payment of a national dividend, a non-work-related, non-means-tested income, to every adult citizen attracted popular support (see Chapters 7, 8 and 9). According to economic orthodoxy the payment of an unearned income to all would be inflationary. In the context of the A + B theorem and the just price, the payment of a national dividend offers an additional mechanism to free the economy from the compulsion to unsustainable growth inherent in capitalist finance.

As Douglas later clarified, in *The Monopoly of Credit*, under capitalism personal incomes derive largely from wages and salaries, with dividends accounting for only a small percentage of the total of personal incomes. Economic processes are, however, carried out by two agencies: first, individual effort and, second, the combined operation of plant, organisation and knowledge resulting from the aggregate efforts of present and past inventors and pioneers. The contribution of the first is rapidly decreasing in relation to the second, which represents real (as opposed to financial) capital and belongs to the community as a whole. Consequently a small, decreasing share of the product accrues to individuals by virtue of their efforts. A larger, increasing amount is due by right to individuals as 'tenants for life' of the communal capital (Douglas 1931b: 79).

The instrument which most clearly demonstrates Douglas/*New Age* economic theory is the national debt. The national debt, which the citizen did not create, should become a national asset reflecting the national capital which belongs to the citizen. The state should lend, not borrow. In this respect the financier currently usurps the function of the state (Douglas 1919b: 119–21).

The technique by which the process could be implemented is best illustrated by the financing of the Great War (1914–18). 'War is a consumer whose necessities are so imperative that they become superior to all questions of legal and financial restriction.' Artificial financial restrictions cannot be allowed to dominate. In peacetime, production follows finance. However, in the exceptional case of war, finance is subordinate to production, which is achieved by creating purchasing power through book entries (Douglas 1924a: 134–5).

The texts note that at the outbreak of war in 1914 the finance to conduct hostilities did not exist in the United Kingdom. The gold standard, upon which British finance was supposedly based, broke down within a few hours of the outbreak of war (Douglas 1924a: 135). The necessary weapons, munitions and supplies for the armed forces were produced by private firms and paid for by the government. Under normal pre-1914 circumstances the government balanced its budget by raising taxation to pay for such products and services. Since it was impracticable to recover the entire costs of the war out of current taxation, the government faced two options. It could create the paper money necessary to pay for increased production, or, using the existing financial system based on the creation of 'credit', it could raise the national debt. It selected the latter option. Between August 1914 and December 1919 the national debt rose from about £660 million to about £7,700 million.

Much of this finance (which did not previously exist) was created through the 'Ways and Means Accounts, and the working of this is described in the first report of the Committee on Currency and Foreign Exchanges, 1918, page two':

> If ten million pounds is advanced at the Bank of England to the credit of Public [i.e. state] Deposits (which simply involves the writing up of the Public Deposits account by this amount), this amount is paid

out by the Spending Departments to contractors in payment for their services.

(Douglas 1924a: 137–9)

The cleared cheques pass to the credit of the contractors' bankers' (joint stock banks) accounts with the Bank of England. These credits with the Bank of England are regarded as cash at call by the joint stock banks. Working on a ratio of four to one between 'cash' and short-date liabilities, the joint stock banks can allow their customers overdrafts up to £40 million. Some customers can buy Treasury bills or war loans with their overdrafts. Alternatively, the banks themselves may take up a proportion of this money, or they may lend to the Bank of England to lend to the government. The overall effect is the same. The government owes £40 million to the banks, through the Bank of England. Had the government provided £40 million in currency notes, at the mere cost of printing it, the effect would have been precisely the same, except that the public now pays 4–5 per cent p.a. interest on the £40 million and holds a debt to the banks which is liable to be redeemed (Douglas 1924a: 137–9).

If holdings under £1,000 and reinvested pre-war assets are disregarded, the bulk of the new loan represents purchases by large industrial and financial undertakings (Douglas 1919b: 120). In effect, this is 'communal capital transferred to private account'. For every piece of ammunition produced and afterwards fired and destroyed, for every aeroplane built and crashed, for all the army stores lost, stolen or spoilt, the financier 'has an entry in his books which he calls wealth, and on which he proposes to draw interest at 5 per cent' (Douglas 1919b: 121).

When the war debt is cancelled, only the interest charges go to the profit and loss account of the bank. However, the repayment destroys the 'credit', i.e. purchasing power, which was available in the community. Since the cancellation of a loan results in the 'immobilisation' of an equivalent amount of price values, fresh purchasing power has to be created through further loan credit, and further interest charges. Hence the insistence on the importance of redemption and the opposition to government-created paper money on the part of bankers and financiers. Only one-sixth of the cost of the war was paid for from public taxation. The other five-sixths was financed through a loan to the public. The repayment of this credit can be justified only on the assumption that public credit correctly belongs to the banks rather than to the community (Douglas 1924a: 139–40).

Significantly, the fictitious 'loans' upon which the increase in the national debt was based did not represent any consumption forgone. Nor did they relate to labour undertaken for the war effort. They did, however, support a novel principle of non-means-tested payment by the state of an unearned income unrelated to employment record or any other tangible contribution to the formal economy.

Furthermore, unearned income from the national debt was drawn against the *future* production of society as a whole. According to the texts, there can be no logical objection to the principle of paying a national dividend, a guaranteed basic income for all citizens unrelated to employment record and non-means-tested on the basis of the 'real' or 'social credit' of society as a whole.

Such payments would involve the conversion of the national debt into a national asset. The state should lend, not borrow, and use the interest earned on its loans to pay the national dividend (Douglas 1919b: 121–2; House of Commons, Canada 1923: 474–5). 'This unearned income rests inalienably on the basis of Capital, not of labour.' Capital derives from, and should be vested in, the community. As members of the community, individual citizens should benefit equally from this unearned increment in the form of a universal dividend (Douglas 1922a: 13–14).

The principle of a universal dividend was recognised as likely to meet considerable opposition, not only from capitalists but also from socialists who abide by the saying: 'If a man will not work, neither shall he eat.' In this scenario 'work' is defined as 'something the price of which can be included in costs and recovered in price'. Such acceptance of capitalist economics 'completely denies all recognition to the social nature of the heritage of civilization'. By its refusal to distribute purchasing power, except on these terms, it allocates to a few individuals selected by the system the right to disinherit the indisputable heirs to the common wealth of society, the individuals who compose it (Douglas 1922b).

CONCLUSION

In raising the question of the relationship between finance and the processes of production, distribution and exchange, the Douglas/*New Age* texts questioned the basis of general equilibrium theory. They drew attention to the fact that bank loans, which form the greater part of the money supply, are not a loan of existing money saved up through abstention from consumption. Nine-tenths of money is bank-created, a ledger entry. A loan for investment purposes does not preclude any savers from reclaiming the money they have saved and paid into the bank. What the loan does is to enable those businesses approved by the banks to invest in goods, produce commodities for profit and repay the loan with interest. The issue of money bears no necessary relation to the supply of goods available on the market at that moment of time. Nor does it relate to the price put upon them, associated with costs deriving from the past period when they were being produced. As Freeman (1995) notes, the sphere of circulation operates in a dynamic relationship with the sphere of production. Decisions determining which commodities can, or cannot, be made are constantly being taken on purely financial grounds. Those decisions, Douglas argued, should rest in the hands of the community rather than with the banks. During the inter-war depression Douglas observed:

> Whatever may be true or untrue about the present situation [1934], it is certainly not true that the productive organisation as it exists, and as it is administered at the present time, cannot produce the goods. In fact, it is very often said that the present crisis is a crisis of overproduction; I have never heard it called a crisis of underproduction (I have heard it called a crisis of underconsumption, but that is a different thing), and yet the financiers, or rather the Bank of England, are saying that the crying need of this country is reorganisation of the productive system. Can there be anything more ridiculous than to suggest that a crisis which is on the one hand described as a crisis of unemployment, and is on the other hand described as a crisis of overproduction, should be cured or could be cured by making industry more efficient, assuming that were to be done?
>
> (Douglas 1934b: 272)

If that were to be done, as Douglas noted, more goods would be produced by fewer people, intensifying the overproduction while simultaneously intensifying unemployment. This was the inevitable result of an over-centralised industrial system operating under the control of institutionally fossilised capitalist finance. Decentralisation of the administration of both industry (including not only manufacturing industry and allied services but also the professions, civil and domestic services) and banking was the only way out of the *impasse*. Douglas concluded that such reform was unlikely to come about through a political system where the vast majority of the 'voters' are 'twenty-five years behind the times' (Douglas 1934b).

3

DOUGLAS/*NEW AGE* PHILOSOPHY

The A + B theorem and its resolution in the just price and national dividend make little sense if divorced from the underlying themes of the Douglas/*New Age* economic philosophy. In the original texts monetary reform was seen as a means to a specific end, the decommodification of labour and the discontinuation of wage-slavery. Shorn of these guild socialist ideals, 'Douglasism' could be dismissed as a mistaken, if idealistic, attempt to find a way out of recurring cycles of depression. Indeed, for most of its history 'Douglasism' was widely regarded as seeking to solve the 'problem' of unemployment by securing full employment and an age of plenty. However, a careful reading of the original texts (as distinct from even the earliest attempts at interpretation by others) indicates that their underlying purpose was to end the exploitation and alienation of labour by creating a socially just, ecologically sustainable economics.

The economics of the Douglas/*New Age* texts is based on the themes woven into politics by William Morris, 'who can properly be called the first English Marxist' (Morton 1979: 21). However, Orage observed that guild socialism would founder so long as the capitalist financial system dominated policy formation. Indeed, socialism in any form was doomed to be the handmaiden of capitalism so long as political decisions continued to be subject to financial controls. True socialism could not live in an economic climate where policy was dominated by the question: 'Can the money be raised, through taxation or other means, to meet the cost of what we want to do?' Through Douglas's observations of the workings of capitalist finance Orage was able to avoid falling into the trap of advocating the abolition of money. Instead, he was able to indicate a route towards the creation of a socialist system of finance tailored to serve socialist, rather than capitalist, ends.

CULTURAL HERITAGE

According to conventional economic theory land, labour and capital are the sources of all wealth. Possession of one or other of these factors constitutes a valid claim to a share of wealth. The Douglas/*New Age* texts suggest that, while this may have been true in pre-industrial times, the 'progress of the industrial arts', described by Thorstein Veblen, is such as to render individual claims based on the orthodox view obsolescent (Douglas 1924a: 49–50).

There is no moral justification for the appropriation of the proceeds of collective industry for private individual gain, whether the claim be based on the ownership of capital or of labour. Production 'is 95 per cent a matter of tools and process'. Since tools and process form the cultural inheritance of the community, the community as a whole is the proper administrator of its resources (Douglas 1919b: 95). The cultural heritage confers value and abridges effort. As Kenner (1972) later explained:

> Imagine one man tending a machine that prints circuits: is the value of the printed circuit his labour time? The value of the printed circuit is design value: the design of the circuit, the design of the machine. Men turn out resistors and capacitors and transistors: these would be utterly worthless curiosities did not designs exist for television sets and computers and amplifiers. Or a Boeing 747 carries twice the load of a 707, but the crew works no harder. What has multiplied the value of their work is design done once and for all. Douglas called it the cultural heritage. It includes many esoterica: the results obtained by mathematicians long dead, the formulae of anonymous metallurgists, even, we may hazard, Brancusi's sense of form, which in a time of motorized box kites anticipated the aluminium cylinders we fly in today.
>
> (Kenner 1972: 311)

Central to any discussion of the distribution of wealth is the question of ownership. Douglas/*New Age* economics sees the common ownership of social resources, both cultural and intellectual, as offering the citizen rights of use unrestricted by powerful capitalists or a dominant state bureaucracy. The collective 'cultural heritage' or 'cultural inheritance' remains the common property of all citizens. People associate together in collective industry to gain the 'unearned increment' of such association. Thus the required goods and services can be obtained with far less effort than by 'isolated endeavour' (Douglas 1920: 19).

Since natural resources are also common property, the means of their exploitation should belong to all (Douglas 1919b: 110). Production depends upon technology. The entire package of tool power and processes forms a cultural inheritance which belongs to the community, since it is largely the result of 'work done by persons now dead'. In consequence, it can be argued that the just return for effort must include a 'dividend' on this inheritance. To be equitable, the dividend should be larger than the direct payment in respect of the relatively minor individual contribution made in the present (Douglas 1922b: 68).

It is possible to imagine an entire country, the inhabitants of which are 'shareholders' in the common property. In their capacity as shareholders the citizens hold the ordinary stock, which is 'inalienable and unsaleable'. It can be seen as supplying a dividend sufficient to purchase the whole of its net production. Consequently, appreciation in capital value (or dividend-earning capacity) is 'a direct function of the appreciation of the real wealth of the community'. Each individual is a 'tenant for life' of the cultural heritage handed down through the generations. The circulation of purchasing power can be made to reflect this situation. It is in each individual's interest to preserve and enhance this heritage. The texts argue that a high wage incentive would be unnecessary. After an initial period of transition, the wage would be small compared with the dividends each individual received as a shareholder (Douglas 1924a: 185–6). In effect, money would be issued first to consumers, who would then call the required goods and services on to the market.

The analysis rests upon the understanding that real wealth exists in undeveloped natural resources and in the 'cultural heritage' of tools and processes, in the *potential* to produce, rather than in the cycle of production, distribution and exchange. It contrasts with other economic theories, from neoclassical to Marxist/radical in which value creation is seen to occur through the process of *production*, followed by distribution and exchange. The Douglas/*New Age* texts took issue with the reduction of 'labour' to a factor of production, rewarded to a greater or lesser extent according to the ebb and flow of the class war. In their view the value residing in cultural knowledge and natural resources was the exclusive property of no section of the community. The cultural heritage constitutes the real wealth of the community, and should be available for communal ends.

CENTRALISATION OF POWER

The twin evils of poverty and servility arise from any system where control is exercised from the apex. The centralisation and concentration of power are, according to the Douglas/*New Age* analysis, a logical extension of the progression from medieval to modern times, bringing with them increasing disempowerment of the individual (Douglas 1919b: 37). In the early stages of industrialisation involuntary poverty arising from 'unemployment' was rare. The craftsman retained considerable independence and took pride in his/her work. But with the advent of machinery the financier appeared on the industrial scene. He provided the financial means for the craftsman to run a workshop on borrowed money, directing the work of others. It was but a small step to the larger factory in which the direction of work ceased to be exercised by the craftsman. With the advent of the limited liability company the direction of policy became still further separated from the craft worker. Finally, large classes of people became mere employees, engaged in tasks on the primary inducement of money, obeying orders and taking no personal responsibility for the outcome of the enterprise. The financial system which now directs production and hence exerts a controlling influence over all aspects of social affairs tends increasingly towards centralisation and concentration of power (Douglas 1919b: 57–8).

The texts note that political control exercised through democratic processes may appear to provide an antidote to the power of commercial conglomerates and industrial amalgamations. Indeed, this is the mainstay of Fabian philosophy. However, observation of national politics in practice reveals only one working principle, that of the 'consolidation of power'. 'The attitude of statesmen and officials to the people in whose interests they are supposed to hold office is one of scarcely veiled antagonism.' Intrigue is prevalent, with 'the easy supremacy of patronage over merit and of vested interest over either' (Douglas 1919a: 51).

Therefore state socialism is no solution; 'potential despots' are just as numerous among 'the careerists of the Labour movement' as they are among the employing class (Douglas 1920: 9). The Labour Party is little more than 'organised complaint'. It has yet to recognise that the idle rich constitute little threat to society. The true champions of the *status quo* are the 'hardworking rich' (Douglas 1920: 13). These are the people who would surface just as surely under class socialism as under capitalism. The texts follow the guild socialist line of opposition to divisive class politics. Neither capitalist nor 'labourist' approaches can operate the classless society envisaged by Morris or Marx. Within five years of a socialist government 75 per cent of the same individuals would hold the same executive positions, albeit under a different 'official title' (Douglas 1923: 5). This passage, published in 1923, strikingly anticipates Orwell's *Animal Farm*, Djilas's *New Class* (1957), Illich's (1971) call for the deschooling of society and Hancock's *Lords of Poverty* (1991).

SUFFICIENCY AND ECONOMIC GROWTH

Preoccupation with the quest for a route out of depression via measures which would stimulate the economy dominated economic discourse in the inter-war years. In the circumstances it is scarcely surprising that proponents and opponents alike took the social credit proposals as being designed to increase production through economic growth. Enthusiastic supporters, including Douglas himself in the 1930s, pandered to the mood of the time by heralding the 'age of plenty'. However, the evidence below demonstrates that the original Douglas/*New Age* economics drew a novel distinction between increased *useful* production and the impetus to *wasteful* production of goods designed to be destroyed and replaced, most notably in the form of production for warfare. The above interpretation of the 'A + B theorem' produces a financial explanation of this phenomenon.

According to Douglas and Orage, the flaw in the capitalist system lies less with the profit motive itself than with 'the delusive accounting system which accompanies it', which creates a false inducement to produce 'in that it claims as "wealth" what may just as probably be waste' (Douglas 1919b: 78). 'The tawdry ornament, the jerry-built house . . . the unwholesome sweetmeat, are the direct and logical consummation of an economic system which rewards variety, quite irrespective of quality' (Douglas 1919b: 84–5). The manufacturer produces 'a new model of his particular speciality' with the object of 'rendering the old model obsolete before it is worn out'. An immense amount of demand is generated artificially through advertising, resulting in 'a demand, in many cases, as purely hypnotic in origin as the request of the mesmerised subject for a draught of kerosene' (Douglas 1919b: 83).

In every industrial country the plant and organisation for manufacturing have been expanded to many times their pre-war (1914–18) capacity. The availability of natural resources may be more difficult to compute than industrial capacity. Nevertheless, although finite, it could (at that time) be assumed that the necessary raw materials to feed into the machines might be available for a 'considerable period' of unlimited activity, 'although by no means indefinitely'. Regardless of the long-term implications, the 'factory system of the world is prepared, to a degree transcending anything dreamt of in the past, to flood the market with any article on which a profit in manufacture can apparently be made' (Douglas 1918: 429–30).

The economic arguments, especially the A + B theorem, provide the technical explanations for the motivation to constant growth in the book value of world production. By 1918 it had already exceeded the capacity to 'absorb or liquidate it' (Douglas 1918: 431). High wages and mass-produced cheap items will not create social stability (Douglas 1919b: 151) or international peace. On the contrary, the 'colossal waste of effort' stimulated by the finance-driven economy so far overtaxed the ingenuity of society to extend production that 'the climax of war only occurred in the moment when a culminating exhibition of organised sabotage was necessary to preserve the system from spontaneous combustion'. Unfortunately, 'if production stops, distribution stops'. Hence 'a clear incentive exists to produce useless or superfluous articles in order that useful commodities already existing may be distributed' (Douglas 1919b: 82).

What is required is a higher degree of economic efficiency, so that economic problems become subordinate to other aspects of social life.

> If by wealth we mean the original meaning attached to the word: i.e. 'well-being', the value in well-being to be attached to production depends entirely on its use for the promotion of well-being (unless a case is made out for the moral value of factory life), and bears no relation whatever to the value obtained by cost accounting.
>
> (Douglas 1919b: 79)

An efficient system for producing real well-being is needed to replace the inefficiency of capitalist accountancy. Modern computing techniques and advances in technology could create an economy capable of meeting a sufficiency of needs with an option to increase material welfare free from the constraints imposed by outdated capitalist finance (Douglas 1919b: 79).

The primary necessities of life – food, clothes, shelter – 'have an important characteristic which differentiates them from what we may call conveniences and luxuries':

> they are quite approximately constant per head of the population. . . . The average human being requires as a groundwork for his daily life a definite number of heat units in the form of suitable food, a definite minimum quantity of clothing and a definite minimum space in which to sleep and work . . . The variation between the minimum and the maximum quantity of each that he can utilize with advantage to himself is not . . . very great. [It is therefore] perfectly feasible (it has already very largely been accomplished) – to estimate the absolute production of foodstuffs required by the world's population; the time–energy units required at the present stage of mechanical and scientific development to produce those foodstuffs; and the time–energy units approximately available. [It can be estimated] that two or three hours of work per day from all adults between the ages of 18 and 40 would amply supply all basic requirements if production for purely financial profit is eliminated.
>
> (Douglas 1919b: 104–5)

Once again the texts anticipate later work, e.g. Maslow's hierarchy of needs and Gorz's (1989) economics of sufficiency. They note that the proper objective of production is to meet the real demand for essentials. First there must be 'a production of necessaries to meet universal requirements; and second, an economic system must be devised to ensure their . . . universal distribution'. Only then should 'the manufacture of articles having a more limited range of usefulness' be considered. The existing machinery of business is highly efficient, and capable of producing such results. However, 'it must undoubtedly be adjusted so that no selfish desire for domination can make it possible for any interest to hold up distribution on purely artificial (i.e. financial) grounds' (Douglas 1919b: 92). It should no longer be possible to take seriously the argument that necessities can be distributed to all if, and only if, production of motor-cars is increased (*New Age*, 25 September 1919).

Industry has a productive capacity far greater, in terms of labour, plant and organisation, than the ability of the nation to consume. It therefore becomes necessary to inflate consumption capacity by artificial means. A favoured mechanism has been the supreme waste of warfare (Douglas 1922b: 79). The obvious beneficiaries of war and excessive consumption are the banks, who have, since 1914, roughly doubled their 'buildings of solid magnificence appropriate to the temples of a great faith' (Douglas 1922b: 129). The inducement to wasteful production is stimulated by a financial system capable of creating artificial scarcities (Douglas 1924a: 44–5).

The Douglas/*New Age* texts note that the orthodox conception of value is 'that quality which gives anything maximum exchangeability'. Exchangeability is stimulated through the creation of scarcity, real or imagined. For example, in order to cross a river a person may require a boat. The boat has utilitarian value in its ability to transport the traveller with a maximum of speed and a minimum of inconvenience. However, the generally accepted notation of its value would be dependent upon the traveller's ability to submit to a financial penalty for the use of the boat. The size of this penalty would vary according to the urgency of the traveller's needs and the availability or absence of other boats. It has nothing to do with the intrinsic value of the boat. The texts acknowledge that there is a certain logic in holding that the value of anything with use value can be enhanced by its scarcity. In such a world it makes undoubted sense to create 'value' by deliberately creating scarcity (Douglas 1924a: 44–5).

However, the ability to restrict access to the material necessities of life, i.e. the basic requirements of food, clothing and shelter, are as menacing as the machine gun as a threat to freedom 'and far more insidious' (Douglas 1920: 145). This may be 'an active conspiracy to enslave the world' or merely the action of 'blind forces . . . at work to the same end'. Whichever form it takes, the tyranny is real and material (Douglas 1920: 145).

WORK, LEISURE AND THE PROBLEM OF 'UNEMPAYMENT'

The Douglas/*New Age* texts noted the commonly held assumption that if people were starving the answer to their problem was to find employment. Hence the provision of employment would end poverty and starvation. However, this 'axiom is now receding into a proposition to be proved' (Douglas 1924a: 109). What people really want when they seek employment is an income, not 'work'. Demands for a minimum wage and recognition of the 'right to work' merely highlight the problems caused by the failure of a distribution system dependent upon the notion of labour as a commodity, subject to the laws of supply and demand (Douglas 1919b: 87–8).

Although it is desirable to reduce enforced and monotonous work to a minimum, work of some kind is essential to well-being. The texts draw a distinction between necessary work – the exercise of hand, eye and brain for productive ends – on the one hand, and the enforced monotony of the work of the wage slave, on the other. It is a vital distinction. The knitting of a jumper or the digging or ploughing of a field can be intrinsically satisfying. The creation of a jumper or a wheatfield can be a fulfilling and healthy activity. However, knitting jumpers or digging and ploughing ten hours a day, six days a week, fifty-two weeks a year in order to obtain the necessities of life is neither healthy nor satisfying (Douglas 1924a: 56).

There is absolutely no concrete difference between work and play . . .
No one would contend that it is inherently more interesting or more
pleasurable to endeavour to place a small ball in an inadequate hole
with inappropriate instruments, than to assist in the construction of a
Quebec Bridge, or the harnessing of Niagara. But for one object men
will travel long distances at their own expense, while for the other they
require payment and considerable incentive to remain at work.

(Douglas 1919b: 88)

Monotonous work is degrading, best undertaken by machines and robots
(Douglas 1919b: 60, 1924a: 57). Scientific progress ought therefore to benefit
society as a whole. However, under the present system of finance, wages
and salaries must be accounted for as costs of production which reappear in
prices. Since these same wages and salaries form the major portion of
society's purchasing power, 'modern scientific progress is the deadly enemy
of Society'. It merely results in 'replacing the persons who now obtain their
living in this way, by machines and processes' (Douglas 1922b: 7). In the
Marxist view the distribution of goods is entirely dependent upon the
performance of labour in their production. In the capitalist view, distribution
is largely dependent upon the performance of labour. Either way, the
introduction of labour-saving techniques has three implications. First, it may
take all the available labour to provide the requisite amount of goods.
Second, an increasing number of persons may not obtain the goods. Or,
third, materials or labour must be 'misapplied or wasted, purely for the
purpose of distributing purchasing power' (Douglas 1922b: 4).

The average standard of living rose during the 1914–18 war because
wage payments were increased, prices and the production of luxuries were
partially controlled and the sabotage of war 'disposed of useless product,
and so kept up wage distribution' (Douglas 1919b: 98). The production of
armaments is the supreme example of wasteful production being deliberately fostered because of its financial profitability. Hence the production
of armaments is a determining factor in world politics today (1920),
because 'millions of men and women get their living, as the phrase goes,
by working in armaments factories'. In a passage which anticipated the
'peace dividend' debate of the 1990s, the texts note that the armaments
business would cease to function if 'millions of human beings' did not
depend on that form of production as a means of access to the necessities
of life. In that event, 'the resources currently wasted in armaments production could be diverted to useful ends' (Douglas 1920: 83–4).

In another class comes the stupendous waste of effort involved in the
intricacies of finance and book-keeping; much of which, although
necessary to the competitive system, is quite useless in increasing the
amenities of life. . . . All these and many other forms of avoidable
waste take their rise in the obsession of wealth defined in terms of

money. . . . [This obsession] obscures the whole object and meaning of scientific progress and places the worker and the honest man in a permanently disadvantageous position in comparison with the financier and the rogue.

(Douglas 1919b: 83–4)

Under the stress of competition for markets it became desirable to reduce the selling price of commodities by standardisation and mass-production techniques. Machinery is substituted for skilled workmanship, and the worker, tempted by piecework schemes, is transformed into a 'machine-like system of which every part is expected to function as systematically as a detail of the machine which he may operate'. As early as 1919 it was evident that 'scientific management systems . . . based on the researches of efficiency engineers such as Mr F.W. Taylor and Mr Frank Gilbreth have resulted in a rate of production per unit of labour, hundreds or even thousands per cent higher than existed before their introduction'. It is a 'stupendous waste of effort' because it fails to benefit even the workers retained in employment, as wages fail to keep pace with rising costs of living (Douglas 1919b: 48–9).

Labourism is no more acceptable than capitalism. In 1920 the *New Age* forewarned of Workfare and other uncongenial forms of forced labour which inevitably follow from the binding link between work and income.

If work is the only just title to food, then it follows that 'work' as arbitrarily defined, must be compulsory and universal. . . . Work must be 'made' if it does not exist. . . . Authoritarianism and materialism . . . are the necessary social consequences of the doctrine that only 'work' entitles the individual to life; and they may be seen under rapid development in Russia today.

(The *New Age* 1920a)

Recently, British workers have become obsessed with a sense of the power of organised Labour. However, that power can be exaggerated and is certainly waning rapidly by misuse. It plays straight into the hands of the enemy in exactly the same way as the Russian workers have been led from the 'tyranny of Czarist Russia into the scientific conscription of Labour now incorporated into the Workers' Republic'. The American Henry Ford 'is credibly reported to have been converted to Bolshevism' by the efficiency of the workers' republic (Douglas 1920: 84–5).

Capitalist and 'labourist' alike have an irrational fear of removing the necessity to engage in paid employment as the primary means of subsistence for the mass of the people. In fact, unemployment as a result of advances in technology would be welcomed were it not 'unempayed' (this term was used by Bardsley 1939). The enforced leisure acquired through 'unemployment' is rendered 'practically valueless by the regulations surrounding it'. Although the 'dole' derives from forced insurance contributions, those in 'work' resent paying taxes and insurance when they see some receiving an income for nothing. The result is an administrative nightmare. An unemployed person performing 'an hour's casual work' is rendered liable to a prison sentence for fraud. The forms required to 'regularise half a day's wood-cutting' for a person registered at a labour exchange make the Russian passport system seem uncomplicated. The 'dole' could more sensibly be regarded as 'a small dividend on the National Income – a forerunner of "Dividends for All"' (Douglas 1924a: 111, 17).

However, proposals to allow the unemployed to be rewarded through the payment of a national dividend are attacked as being both 'immoral' and likely to 'demoralise' recipients, i.e. 'render them unsuitable for subsequent employment'. The evidence suggests otherwise. Some of the most valuable contributions during the war (1914–18) were made by the idle rich, young men and women who might, by that argument, have been expected to laze about doing nothing. The texts recognise that it might be difficult to persuade people to return to 'long hours of mechanical drudgery, offering no prospect of improvement or release' once they have experienced the 'expanding influences of increased freedom of initiative'. Employers operating in the traditional mode might be suspicious of any scheme offering security of income, and hence the option not to seek employment. However, such a circular argument is low on facts and illogical (Douglas 1924a: 17).

Once basic needs are met, there are more creative ways to work than under a factory regime. Furthermore, new ideas and technological innovations do not flow from the stifling compulsion of enforced labour. The vast majority of ideas and inventions to which the human race is indebted are attributable to people who were freed from the restraints of wage slavery as a means to secure subsistence. Douglas illustrates the point by drawing an analogy with a racing stable.

> [E]very racing stable produces a higher percentage of 'weeds' than potential Derby winners; but he would surely be foolish who would suggest that the way to get more Derby winners would be to work horses of every description at the plough.
>
> (Douglas 1924a: 115–17)

It may well be necessary to end the state of artificial scarcity and enforced labour gradually, to give people time to learn how to use their newly found freedom. However, it seems spurious to argue that an obsolete system of organisation must be preserved because of a hypothetical risk that people may face problems in adjusting to a new situation. Such a policy is analogous to refusing to develop a railway because it might have detrimental effects upon the stagecoach (Douglas 1924a: 115–17).

One must conclude that objections to unemployment with a guaranteed universal income are 'Moral' rather than 'Economic'. Attacks on the 'dole' focus upon the 'demoralisation' of the recipient. The financial reasoning behind the system as a whole never comes into focus (Douglas 1924a: 117, 201). From the outset it was envisaged that the national dividend would be paid to 'every man and woman', i.e. that the unit of assessment would be the individual and not the household. It was also recognised, however, that a reformed monetary system would have implications for foreign trade.

EXPORTS AND INTERNATIONAL TRADE

After the end of the war (1914–18), Douglas noted, schemes adopted by the government to stimulate trade and investment also benefited powerful financial interests. Proposals for dealing with 'unemployment' were based on an export credit scheme, buttressed by relief works financed out of taxation. Some £25 million of public credit was pledged to the production of machinery for export.

Lloyd George was reported as advocating the production of capital goods, machinery and transport for export in order to stimulate trade and create a strong economy. Consequently, the production of consumer goods had to be delayed. However, Douglas observed, 'the productive capacity of the industrial nations' was already greater than ever before. It would make sense for the millions of unemployed in the United Kingdom and the United States to obtain 'maximum benefit' from existing plant, rather than producing further plant 'to be exported in competition with countries similarly situated' (Douglas 1922b: 153–4).

The proposal (in 1922) was to pay out £25 million in wages, salaries and dividends in respect of the production of capital goods without any increase in the supply of consumer goods. The Douglas/*New Age* texts predicted that the result would be inflationary. The general public would pay in higher prices for the export of goods which were no use to them. When the credits came to be repaid their destination would be the banks who financed them. In general, international competition over exports serves to destabilise international relations while providing few tangible benefits to the ordinary citizen (Douglas 1922b: 154–5).

Powerful financial interests are the source of the insistence on the 'necessity' of super-production. They do not advocate the necessity of housing, clothing and specific essentials, merely 'increased production' along with the duty to consume less because of the 'need' to increase exports and 'restore the exchange rate'. Few can comprehend the workings of such a system. Virtually every action in the civilised world is inspired by money or has some relation to money. 'Seventy-five per cent of the business world lives for money, dreams of money and will die and condemn millions of others to death for money.' However, few people can conceive how 'modifications in the money system can and do divert the current of productive energy supplied by skill, science and labour into alternative channels of enterprise' in much the same way 'as the manipulation of more concrete materials by the civil engineer may modify the course of a great river' (Douglas 1919a: 368).

> The important point to grasp is that the problem of exchange is a problem which is raised solely by the treatment of money as a commodity. . . . [B]ecause of the immensely powerful interests behind the whole system of money broking and credit issue, an attempt is being made once more to fasten on the world at large, and this country in particular, a form of society which, in combination with an international political system forming its complement, is directly responsible for the misery and unrest in the world today. . . . If the super-production for export policy gets its way [it will lead to war between continents and perpetual conflict of] the controllers of production with their dupes, the consuming community. Under the present system of unregulated currency and credit, administered in their own interests by international groups of financiers and super-industrialists, the cost of living measured in terms of intensity of effort will rise, and the standard of life measured in terms of security, leisure, and freedom will fall until the crash comes.
>
> (Douglas 1919a: 369)

Bankers and financiers clothe exchange in mystery. It is, however, 'a simple enough matter'. To the exchange broker, different sorts of money are 'different varieties of merchandise', subject to the laws of barter.

> As a result, the 'price' of the money of any specific variety, e.g. English pounds sterling expressed in terms of the money of any other variety, e.g. American dollars, varies directly as the dollar demand for English pounds, and inversely as the quantity of English pounds is available. That is all. Now this clamour for super-exports as a means of 'stabilising' exchange is based on a desire to raise the price of English pounds in the international money market for exactly the same reason that the fruit merchant wants to raise the price of plums in the fruit market – because there is more profit for him. *It is not based on a desire to increase the purchasing power of the consumer expressed in terms of American goods, because the demand that American goods shall not be allowed to enter this country comes from the same quarter.*
>
> (Douglas 1919a: 370, original emphasis)

The viability of the system requires consumption in general, and the consumption of foreign goods in particular, to be reduced. Since imports of ultimate consumer goods must be restricted, imports must take the form of 'raw materials for manufacture for re-export'. The citizen does not have the option to select a comfortable standard of living and increased leisure so long as a small group holds control over industrial decision-making (Douglas 1919a: 370). From this early date (1919), in *Economic Democracy*, it was noted that the 'super-production-for-export-policy' was socially and ecologically unsustainable over the long run. Again the texts anticipated the 1990s environmental debate.

> The effect of this on the worker is that he has to do many times the amount of work which would be necessary to keep him in the highest standard of living, as a result of an artificial inducement to produce things he does not want, which he cannot buy, and which are of no use to the attainment of his internal standard of well-being. [There is a] good sound reason for the international financiers' hatred of economic nationalism; failing interplanetary commerce, he will have nowhere to export to, and will be faced with the horrible prospect of dividing up the world's production amongst the individuals who live here. In which case a larger number of people than at present will agree that it is possible to overproduce gunboats.
>
> (Douglas 1922b: 50)

First published in the *New Age* (2 January 1919), the article anticipated 1990s' debates on international debt, European Union, GATT and the New Protectionism (see Lang and Hines 1993) and armaments exports to repressive regimes.

In 1922 the United Kingdom could produce sufficient food to feed its population from its own land acreage. However, under the present financial system it would not be good business for it to make the attempt. A given amount of foreign wheat is normally contracted for this country. The wheat is bought on 'futures' by grain brokers whose price fixes a 'datum line for home-grown wheat' (Douglas 1922b: 70–1). World prices rise when wheat is in short supply relative to demand. Producers may benefit, but dealers certainly do. The farmer's criterion of a satisfactory output bears no relation to the amount of wheat the public requires. In all circumstances he must avoid throwing grain on to the market in any quantity which will lower prices. As transport improves and grain can be moved from 'other markets' the farmer is driven to produce perishable goods (eggs, butter, milk, vegetables) for local markets or livestock which is risky and expensive to transport for sale (Douglas 1922b: 72). The sole beneficiaries are the international financiers (Douglas 1922b: 74–5). In the early 1920s the commercial food industry was still in its infancy. Again the texts anticipate future developments. Later in the century sophisticated refrigeration and food-processing techniques turned the provision of the most basic necessity, food, into a highly profitable business. Small-scale farming, in which the working farmer controlled decision-making, was progressively rendered 'uneconomic'. In the production of 'convenience' foods through process, packaging, transport and clerical work, decision-making was centralised and the scope for intrinsically satisfying work reduced.

The Douglas/*New Age* texts had, by 1924, mapped out an alternative economic route. They noted that an economic system which involves the 'forced extrusion of product' from industrialised countries to 'under-developed' countries as an 'integral component of the machinery for the distribution of purchasing power' will lead to long-run political instability. The 'logical and inevitable consequence of economic competition is war' and such a war is 'not only a crime but a blunder' (Douglas 1919b: 136–7). This section of *Economic Democracy* concludes with the observation that an alternative exists, in which international trade ceases to be based upon financial competition. When each country meets its own subsistence needs international trade can be conducted in a spirit of mutual co-operation.

THE DRAFT MINING SCHEME

Douglas and Orage collaborated to produce 'A Practical Scheme for the Establishment of Economic and Industrial Democracy' in the form of a 'draft scheme' and detailed commentary. Published within months of the introduction of the National Building Guilds experiment, the scheme offered the potential to create a guild system based upon non-capitalist finance. Reckitt and Bechhofer speculate that in selecting the coal industry as their subject the authors' intention may have been to secure the backing of leading trade union executives for the proposal to secure economic control of capital on an industry basis (1918: 265).

The Draft Mining Scheme was an outline of an economic model directly responsive to the needs and wishes of consumers and producers, free from the distortions which stem from dependence upon a predatory, competitive financial system. The scheme proposed 'producers' banks' in conjunction with a national clearing house capable of providing the financial mechanisms necessary to support a decentralised system of production and distribution. In this model decision-making specific to industry and locality would replace large-scale private or state-controlled structures.

The Mining Scheme, designed to provide an example of the type of interim measures which might be employed in the transition to the new economic order, was first published as an appendix to *Credit-Power and Democracy* (Douglas: 1920 147–211). It appeared in pamphlet form and was widely discussed by trade unionists and Labour Party members, giving rise to widespread pressure on the Labour Party leadership to make a formal assessment of the 'Douglas/*New Age*' economics. The report *Labour and Social Credit* (Labour Party 1922) contains only passing and misleading reference to 'The Mining Scheme'. The original proposals are reproduced below, the sections in different type being taken verbatim from the original. The comments which follow each proposal are a condensed paraphrase of the explanatory text written by Orage.

I (1) For the purpose of efficient operation each geological mining area shall be considered as autonomous administratively.

Decentralisation is advocated because 'uniform conditions cannot be imposed upon industrial areas differing widely in natural and other respects without involving all the evils and waste of regimented bureaucracy' (pp. 153–4). Local administration will respond to local needs and local resources.

I (2) In each of these areas a branch of a Bank, to be formed by the M.F.G.B. [Miners' Federation of Great Britain] shall be established, hereinafter referred to as the Producers' Bank. The Government shall recognise this Bank as an integral part of the mining industry regarded as a producer of wealth, and representing its credit. It shall ensure its affiliation with the Clearing House.

Orage explains the terms 'real' and 'financial credit' (as defined in Chapter 2) and adds, 'Real Credit depends on an ability to produce and a need to be satisfied' (p. 157). Real credit is social or communal in origin. 'It belongs neither to the producer nor to the consumer, but to their common element, the community, of which they each form a part' (p. 158). The state is the custodian of the real credit of the community.

(a) Financial credit is 'based on goods only through the medium of money'. Its function is to set real credit in motion. Money is needed to buy raw materials and to pay wages so that the worker can buy existing food and necessities for survival. At present this money is advanced by a bank only on consideration of the likelihood of a financial return. The bank is not concerned about whether the producer can produce 'boots for the luxurious few or for the needy many'. The only consumer who 'counts' is one with purchasing power. Whether the consumer needs more or the producer could produce more is irrelevant to the bank. 'The Bank is concerned with money, and only with goods as they are or can be related to money' (pp. 161–2). In theory the answer is to extend financial credit indiscriminately. In this event the proposals of 'men like Sir Oswald Stoll and Mr Arthur Kitson would be realised'. Evidently the results would be wildly inflationary and would lead to a fall in the effective demand of consumers (pp. 162–3). This is the inevitable result of the disharmony between real credit and financial credit ' – Social Credit, that is to say, from Financial Credit privately controlled' (pp. 165–6). Orage and Douglas used the term 'social credit' for the first time in this document.

(b) The MFGB is an organisation of men engaged in the production of coal, at that time a vital sector of the national economy. Without the labour of its members, coal production would cease. Hence 'the M.F.G.B. is *at least* equally entitled with Capital to a share in the Financial Credit that rests, in the last resort, on Real Credit' (original emphasis) (p. 167). Equally the public 'as representing the ultimate reason for the existence of the

73

Mining Industry is also a factor in its Credit'. Depositors in the bank are members of the public.

(c) A bank issues financial credit against real credit in the form of money. 'The Producers' Bank herein suggested is the representative . . . of the power inherent in the Real Credit contributed to the Mining Industry by the workers engaged in it.' Second, the function of the producers' bank is to issue 'Financial Credit against the Real Credit inherent in the ability of the M.F.G.B. to produce coal, and the need of the public for coal' (pp. 167–8).

(d) The producers' bank is brought into relation with the financial credit of the community as a whole through affiliation with the clearing house (p. 168).

I (3) The shareholders of the Bank shall consist of all persons engaged in the Mining Industry, ex-officio, whose accounts are kept by the Bank. Each shareholder shall be entitled to one vote at a shareholders' meeting.

The producers' bank abolishes the distinction between labour and capital, and between wage and salary earners. Provision is made for those who leave the industry to continue as members. The body of equal members decides policy.

I (4) The Bank as such shall pay no dividend.

The bank represents the real credit of the industry: it exists to facilitate the formation of real capital in the industry.

I (5) The Capital already invested in the Mining properties and plant shall be entitled to a fixed return of, say, 6 per cent, and, together with all fresh Capital, shall continue to carry with it all the ordinary privileges of Capital administration other than Price-fixing.

This clause avoids the political and economic disadvantages of confiscation without compensation, or the financial disadvantage of the payment of annuities to dispossessed owners. Further, the 'fresh Capital' which is the direct property of the producers will provide the major benefits and hence reap the rewards. 'It is not Capital that is evil, but capitalism' (pp. 175–6). 'The Scheme looks forward to the time when everyone will draw a dividend by virtue of his sharehold in the communal enterprise' (p. 177).

I (6) The Boards of Directors shall make all payments of wages and salaries direct to the Producers' Bank in bulk.

This clause follows from the system recently adopted by Lever Brothers to make 'a bulk-payment of wages and salaries through a local bank in their works in the North of England' (p. 177). These payments, partly in cash, partly in cheques, would provide the working financial capital to conduct business.

I (7) In the case of a reduction in cost of working, one half of such reduction shall be dealt with in the National Credit Account, one quarter shall be credited to the Colliery owners, and one quarter to the Producers' Bank.

Thus the colliery 'owners' are required to take account of the MFGB. The interests of the community were represented in the national credit account. Cost savings resulting from new technology arise from the community and correspondingly benefit the community as a whole. There is an incentive to economise on energy and 'produce as much as possible at the smallest possible cost, a proceeding in direct antithesis to the existing state of affairs' (p. 181).

I (8) From the setting to work of the Producers' Bank all subsequent expenditure on capital account shall be financed jointly by the Colliery owners and the Producers' Bank, in the ratio which the total dividends bear to the total wages and salaries. The benefits of such financing done by the Producers' Bank shall accrue to the depositors.

In the mining industry the allocation of costs between the direct producers and the owners of capital is estimated as 9:1. All fresh capital creation will reflect this ratio. Hence the producers' bank will acquire a controlling interest in the capital of the industry within ten years, satisfying the avowed claims of labour to a share in the control of capital.

II (1) The Government shall require from the Colliery owners a quarterly (half-yearly or yearly) statement, properly kept and audited, of the cost of production, including all dividends and bonuses.

This periodic statement of costs is 'an indispensable element in the National Bookkeeping of the National Credit Account'. It will for the first time establish whether 'we are wealthy beyond the dreams of avarice . . . [or] a poor nation on the verge of bankruptcy' (pp. 186–7).

II (2) On the basis of this ascertained Cost, the Government shall by statute cause the Price of domestic coal to be regulated at a percentage of the ascertained Cost.

The government's function is to compile statistics and to publish the results (pp. 187–8).

II (3) This Price [of domestic coal] shall bear the same ratio to Cost as the total National Consumption of all commodities does to the total National Production of Credit

That is:

Cost : Price : :Production : Consumption.

$$\text{Price per ton} = \text{cost per ton} \times \frac{\text{cost value of total consumption}}{\text{money value of total production}}$$

(Total national consumption includes capital depreciation and exports. Total national production includes capital appreciation and imports.)

Real credit represents 'a resource of power over and above that necessary to supply today's needs' (p. 190). The commodities produced every year represent only a fraction of the real credit produced in the same period. Hence national production cannot be measured solely in terms of the amount of commodities produced. 'Our Total Balance Sheet may therefore be said to run as follows: Credit, actual goods produced, plus Capital appreciation plus Imports. Debit, actual goods consumed plus Capital depreciation plus Exports. The balance one way or the other would show whether as a community we had done well or badly. The whole would constitute our National Credit Account' (p. 193). Hence, to fix price, we calculate the proportion of real credit in existence which is actually consumed. If it is 4:1, price must be a quarter of cost (pp. 195–6).

This price applies only to domestic coal sold to the consumer. It does not apply to coal used for further production, nor does it apply to exported coal. Thus a share of the total national production of credit accrues to consumers (p. 201).

II (4) Industrial coal shall be debited to users at Cost plus an agreed percentage.

Price is confined to the means of transferring ultimate goods to the consumer. Exchange within the manufacturing process is merely an accounting procedure. The industrial user is charged at the full cost, which enters into his general costs and adds to credit. The final output of all industry will, in due course, be sold 'below cost'. This is justified because production is intended to meet the needs of the consumer rather than the requirements of an outmoded financial system (pp. 202–3).

II (5) The price of coal for export shall be fixed from day to day in relation to the world-market and in the general interest.

By 'the general interest' is meant 'the value to ourselves or the use we can make on the exchange' (p. 205). If our own use of coal is 'so skilful' there may be nothing worth exporting it for.

II (6) The Government shall reimburse to the Colliery owners the difference between their total Cost incurred and their total Price received, by means of Treasury Notes, such notes being debited, as now, to the National Credit Account.

Although the stipulation may appear inflationary, representing a subsidy to the coal user, the credit advanced will already have been spent. Prices cannot rise, owing to clause II (3).

The proposals end by posing the rhetorical question: if this scheme appears complex and incomprehensible, is it any more so than the present financial system? The use of the term 'Social Credit' in the blueprint cements the link between 'Douglasism' and guild socialism.

CONCLUSION

Douglas/*New Age* political economy presented an alternative analysis of economic 'progress'. As machinery replaces human effort it becomes necessary to seek alternative means to distribute the proceeds of the machine age justly and efficiently (Douglas 1919b: 109–10). The present system, founded on outmoded financial mechanisms, dictates economic growth based on the wasteful use of natural and material resources. It was necessary to decide

> whether you wish the economic system to be made the vehicle for an unseen government, over which you have no control, which you did not elect, and which you cannot remove so long as you accept its premises; or whether, on the other hand, you are determined to free the forces of modern science, so that your needs for goods and services may be met with increasing facility and decreasing effort . . . [This would permit] humanity to expend its energy on altogether higher planes of effort than those involved in the mere provision of the means of subsistence.
>
> (Douglas 1923: 12)

'No financial system by itself affects concrete facts.' However, 'the object of measures of the character indicated is the provision of the right incentive to effort and the removal of any possible incentive to waste' (Douglas 1919b: 132).

Underlying the texts was a belief that waste of human effort and natural resources was inherent in capitalist finance. Furthermore, political reform which fell short of the decommodification of labour would be rendered ineffective through the internal logistics of capitalism. The correctly named 'Draft' Mining Scheme was a revolutionary proposal to bring industry under the economic control of workers' banks, monitored by a central clearing house scheme. The abolition of the traditional antagonism between capitalist and worker combined with social control of prices was a novel concept. To most, including leading thinkers like Cole, the familiar language of reformist politics appeared to indicate a more practical route to socialism (Reckitt and Bechhofer 1918: 266). Douglas and Orage were aware that their work constituted an introduction to a new political economy. The development of a working blueprint would require the co-operation of leading thinkers, the trade unions and the wider community over an extended period. In 1922 Orage recognised the impossibility of further development in the short term.

Part II

In the decades following World War II Douglas has been dubbed a crank whose 'funny money' proposals were an attempt to solve depression in the inter-war years. The volume of material deemed necessary to refute an elementary error is inconsistent with this analysis. The Labour Party, Fabians, other socialists and academics, including Keynes, read and commented upon the texts, some at considerable length. In the following chapters reactions are categorised in order to summarise the debate. To some extent the categories overlap. For example, some members of the Labour Party committee of 1922 (Chapter 5) made individual contributions and hence appear in Chapter 6. The Douglas/*New Age* analysis and policy proposals formed a coherent alternative not only to orthodox economics but also to contemporary socialist economic policies, which were based upon acceptance of the essential tenets of orthodoxy. Under these circumstances their failure to influence practical policy formation is less remarkable than is the extent to which they engendered an extensive and often heated debate.

Reaction was largely concentrated within two periods. First, the early 1920s, when the Douglas/*New Age* texts outlined in Part I were originally published. Second, throughout the 1930s debate centred on a search for alternative solutions to trade depression and large-scale unemployment. In both periods the 'disproof' of the A + B theorem, in terms of orthodox neoclassical analysis, was the main focus of appraisal.

Two factors influenced the character of the debate. First, 1922 saw the end of the close co-operation between Orage, the guild socialist, and Douglas, the practical engineer, on the resignation of Orage as editor of the *New Age* and his departure from the United Kingdom. Second, Douglas continued as a prolific writer and publicist throughout the 1920s and 1930s, travelling widely in the United Kingdom and the dominions until his death in 1952. In addition to a profusion of journal articles and pamphlets, he published *Warning Democracy* (1931), a compilation of texts previously published in the 1920s, and *Monopoly of Credit* (1931), his last major text. Douglas had neither the personality nor the desire to act as leader of a mass movement: he provided *faux de mieux* the focal point of the social credit movement which arose out of his original collaboration with Orage. To some extent reactions were a response to the existence and evolving character of the social credit movement. Additionally, the original texts presented by Douglas and Orage from 1918 to 1922 aroused serious debate among leading academics and socialists.

The UK 'social credit movement' can be described as three movements which coexisted in an uneasy relationship. First, a self-appointed 'Social Credit Secretariat', loosely formed as early as 1921, produced material for study groups which sprang up throughout the United Kingdom. Finlay estimates that by late 1922 thirty-four study groups had been formed across the United Kingdom, centred largely on guild socialism (Finlay 1972: 122). Douglas was drawn into reluctant co-operation with this secretariat in the absence of any other prominent figure. Second, the informal Chandos group encompassed a number of leading artists, journalists and Church figures who shared common links with Orage. Third, John Hargrave and his Green Shirts movement popularised social credit ideas among the disaffected and unemployed in the United Kingdom.

The character of the social credit movement, covered in detail in Part III, heavily influenced the nature of reactions, particularly in the 1930s, when its widespread popularity was perceived as threatening to the established political scene. Indeed, reactions are more accurately described as responses to elements in the publicity and propaganda of the social credit movement than to the Douglas/*New Age* analysis as a whole. This, coupled with the search for solutions to problems of the time from various vantage points in society – the orthodox liberal economists seeking solutions to depression, the Labour Party seeking political credibility, the unemployed and low-paid seeking explanations and deliverance – obscured the holistic character of the original texts.

Had the texts contained merely the maverick meanderings of a single mind, the subsequent fate of the ideas would be of little consequence. It is contended here that the Douglas/Orage collaboration synthesised into a coherent framework a constructive alternative view of the relationship between economics and society. The ideas propounded by Orage and Douglas had considerable impact on Meade, Keynes and other major figures in politics and economics in subsequent decades. The central theme of the *detrimental* impact of the impetus to economic growth and its relentless drive towards the production of armaments and waste arising from a debt-driven financial system was often neglected, even by leading advocates of social credit. In the ensuing debate, proponents and opponents alike failed to acknowledge an alternative framework for freeing the productive capacity of developed nations from exploitation for individual greed and competitive gain.

It was easy to turn the A + B theorem around in order to argue that the 'age of plenty' failed to materialise because of the Machiavellian character of the financial system. Douglas's original texts were often obscure to the point of incomprehensibility. Indeed, it is difficult to disagree with Mehta's observation that 'no writer in economics has made his thought so opaque to the reader' (Mehta 1983). From 1922 onwards the guild socialist origins of social credit were largely forgotten as enthusiastic interpreters canvassed an implausible underconsumptionist theme. This variation on the Hobsonian 'over-investment' theory presented a simplistic method of creating additional money (credit) so that all goods capable of being produced could be consumed. In his quest for active support for his ideas Douglas often failed to correct this misrepresentation, resorting to vague references to the 'technical' details underlying his proposals. Nevertheless, elements of contemporary reactions, summarised below, suggest that an alternative approach to the allocation of resources would have been economically, if not politically, feasible. For the sake of linguistic clarity in dealing with contemporary quotations, in this and the following chapters we revert to the convention of regarding Douglas as the sole author of the texts published in his name.

4

ORTHODOX/NEOCLASSICAL REACTIONS

REACTIONS IN THE 1920s

In the early 1920s the Douglas/*New Age* texts were considered sufficiently substantial to attract the attention of economists at Cambridge. R.F. Harrod reports a conversation between Keynes and the philosopher H.W.B. Joseph which took place in 1921. Keynes endorsed Joseph's 'long and complicated refutation of Douglas' arguments' as 'the most clear and admirable exposure of Major Douglas' fallacies I have ever heard' (quoted in King 1988: 143). Meade later claimed (in an interview with one of the authors on 17 November 1993) that the Douglas texts were 'an element' in the development of Keynes's theory of demand management, lending support to King's (1988) view that in economics, as in other disciplines, the provenance of their author affects the acceptability of theories.

Exactly which version of the Douglas/*New Age* texts formed the subject of these discussions is not known. A publication by Ramsey (1922) clearly drew on an early misinterpretation, *Dividends for All*, which Ramsey describes as 'a sixpenny pamphlet possessing distinct advantages both in brevity and clarity over the exposition of Major Douglas himself, who is always obscure and often absurd' (Ramsey 1922). Unfortunately, however, the 'sixpenny pamphlet' reverses the A and B payments and demonstrates only partial comprehension of the texts summarised in Part I. In the same article Ramsey admits that

> Mr W.A. Orton, late of Christ Church . . . regards the Douglas–Orage analysis as the most searching critique of the existing order which has appeared, and there is no doubt that the enthusiasm aroused in certain quarters by the two books *Economic Democracy* (6/–) and *Credit Power and Democracy* (7/6) requires some explanation.
>
> (Ramsey 1922: 74)

Presumably, unlike Ramsey, Orton had taken the trouble to undertake a critical reading of the original texts. Ramsey proceeds to attribute the popularity of the 'Douglas Scheme' to the 'journalistic genius of Mr Austin

Harrison [editor of the *English Review* who published Douglas's first articles in 1918–19] and Mr Orage' (Ramsey 1922). These comments provide an early example of the resistance to innovation displayed by economists towards the Douglas/Orage proposals. Other forms of 'scepticism concerning basic principles' (King 1988: 7) have continued to the present time. King's chapter is entitled 'Economic Heresy as Deviant Science'.

Ramsey dismissed the Douglas/*New Age* economics by using the then novel tool of integral calculus to explore the relationship between the selling prices and cost prices of consumable goods. He established that in a stationary state the relationship would be unity. He added: 'Since the ratio is unity for a stationary state, it is unlikely that in the present state it differs greatly from unity, for the present state is not so very far from a stationary state' (Ramsey 1922: 75). This conclusion is drawn on the curious basis of rejecting Douglas's original texts, which assume a dynamic economy, in favour of Young's misleading statement 'It is contended that the Wages, Salaries and Dividends issued in any unit period of time are never sufficient to buy the ultimate goods released for sale during the same period' (quoted by Ramsey 1922: 74). A thoughtful perusal of the original texts would have revealed the elementary error.

Ramsey proceeded to demonstrate two special circumstances in which the ratio of price to cost may not equal unity: that of a socialist state paying no interest, and when the rate of interest on new investment is less than the rate of interest which is incorporated in (past) costs. Both of these circumstances are irrelevant, Ramsey declares, to 'Douglas' contention that "just price" is today a quarter of cost' (Ramsey 1922). Having devised the rules which designated the terms of the debate, orthodoxy declared game, set and match against the Douglas/*New Age* economics.

Future rejections of 'social credit' may well stem from Young's fundamental misrepresentation of 'A + B'. If indeed 'wages, salaries and dividends issued in any unit period of time are never sufficient to buy the ultimate goods for sale during the same period', as Young definitely states, the economy could not function at all. Clearly, this is not the case. It is merely necessary to show that wages, salaries and dividends are constantly being paid out not only in respect of the production of 'ultimate products' (consumer goods) but also in respect of the manufacture of intermediate goods which form the basis of future production to demolish the argument as presented. Given the inadequacy of such expositions of the A + B theorem it is not remarkable that they were so easily dismissed. What is remarkable is the frequency with which it was deemed necessary to restate the apparently elementary proposition in a variety of forms over the two succeeding decades.

Equally remarkable is the extent of positive orthodox academic interest in the Douglas/*New Age* texts. The two earliest books, *Economic Democracy* and *Credit-Power and Democracy*, were 'set as text books for

Economic Honours at Sydney University in 1921' (Gaitskell 1933: 348n.). In their treatise on *Money* Foster and Catchings (1923) make full and precise reference to the Douglas/*New Age* texts, citing the three extant books and the Douglas/Hobson debate in the *Socialist Review* (Douglas 1922c) in addition to Young (1921) and Cousens (1921). They doggedly pursued the 'standard interpretation' (Mehta 1983) employed in refutation of the texts: if the financial system worked well enough most of the time there could be no inherent flaw in it. However, the similarity between their description of the factors affecting economic growth presented in *Profits* (Foster and Catchings 1925) and the analysis of the A + B theorem in the original texts is so strong as to be, perhaps, more than coincidental. The determination of academia to limit debate on economic questions is illustrated, for example, by Pigou's passing reference to the failings of guild socialism. In a footnote he refers to Reckitt and Bechhofer's *The Meaning of National Guilds*, observing that proposals for National Guilds were admirable in spirit. However, 'schemes of industrial reorganisation on these lines are exposed to serious practical difficulties, which their authors do not as yet seem fully to have faced' (Pigou 1929: 17). Although Pigou does not expand upon the 'practical difficulties' it must be surmised that they relate to financial viability and the motivation of labour. The key proposals in the Douglas/*New Age* texts for the reform of finance and the decommodification of labour apparently remained outside Pigou's purview.

Further 'official' interest was taken in the Douglas/*New Age* approach to banking and credit creation when Douglas was invited to present evidence to the Select Standing Committee on Banking and Commerce of the Canadian House of Commons in Ottawa in 1923. Douglas introduced his theories in over eighty pages of closely typed text and amplified upon them under questioning. Speaking largely without notes, Douglas presented a prestigious body of experts with a remarkably coherent account of the basic concepts as described in Part I (above) (House of Commons, Canada 1923).

REACTIONS IN THE 1930s

The range and vigour of debate on social credit in the 1930s has been attributed to the quest for solutions to the collapse of the world economy (Gaitskell 1933: 347–75; King 1988: 146). Two propositions are here implied. First, that social credit was merely examined out of desperation. Second, that social credit ideas would have gained little credence but for the circumstances of the time. It is contended here that social credit attracted more serious and widespread attention, both popular and academic, than other coherent monetary heresies, e.g. those of Soddy, Gesell and Eisler (Gaitskell 1933) which specifically sought to overcome economic stagnation.

Douglas continued as a prolific writer and speaker on an international scale. Although he continued to propound some of the socialist themes

85

arising from his pre-1922 collaboration with Orage, these aspects of the theories were never further developed. By the late 1920s, in response to contemporary reaction and the predominance of concern at encroaching depression, Douglas emphasised his financial and technical arguments for social control over the issue of credit so that the technological age could be distributed equitably while all were freed from wage slavery.

However, after 1922 partnership between the Labour Party and the trade unions precluded the possibility of guild socialism being realised through the trade unions. Indeed, 'social credit' ceased to be clearly identifiable as an alternative form of socialism as traditionally defined. It proved attractive to *petit-bourgeois* small farming interests in the dominions and the disaffected urban unemployed, both of which groupings had a tendency towards xenophobia and antisemitism (Irving 1959). Douglas's attacks on international trade and international finance fell on fertile ground, generating a groundswell of popular support well beyond the United Kingdom.

The range and extent of public reactions to social credit in the 1930s reflect elements in the evolving character of the social credit movement as well as Douglas's later development of particular aspects of the original themes. Although Douglas and his followers continued to publicise the earlier texts, which were frequently reprinted, the advisability of *restraining* material output and increasing leisure time ceased to be the dominant theme. In short, reactions in the 1930s reflected the decade's social credit phenomenon. They owed more to the interpretations placed on the original ideas by social credit activists in the light of the events of the 1930s than to the early texts. Subsequent historical presentations of sociological and psychological interpretations of the social credit movement treat the political economy of the original texts as little more than incidental (Macpherson 1953; Irving 1959; Finlay 1972; Finkel 1989).

ACADEMIC AND OFFICIAL REACTIONS IN THE 1930s

Douglas was invited to give evidence to the Macmillan Committee on Finance and Industry which reported in 1931. His evidence was at times muted and confused, lending credence to the view that social credit was an incoherent doctrine and that Douglas himself possessed no clear concepts. In the specific circumstances such an assessment may well be accurate. The Douglas/*New Age* economics, outlined in Part I, was not designed to enable free-market capitalism to survive a recession. Questions requiring Douglas to justify the texts as solutions to problems as perceived by orthodoxy were inevitably difficult to answer coherently.

Nevertheless, in giving evidence to the Macmillan Committee Douglas attempted to present social credit as a remedy for industrial depression and 'the consequent unrest', arguing that its cause was 'financial'. 'It is due to lack of power to buy, not to lack of political will to produce,' he argued in his written evidence, presented to the committee and reprinted as an appendix to *Monopoly of Credit* (Douglas 1931b: 123). The statement is consistent with the texts outlined in Part I, but appears to be a naïve basis for a coherent strategy worthy of serious consideration *within* the framework of orthodoxy. Keynes asked several of the committee's theoretical questions (Macmillan 1931: qq. 4470–88, 4499). His probings revealed the familiar inconsistencies in the A + B theorem as commonly interpreted. His further queries on the potential of vertical integration as a solution, or for the financial system to maintain an equilibrium volume of credit, indicate Keynes's considerable familiarity with the original texts. Nevertheless, Douglas's presentation of the 'small is beautiful' approach to economic stability (Douglas 1931b: 112) appears to have held no attraction for Keynes or the rest of the committee.

The Macmillan Committee had its own narrowly defined terms of reference: it sought concrete proposals to overcome the inadequacies of the existing financial system. Douglas insisted that he was not attempting to provide a definitive blueprint for an alternative to that system (Macmillan 1931: a. 4518). His object was to demonstrate that the financial system *could* be changed so that the industrial system no longer had to 'follow the financial system'. Rather, the financial system should 'serve the necessities of the industrial and social system' (Macmillan 1931: a. 4433). He wished to present possibilities rather than a final scheme (Macmillan 1931: a. 4438). That could not be provided on an *ad hoc* basis, but 'it is inconceivable that you cannot get a mechanism which will enable you to equate purchasing power to the capacity to deliver' (Macmillan 1931: a. 4469). Although the Macmillan Committee found Douglas's ideas confusing and unfamiliar, the fact of his being asked to give evidence to so prestigious a body raised his profile among academic economists, actual and potential social crediters and the public at large.

However, the concept of a value-added subsidy (a kind of inverse VAT) to regulate the production and distribution of the product of increasingly complex and extended technological processes failed to elicit the comprehension not only of the members of the Macmillan Committee but also of other academic figures of the 1930s. By no means entirely negative, the sheer volume of academic debate is itself significant.

Douglas's sixth book, *The Monopoly of Credit*, was reviewed in the *Economic Journal* (Biddulph 1932). The reviewer echoed the standard theme: Douglas was mistaken in his belief in an inevitable shortage of purchasing power, since no such shortage existed. However, the *Economic Journal* accorded Douglas a certain respect by spending over two pages to make this elementary statement. Lionel Robbins classified Douglas along with J.A. Hobson and other underconsumptionists, and assumed that in arguing for an increase in consumers' purchasing power Douglas had made a correct assessment of the relationship between turnover costs and distributed incomes (Robbins 1932, quoted by King 1988: 157).

R.G. Hawtrey corresponded at some length with Douglas in 1933 and 1937, taking a more positive approach. He debated with Douglas in Birmingham in 1933, included Douglas in his lectures and devoted a chapter in *Capital and Employment* to Douglas alongside Keynes, Hayek, Pigou and Harrod (Hawtrey and Douglas 1933; King 1988: 158; Hawtrey 1937). His theory that depreciation differs from other costs in that it does not generate income derived, on his own acknowledgement, from Douglas (King 1988: 153).

In his debate with Douglas (Hawtrey and Douglas 1933), Hawtrey reiterates the familiar argument that Douglas exaggerates the value and significance of 'B' payments in the formulation of costs and hence of prices. 'B' payments do not mysteriously disappear from the system, causing a chronic shortage of purchasing power. On the contrary, the ability of banks to generate purchasing power to be distributed in the form of wages and salaries *before* the final products appear on the market enables the economy to function. Although Hawtrey states specifically that he agrees with Douglas that banks create money and that incomes arise out of production, Hawtrey's appreciation of Douglas's central argument is lost at this point in the process of adversarial debate.

Supporters of social credit at the meeting attacked Hawtrey, the orthodox economist, on the grounds that he failed to place income generation at the centre of his argument. That this was the case, and that neither he nor indeed Douglas detected the significance of his acceptance of the central thesis of the Douglas texts, can be attributed to the circumstances under which the debate was conducted. Orthodoxy dictated its terms, which were to discover whether heresy had any solutions to offer to the *temporary* observable problems in the system. Once such problems were corrected the *existing* system could function smoothly. That the economy operated on a permanent basis of a series of unsustainable speculative gambles was inadmissible. That an alternative science of economics could potentially evolve (see King 1988) was unthinkable.

In his radio debate with Douglas, Dennis Robertson (Douglas and Robertson 1933) provided a convincing illustration of Keynes's maxim that 'the difficulty lies not in the new ideas but in escaping from the old ones which ramify . . . into every corner of our minds' (Keynes 1936: viii). Robertson contrasts himself, the practical university don, with Douglas the 'poet and dreamer', the pedlar of 'bright ideas' for improving existing financial arrangements, ideas which are 'completely fallacious'. He ignores the substance of Douglas's earlier contribution to the debate and proceeds to criticise the hypothetical thesis which he imagines Douglas to have presented. Douglas himself summed up during the debate: 'If I am not misrepresenting him, he agrees with me up to a certain point, but at this point he very kindly makes a completely new speech on my behalf which consists . . . of his own interpretation. He then expresses his own disagreement with his own paraphrases.' Douglas's comment is a fair reflection on Robertson's presentation.

However, the protagonists at the Birmingham debate agreed on two points. First, some adjustment in the system of private enterprise was necessary if the leisure resulting from the introduction of new technologies was to be distributed equitably as increased wealth. Second, Robertson recognised the validity of Douglas's view of the world instability which would result if industrialised countries attempted to export more than they imported indefinitely into the future.

In the radio discussion Robertson could not envisage an alternative financial system which would not undermine confidence and stability, despite Douglas's coherent opening summary. In his view, the economy was subject to only temporary setbacks. Although it might be necessary to rectify a *temporary* gap between incomes and costs, no permanent discrepancy existed. To provide an additional supply of purchasing power would be inflationary. If the credits offered to producers were not to operate as money in the 'normal' way, they would be rejected as 'bogus' money (Douglas and Robertson 1933). Robertson either failed to comprehend or elected to ignore the substance of Douglas's argument that the existing financial system was a contrived construct and as such capable of adaptation.

Robertson's view that the issue of additional purchasing power might provide a temporary solution to a temporary trade depression *within* the existing financial system was later echoed by James Meade (1938). In his proposal to issue 'consumers' credits' in the event of 'depression unemployment' (i.e. cyclical, as opposed to structural, unemployment) Meade was at pains to dissociate himself from 'the Social Credit schemes of such authors as Major Douglas' (Meade 1938: v). Meade envisaged grafting consumer credits on to the existing financial system in order to stimulate consumption. There was a danger, however, that if issued as cash and treated as such by commercial banks, consumer credits could act to swell bank reserves beyond the amount which could be reflected in loans and investments at the normal 1:9 ratio. The effect would be to thwart Bank of England control when contraction in the money supply became necessary. Meade's consumers' credits had therefore to be a form of 'bogus' money, hedged with unfamiliar regulations (Meade 1938: 53–63, 80–92).

The complexities and anomalies of persisting in the maintenance of a predominating link between employment and income are demonstrated, albeit inadvertently, by Meade's proposals. Meade's consumers' credits are based on contributions in respect of insured workers in employment, graduated in line with unemployment (as unemployment increases, the payments increase). Beneficiaries are all insured workers and their wives, widows and dependent children, and old-age pensioners over the age of 65 years. Calculations from available statistics enabled Meade to estimate that 77.6 per cent of the total population would be eligible (directly or indirectly) to receive his consumers' credits, which would be paid when necessary to counteract the decrease in purchasing power resulting from excessive unemployment. Taking 1931 as an example, out of a total population of 45,831,000, 34,800,000 individuals would have been eligible for payments under the scheme, while 11,031,000 (22.4 per cent of the population) would have fallen completely outside it.

This was the era of the continued quest for a 'living wage' for the male manual worker, who was assumed to provide for his wife and children. It was customary, then and now, to regard the insured male worker of 16–65 years as 'normal'. Being female and married or widowed (with or without dependent children), a child under 15 or an old person over 65 years was classed as 'abnormal'. On Meade's figures, insured males (employed and unemployed) of 16–65 years totalled 11,529,000, roughly the same figure as the most highly 'abnormal' who fell outside the scheme altogether (11,031,000). Additionally, he estimated a total of 5,550,000 insured single women; 6,143,000 women were insured, but a proportion of these would be wives of insured workers or over 65 years and would therefore not enter the statistics in their own right. Out of a total population of 45,831,000, this gives 17,079,000 individuals in the 'normal' situation of being insured workers (i.e. actually or potentially in employment) and 28,752,000 individuals (60 per cent of the population) in the 'abnormal' situation of being dependants of insured workers, in receipt of pensions or otherwise outside the 'labour market'.

In this light, an equitable scheme to provide income security based upon some form of national insurance derived from employment appears problematic. The Beveridge provisions which followed were based upon the normative view of a male breadwinner earning a family wage through constant employment between the ages of 16 and 65, bringing in sufficient to provide for his wife and children. Under this scheme the income security of married women (the majority of women) is doubly jeopardised, in that they remain dependent upon a man's wage, and on whether or not he is in employment. A study of Meade's statistics indicates that under any such scheme most women would spend most of their lives in a high degree of income insecurity. Recognition of the implications of this fact, particularly for provision for children, gave rise to the campaign for non-means-tested family allowances payable to the mother. Anomalies of this type are endemic in a reformist approach to social justice.

In 1931 unemployment, i.e. the unemployment of *insured* workers, was 21 per cent (Meade 1938: 106), converting the percentage in employment to a mere 30 per cent of the total population. Hence 70 per cent of individuals were dependent for subsistence on some source other than a personally earned income. In comparison with Meade's scheme and contemporary practice, the Douglas/*New Age* proposals to adjust the work/income relationship in the light of economic realities carries the hallmark of sense and simplicity.

Challenged by Hawtrey to recognise his debt to Douglas for his analysis of company sinking funds, Keynes claimed that the resemblance was very slight (King 1988: 153). He omitted specific references to Douglas in *The Treatise* but included him in *The General Theory* alongside Marx (to the irritation of Marxists), Mandeville, Malthus, Gesell and Hobson as belonging to the underworld of economic heretics (Keynes 1936). His inclusion of Douglas in his section on the history of the theory of effective demand is, according to King, of some significance (King 1988: 153). According to Keynes:

> The great puzzle of effective demand with which Malthus had wrestled vanished from economic literature. You will not find it mentioned even once in the whole works of Marshall, Edgeworth and Professor Pigou, from whose hands the classical theory has received its most mature embodiment. It could only live on furtively, below the surface, in the underworlds of Karl Marx, Silvio Gesell or Major Douglas.
>
> (Keynes 1936: 32)

King (1988: 147) also states that Hayek mentioned Douglas briefly.

Geoffrey Crowther's standard textbook on money, published in 1940, made reference to Douglas and included an appendix on Douglas in the numerous editions published up to, and including, 1946. The appendix on social credit in the standard text on money for a generation of economists offers an excellent 'case study' of the history of the Douglas/*New Age* texts. The material in the appendix first appeared in 1934 as a series of articles published in the *News Chronicle*, indicating that for over a decade social credit remained an issue for orthodoxy to contend with. The tone and content of this appendix illuminate the tone and content of the overall debate.

Basically, Crowther speaks for orthodoxy, assuming the high moral ground in terms of authority. He questions the motives of those members of the general public who have the audacity to venture into 'the extremely difficult and technical subject of money'. One should be 'naturally suspicious' of a theory which promises:

> 'the abolition of poverty, the reduction of the likelihood of war to zero, rapidly diminishing crime, the beginning of economic freedom for the individual, and the introduction of the leisure State' – and all by means of simple bookkeeping.
>
> (Crowther 1946: 432)

Although one hears 'little' of the movement in the press, it has 'an evident popular appeal'. Crowther is 'reluctant' to conclude that the remedy Douglas proposes is likely to 'do more harm than good' (Crowther 1946: 433, 445). His slight variation on the 'standard misinterpretation' is followed by: 'The final conclusion at which I arrive is not that Major Douglas is wrong. Far from it – I believe there is much that is valuable in his theories'

91

(Crowther 1946: 444). The fault, according to Crowther, is that it has all been said before, by orthodox economists, but without the same conclusions being drawn. Crowther finds it 'distasteful to disagree with enthusiastic idealism, especially when the objectives of the movement are so admirable' (Crowther 1946: 445).

In the debate with academics, how closely Douglas related to orthodoxy emerges as less relevant than how closely he or orthodoxy related to fact. Although uneasy with certain elements of neoclassical thought, Hawtrey, Robertson and Meade observed the convention of distancing orthodoxy from heresy. Douglas and his supporters were therefore deemed mistaken to imagine that industry existed to produce a necessary minimum of goods for all, to reduce work and to decrease waste. In the depression years Douglas's theories were examined in the quest to ameliorate a temporary economic malaise. The depression, although severe, was perceived by orthodoxy as a temporary aberration in an otherwise sound system. No inherent flaws existed in the financial system. Orthodoxy was therefore under no obligation to review its basic tenets.

In debates during 1933 Douglas accused orthodox economists of living in the past in their understanding of the role of finance in the economy. Their stylised view of finance coincided well with 'single-stage production' methods which antedated the industrial revolution. Under the complex system of production developed in the later industrial revolution, however, finance played a more complex role. Economists could not decide 'whether the money system is a system of government or an accounting system' (Douglas and Robertson 1933). By a 'system of government' Douglas implies a system which is in overall control of economic decision-making. In the contemporary monetary framework, financing the production of 'unsuitable products' in order that purchasing power should be created and circulated is considered sound practice (Douglas and Robertson 1933). To 'the engineer' (as opposed to the economist) it does not make sense to stimulate demand

> by making a large quantity of goods which are not intended to be sold to the public [so that] . . . the purchasing power distributed in making these goods [can be used] to buy consumable goods. . . . I do not regard it as being a sane system that before you can buy a cabbage it is absolutely necessary to make a machine gun.
>
> (Hawtrey and Douglas 1933)

CONCLUSION

To conclude, the evidence suggests that the Douglas/*New Age* texts were widely debated and well read by orthodox economists, who often adapted the theories for their own purposes. Indeed, the points of similarity between the Douglas texts and, for example, Meade's *Consumers' Credits and Unemployment* and his later 'Agathotopian' proposals are more than coincidental. Meade was introduced to the Douglas/*New Age* texts as a young student by an aunt who subscribed to the *New Age*. He described himself as a 'social crediter' in the early 1920s, and the theories were instrumental in attracting him to the study of economics. However, in order to become a *bona fide* practitioner of the orthodox science of economics it was necessary for him to dissociate himself from the 'heresy' of social credit (Meade 1938, 1993; interview with one of the authors, 17 November 1993; see also King 1988: chapter 1, on orthodoxy).

As the Western world view has emerged to full hegemony during succeeding decades of this century it has been increasingly necessary to distance the orthodox from the heretic, the professional from the amateur. The emergence of the career economist, dependent on his/her profession for a livelihood and under pressure to conform to preserve it (King 1988: 12–13), restricts validation of economic theory to areas which conform with prevailing financial jurisdiction. Orthodox economics is *an* accepted set of axioms from which analysis proceeds. To paraphrase Orage (Douglas 1922a), the orthodox economist need merely declare the treatise on the game of cricket invalid on the grounds that it does not conform to *the* generally accepted view on stool-ball. There is no requirement to provide scientific proof of the validity of orthodoxy's preference for stool-ball.

5

THE LABOUR PARTY AND SOCIAL CREDIT

SIDNEYWEBBICALISM VERSUS SOCIAL CREDIT IN THE 1920s

In 1922 a committee appointed by the Labour Party reviewed 'The Douglas–*New Age* Scheme' and concluded that it was 'out of harmony with the trend of Labour thought, and . . . indeed fundamentally opposed to the principles for which the Labour Party stands' (Labour Party 1922). The rejection of its analysis by the Labour Party in 1922 proved decisive to the subsequent history of the Douglas/*New Age* economics. To Douglas, Orage and many guild socialists at the time, the alternative economic framework presented in the Douglas/*New Age* texts was in close accord with a socialist critique of capitalism. 'Labourism', as propounded by the Labour Party, challenged 'not a single proposition of the capitalist system'. Rather, 'every strike has been a fight for position in the system', with individuals aspiring to posts of status and power within a system which they might as socialists have been expected to challenge (Douglas 1922b: 152). Throughout World War I 'Guild Socialist Fabian researchers' worked in a close but uneasy relationship with 'what *Punch* called "Sidneywebbicalism"' (Cole 1940: 160). By 1918 the statistical paternalism of Clause IV nationalisation held sway in the Labour Party in alliance with the trade unions.

Later, Orage perceptively noted that career politicians emerging from the ranks of the trade union movement were easily sidetracked from socialism by the prospect of public honours. Flattered by the 'English governing classes', they were treated with the 'condescending courtesy meted out to ex-butlers who have come into a moderate fortune'. Most artful of all, the wives of newly elected Labour politicians were 'patronised and begged by dowagers, in the name of their common class, to dissuade their husbands from ruining the country' (Orage 1926: 378). Writing in 1979, Margaret Cole made similar observations on the lengths to which Labour politicians went to convince the ruling classes that they were 'fit to govern' (Cole 1979).

According to Douglas and Orage, by opting for class-based confrontational politics the Labour Party failed to capitalise on the lessons of the

1914–18 war. A socialist political economy offering the potential for a united society, and international peace could have been developed from close observation of the workings of the wartime economy. As Orage later commented, 'In creating the Labour Party Socialism has created an obstacle to its own realisation greater perhaps than any obstacle that had previously existed' (quoted in Steele 1990: 70).

When it emerged as a major political force the Labour Party might well have opted to present a radical critique of economic liberalism, and to offer alternative policies on banking and finance. Instead, the right and duty of individuals to be offered and to find work as a condition of subsistence formed the dominant consideration. The Fabians sought modifications of the existing system on grounds of greater efficiency. As Booth (1983) explained, the role of finance in the capitalist system was, at that time, neither understood nor questioned. *Labour and the New Social Order* (1918), based on Fabian philosophy as developed within the framework of the *Fabian Essays in Socialism* (1889) (McBriar 1962), presented a programme of minimum wage legislation and social planning which demonstrated a failure to grasp the elements of capitalist finance or external trading relations. 'Until Labour understood the financial workings of capitalist economics, its programme of transition to socialism could always be threatened by capitalist crises' (Booth 1983).

Orage's championing of alternative economic ideas through the *New Age* was, however, complemented by pressures from within the Labour Party. At its annual conference in 1919 Philip Snowden advocated a 'National Bank for national service with branches in all centres', following the inept handling of wartime finances whereby 'fictitious credits' had been created, and thousands of millions of pounds borrowed at high rates of interest. Snowden's resolution was adopted, along with a resolution to examine the 'state bonus scheme' advocated by Dennis Milner (Finlay 1972: 196–7). Milner's scheme, which contains proposals similar to Douglas's national dividend but with a 'workfare' element and without the wider financial analysis, is detailed by Van Trier (1991: 5–16). Despite popular support among Labour Party members for a system of basic remuneration by virtue of citizenship rather than a guarantee of the right to employment, the Labour Party executive rejected further consideration of the Milner scheme in 1920 (Finlay 1972: 196–7).

Following publication of the Draft Scheme for the Mining Industry in 1920 (Douglas 1920), calls from throughout the United Kingdom for the Labour Party executive formally to consider the 'Douglas Credit Scheme' were articulated by the Scottish Miners and the South Hampshire Divisional Labour Party (Finlay 1972: 197). A formal request first came in January 1921 after discussion between Douglas and a sub-committee of the Scottish Labour Advisory Committee, which received Douglas's proposals favourably (Finlay 1972: 198; Scottish Labour Party 1920). Although the proposals were widely discussed it was not until 24 May 1921 that Douglas and Orage received an offhand invitation to attend a meeting of the specially appointed committee the following week (Douglas 1922a: appendix II, p. 37).

The Labour Party sub-committee presented its negative report on *The Labour Party and Social Credit: a Report on the Proposals of Major Douglas and the 'New Age'* (hereafter referred to as 'The Labour Party Report' to distinguish it from the commentary on the report by Douglas and Orage) in 1922. The composition of the sub-committee, its method of approach and the perfunctory nature of its report lend support to the conclusion expressed by Orage and Douglas in the pages of the *New Age* and summarised in *The Labour Party and Social Credit* (Douglas 1922a) that the executive of the Labour Party never intended to give the proposals serious consideration. This becomes apparent in view of three considerations.

In the first place, the terms of reference and approach lacked coherence. The Labour Party had originally been asked by the Mining Federation of Great Britain to investigate the Draft Mining Scheme, following detailed discussions between Douglas and the Scottish Labour Committee (Finlay 1972: 198). The interest here centred on a novel approach to financial reform, via the guild system. The 'scheme' to be discussed by the committee turned out, as Orage correctly surmised, to be Douglas's monetary reforms shorn of their guild socialist implications. Second, only at the first meeting of the sub-committee on 24 May 1921 was any decision taken to invite Douglas, via Orage, to explain 'The Douglas Credit Scheme', offering barely a week's notice of the intended meeting. In their joint reply Douglas and Orage named the subject of the inquiry as 'The Douglas–NEW AGE Scheme' (referring to the Mining Scheme) and asked for clarification. Was the committee to investigate the 'social aspects' of the scheme – 'the results of putting it into operation' – or the 'technical aspects . . . concerned with its feasibility and the theory on which it is based?' They declined the invitation to attend the hearing at such short notice and on such vague terms. Finally, following disagreement over the composition of the committee, no further invitation was extended to the authors of the 'Scheme' to participate in the deliberations or elaborate on its significance (Douglas 1922a: 37–42). Subsequently the full text of the correspondence between Arthur Greenwood, secretary of the Labour Party, and Douglas and the editor of the *New Age* was printed as an appendix to *The Labour Party and Social Credit* (Douglas 1922a). Although published under Douglas's name alone, the section of this pamphlet dealing with the Labour Party and social credit, and the letters in appendix II, are written in the distinctive style of Orage.

As a central figure in the socialist movement Orage was well placed to forecast the outcome of the inquiry. Subsequently, in July 1922, he published a 'Who's Who' of 'the Labour Party Committee of Inquiry into the Douglas–NEW AGE Scheme' (*New Age* 1922a, 1922b) with a critical commentary on the track record and interests of its members. A condensed version follows.

The committee consisted of:

1 *Sidney Webb*, Fabian since 1885, principal founder of the London School of Economics, Professor of Public Administration, chairman of the *New Statesman* Publishing Company and author of innumerable statistical reports on all manner of 'poverty and distress' (the latter listed in detail).

2 *Arthur Greenwood*, former lecturer in economics (Huddersfield, Leeds), Labour Party General Secretary and Fabian.

3 *J.A. Hobson*, writer and publicist, author of *Economics of Distribution* and *Imperialism* (1902), until recently the recognised exponent of 'Social Reform Liberalism'. Hobson was frequently attacked by orthodox economists for his theory that too rapid accumulation of capital goods (too much 'saving') leads to industrial slumps through underconsumption. 'No further progress visible.'

4 *R.H. Tawney*, lecturer at LSE on economic history, author of books on economic history and the minimum wage and of *The Acquisitive Society*. A Fabian Society member and parliamentary candidate. A 'Change of Heart Man', i.e. belonging to the school of thought which imagined that capitalism would capitulate to reasoned argument.

5 *C.M. Lloyd*, barrister, Fabian Society member, lecturer at LSE and author of a book on trade unionism.

6 *Sir Leo G. Chiozza Money, Kt*, Fabian, member of various government committees, parliamentary secretary during the war, 'a fervent nationaliser', but might have been expected to disagree with part of the report which states that banking is a process of 'collecting funds from depositors and handing them over to borrowers' (Labour Party 1922: 11): in *The Future of Work and other Essays* (1914) Money had written, 'When a bank gives an overdraft to a creditable customer, it in effect coins credit, and it should be remembered in this connection that the greater part of the enormous so-called "deposits" with British banks consist of such coined credits.'

7 *Frank Hodges*, educated at Ruskin College, South Wales miner, member of the Coal Industry Commission. Hodges played a 'decisive and tragical' role in the negotiations on the eve of the 1921 coal miners' strike and was the author of *The Nationalisation of the Mines*.

8 *F.B. Varley*, Notts miner, elected to the Labour Party executive in 1922, 'otherwise and thereafter a blank'.

9 *R.J. Davies*, 'originally a miner', now an MP.

10 *Hugh Dalton*, reader in commerce at LSE, barrister.

11 *G.D.H. Cole*, tutorial class tutor, guild socialist and author of fourteen books on trade unionism, guild socialism and sociology, 'thousands to follow' (*New Age* 1922a, 1922b).

12 An unnamed 'experienced bank official' also assisted the committee (Labour Party 1922).

Douglas and Orage were convinced from the outset that the Labour Party had no intention of giving their proposals a reasoned hearing. As they observed in the exchange of letters with Greenwood during the course of the inquiry, no member of the committee except Hodges had any direct knowledge of the coal-mining industry (to which the scheme specifically referred), or any practical experience of business management or finance. At least three members of the committee had already publicly pronounced against the scheme and at least two were determined not to face up to the implications of industry's 'decreasing requirements in respect of active labour' (Douglas 1922a: 38–9). Furthermore, the decision to secure the advice of a banker in preference to that of the authors of the proposals suggested that the report was intended as a publicity exercise for orthodox Labour policy.

The Labour Party and Social Credit is a sixteen-page document purporting to examine 'The Douglas–*New Age* Scheme'. Almost six pages are devoted to a description of the existing system of banking and finance. This section of the report is intended to substantiate the claim that the Labour Party would operate the existing system more efficiently through nationalisation and municipal (decentralised, democratic) control of the banks. While these proposals might well make traditional banking more accessible to the wage earner, they would do nothing to end wage slavery.

The remaining ten pages of the report which constitute Part 1 set out the Labour Party's reasons for rejecting Major Douglas's 'Scheme for the Control of Credit and the Fixing of Prices', as 'propounded' in articles in the *New Age, Economic Democracy, Credit-Power and Democracy*, and by various 'supporters' of the 'scheme'. The committee concludes that the most useful aspect of the scheme is in drawing attention to the 'importance of credit and banking to the Economic System' (Labour Party 1922: 1). Close reading of the report in the light of the original texts, as outlined in Chapters 2 and 3, suggests that the general comments and specific response of Douglas and Orage as published in the pamphlet *These Present Discontents and The Labour Party and Social Credit* (Douglas 1922a) present a reasonably accurate assessment of the context and content of the report.

BACKGROUND TO THE LABOUR PARTY REPORT

In *The Labour Party and Social Credit* (Douglas 1922a) Douglas (or Orage?) summarises the fundamental misinterpretation of the 'scheme', adopted in the report, before setting the report in its historical context. A detailed analysis of the report is included in appendix I, which clearly bears the hallmarks of Douglas's style of writing. Since the entire pamphlet is published as authored by Douglas, for the purpose of this analysis we refer to the author as Douglas. The pamphlet was the product of a close collaboration between Douglas and Orage.

Before analysing the specific objections to the 'Douglas–*New Age* Scheme' as voiced in the Labour Party report, Douglas and Orage suggest that the subject matter of the report itself is of less significance than the circumstances surrounding its publication. The origins of the report, the composition of the committee, the date of publication and the general tenor of the report are of more significance (Douglas 1920: 20).

The origins of the report

Douglas points out that in 1920, following the shelving of the Sankey Report, 'Scottish Labour Groups' were in a state of general disaffection. They foresaw the drift towards wage reductions and blamed the situation on the agitation for nationalisation. For these reasons the Draft Scheme for the Mining Industry, drawn up by Douglas and 'most ably expounded by Mr A.R. Orage in the first place', created a great deal of interest. As a result, in January 1921 the Scottish Labour Advisory Committee (SLAC) requested the Central Executive Committee of the Miners' Federation to investigate the 'Mining Scheme'. Although not prepared to endorse all of 'Major Douglas's views' the SLAC accepted that bank credits were one of the main constituents of prices, and that the issue of credit and the fixing of prices should come 'under the community's control'. The matter required further examination.

In other words, as Douglas observes, the Labour Party committee had not accepted the recommendation of the SLAC, which expressed itself as satisfied with the background theory and was asking the Central Executive of the Miners' Federation to consider the practicalities of the Draft Mining Scheme. The Miners' Federation had referred the whole matter to the central Labour Party executive, which had appointed the committee in question. Douglas notes that this body made no reference to the SLAC. The recommendation of the SLAC had not been accepted, and its opinion had been disregarded. Douglas speculates that, since the composition of the Labour Party committee was such that it could by its very nature come to no other conclusion, the SLAC would not, had it been consulted, have agreed to its composition.

The composition of the committee

After listing, briefly, the members of the committee, Douglas notes that there is no indication that the report was agreed unanimously, and no individual members have signed it 'as published'. The suspicion was that a number of the committee knew nothing whatsoever about 'the subject of

Credit . . . [and] proposed to have as little as possible to do with it'. Furthermore, apart from the trade unionists, who might be expected to have worked at a trade at some time, most of the committee had no first-hand knowledge of 'economic production'. Although Sidney Webb had written a book on the 'Works Manager', a works manager might experience some difficulty if 'called upon to find a use for Mr Webb in his work'. Since the proposal was for 'economic democracy' in the form of worker control over the process of production, this oversight was more than a mere technical quibble. Furthermore, lacking any practical knowledge or theories of finance, the committee had co-opted an unnamed 'experienced Bank official'. This, as Douglas points out, is very different from a well-informed committee asking for evidence in support of their inquiry. Such evidence would, indeed, be valuable.

Douglas and Orage conclude that neither in practical matters associated with 'Real Credit' nor in the complexities of 'psychology, business procedure, and politics' associated with 'Financial Credit' was the committee equipped to judge the complexities of the scheme. The failure to seek relevant evidence was all the more surprising in view of the presence of barristers on the committee. However, the Webbs and the Fabians as a whole were 'notably successful in intercepting, sterilising and misdirecting intelligent enquiry into the causes of social unrest'.

Observing that the London School of Economics (LSE), founded by the Webbs, is an 'unimpeachably orthodox institution' turning out candidates for the Treasury and the banks, Douglas notes the lack of any fundamental conflict of interest between the ideal Fabian state and the banking interests. Both would no doubt consider themselves to be 'actuated by the highest motives' but both rely upon 'economic slavery' to achieve their ends.

The date of issue of the report

The committee first met on 24 May 1921. Following reports of disagreement, the *New Statesman* advised that no report would be published. Douglas notes that Sidney Webb was at that time chair of the Statesman Publishing Company, and hence in a position to advise. The following year, however, in March 1922, the crisis in the mining industry revived interest, and an unsigned and undated report was published immediately prior to the Miners' conference, but with insufficient time for it to be read and discussed. The review of the report in *Financial News* made no mention of the social credit proposals, and focused exclusively on the suggested nationalisation and municipalisation of the banks.

The impression the report is intended to convey

Douglas argues that the report succeeds in maintaining the orthodox formula of the relationship between cost and price as determined by the existing financial system. In this light, any defects in the system can continue to be blamed upon 'wicked employers making undue profits'. In this way, employers and employed working in the same industry are set in opposition to each other, whether in large companies or in small enterprises.

At the same time, Douglas argues, the report demonstrates that worker control over policy and conditions and an 'incomparably wider outlook on life' were, in the words of the report, 'fundamentally opposed to the principles for which the Labour Party stands'. Instead, the report advocates the outright abolition of the shareholder, coupled with appropriation of ownership from the banks without any clear strategy for the construction of an alternative system.

In presenting this detailed review of the background of the report Douglas and Orage sought to demonstrate the superficial nature of the Labour Party publication. Had there been evidence of full and detailed consideration of the 'Douglas/*New Age* Scheme' by a committee containing many eminent figures, subsequent claims that it had been examined and found wanting would have held substance. In their analysis Douglas and Orage note that several individuals on the committee had on previous occasions declared their opposition to the proposals. These individual reactions are considered in more detail in Chapter 6.

THE DOUGLAS/ORAGE CRITIQUE OF THE REPORT

In appendix I of the pamphlet *These Present Discontents and the Labour Party and Social Credit*, Douglas (and Orage) rehearse the argument that the Labour Party report is nothing more than a defence of the existing banking and financial system. The Labour Party appears to use the occasion to assert that its 'motives, intelligence and general equipment' qualify it to claim the ability to run the existing system better than its present administrators.

The Labour Party and 'High Finance' appear to be agreed on four points. First, by misusing the word 'capital' (as in 'production capital appreciation' on p. 6, 'additional capital required . . . by existing capitalist employers' and 'share capital of the colliery companies' on p. 7) they demonstrate a belief that financial credit is a 'concrete thing conditioned by limitations inherent in itself'. Second, that the banking system cannot and does not create financial credit. Third, that price is always and only determined by the market (i.e. that goods exchange only at equilibrium prices). And fourth, that 'the objective of the industrial system is employment'.

By way of contrast, Douglas presents the premises of the 'Social Credit Movement'. First, financial credit is a 'mere device' which should have no economic significance separate from real credit, 'the correct estimate of the ability to deliver goods and services as and when desired'. Second, that banks do create financial credit and manipulate it in order to use the power inherent in the real credit of the community. Third, that the price of an article should be such as to ensure it is produced and delivered in the quantity desired by the community. And fourth, that the object of the industrial system should be the delivery of goods and services to individuals. Neither the Labour Party nor 'High Finance' should be in a position to arbitrate over what is, or what is not, 'useful work'. Nor should they be in a position to use this arbitrary decision to withhold a share in the fruits of the economy from 'non-workers' as so arbitrarily defined.

Douglas proceeds to examine the report in detail, paragraph by paragraph, pointing out the misleading paraphrases which add up to a parody of the original texts. For example:

> Page 3, line 42: 'Further, all payments – wages, interest, salaries and everything else *eventually* go to individuals.' Wages and salaries came out of credit and *originally* went to individuals, and *eventually*, together with profits, are recovered in prices out of which dividends are paid.
>
> (Douglas 1922a: 32; Douglas's emphasis)

This statement of the essence of 'social credit' is followed by a number of criticisms in similar vein of the subsequent pages and paragraphs, demonstrating the inadequacies of the report as a serious examination of the original proposals.

One paragraph of the report (the final paragraph on p. 4) clearly confuses the credit which induces production of capital goods with the capital goods themselves. J.A. Hobson, a member of the committee, had previously argued that financial credits, i.e. bank deposits, were 'savings'. Since the plant indicated in the words 'Capital employed in production' quite evidently did not come into existence until after the credit (bank loan) which had 'induced its production', Douglas speculated that Hobson probably dissociated himself from this 'singularly incompetent' paragraph.

In the same vein, p. 7 of the report objected to the 'price-fixing scheme' (the very reverse of the core theme of *Economic Democracy* and *Credit-Power and Democracy*) while claiming that the proposals would be inflationary, again, the result of a misreading of the proposals.

It is in its attitude towards the trade unions, as organisations of producers, however, that the report reveals the hierarchical nature of the relationship between the Labour Party and labour organisations. In this relationship 'money' has a higher profile than goods and services or those who produce them (Douglas 1922a: 35). One spurious argument advanced in the report was the cost of administration of locally controlled producers' banks. Douglas concludes that this criticism:

> may charitably be ascribed to ignorance of commercial procedure in the payment of wages, etc., at present. By combining the credit-keeping and the wage-paying organisation in one, not only would a

considerable amount of labour [!] ensue, but the practical inconvenience of 'pay-day' to everyone concerned would be eliminated.

(Douglas 1922a: 36)

In summary, in eleven pages the Labour Party dismissed the proposals, discounting the A + B theorem on the same misunderstanding as Ramsay's analysis. The concept of producers' banks was declared unworkable, on the grounds that it did not accord with current banking practice and would prove inflationary. Part II of the report argued that it would not have 'effectively refuted Major Douglas' proposals' unless it could be shown that 'the Labour Party had a policy for dealing with the admitted dangers of the control of credit by profit-making interests'. Nationalisation of the banking system and the development of municipal banks were proposed, although the method by which these proposals would effectively alter the relationship between production and distribution was not examined. The report persisted in the belief that redistribution of the profits paid to shareholders would miraculously transform the relations of production. As Reckitt later noted, this rejection marked the end of the close collaboration between Orage and Douglas. Although Orage continued to promote social credit, from that point in time 'social credit became less and less social and more and more concentrated on the technical aspects of finance' (Reckitt 1941: 189).

Despite their rejection by leading labour theorists, the Douglas/*New Age* texts were popular and widely read. The first three books, originally presented in the *New Age*, found external publishers and went into multiple reprints. Although the *New Age* was the central periodical in the debate, discussions appeared in a wide range of journals. Even the *New Statesman* was stung into a response, albeit derogatory, through pressure of readers' letters (*New Statesman* 1922). Douglas's impenetrable style facilitated the debunking of 'Douglasism' through the simple expedient of juxtaposing two incomprehensible sentences and indicating apparent inconsistencies almost at random. Hence in the *New Statesman* article 'Douglasism' is described as 'the most harmless religion that has ever invaded these islands' (*New Statesman* 1922). The unknown author (Sidney Webb?) admits that the power of banking and finance over the mechanisms of production and distribution may well be excessive but fails to attempt a reasoned critique of the 'Draft Mining Scheme'.

Rank-and-file Labour Party interest in Douglas's texts was encouraged by such publications as Cousens's *A New Policy for Labour: an Essay in the Relevance of Credit Control* (1921). Cousens argued that Labour should not neglect finance just because it was mysterious and 'an unsuitable subject for an Albert Hall demonstration' (Cousens 1921: 21). Despite the impressive line-up of talent on the 1922 committee, the report was not reissued. It rated only a passing reference in the 1935 Labour Party report on social credit.

BACKGROUND TO *SOCIALISM AND 'SOCIAL CREDIT'* (1935)

The range and vigour of debate on social credit in the 1930s has been attributed to the quest for solutions to the collapse of the world economy (King 1988: 146). Two propositions are here implied. First, that social credit was merely examined out of desperation. Second, that social credit ideas would have gained little credence but for the circumstances of the time. It is contended here that social credit attracted more serious and widespread attention, both popular and academic, than other coherent monetary heresies. In general, monetary reformists took the simplistic view that monetary reform would automatically result in social equity. They joined politicians in viewing economic stagnation as the great evil.

Douglas continued as a prolific writer and speaker on an international scale. Although he continued to propound some of the socialist themes arising from his pre-1922 collaboration with Orage, these aspects of the theories were not further developed. By the late 1920s, in response to contemporary reaction and the predominance of concern at encroaching depression, Douglas had cultivated his financial and technical arguments for social control over the issue of credit so that the technological age of plenty could be realised.

Social crediters with a guild socialist background continued, with diminishing optimism, to argue the case for the social implications of social credit economics. Reckitt, editor of the *New English Weekly*, describes this period in some detail. Writing after the outbreak of World War II, he notes that the main task of the *New English Weekly*, founded by Orage in 1932, was to seek to 'integrate the truths of social credit into a sufficient social synthesis' (Reckitt 1941: 178). Describing social credit as 'the truth about economics', Reckitt argued that by 1936 the movement had come to embrace 'the philosophy of abundance' and the economic theory was no more than a 'quantitative mechanism' for supplying material goods in abundance. He attributes the disintegration of a movement which 'half a dozen years ago could fill the Albert Hall and count adherents all over the country by thousands' to the subordination of its cultural and spiritual aspects. Acknowledging that many social crediters may disagree, he observes that adherence to mere monetary reform is no different from arguing that human hearts and minds should be subordinated to the rules of 'Sound Finance'. He attacks the suggestion that all that society needs to cure its ills is a 'vastly accelerated output of the very things it now spills out so copiously to those who can afford to buy them'.

> To a world suffering from the accumulating devastations of mass production, mass publicity, mass creation, and mass recreation, the addition of mass consumption may seem only likely to make our spiritual confusion more confounded . . .

> A particularly revealing sign of the materialistic outlook which has dominated and impaired much [recent] Social Credit propaganda is the curious argument which justifies the Douglas Proposals on the grounds that without their application it is impossible to run modern industry at full blast.
>
> (Reckitt 1941: 175–8)

This attack on the purely 'technical' approach to social credit was originally published in an article in the journal *Purpose* in April 1936. In the previous year, when the popularity of social credit was at its height, the Labour Party considered it necessary to publish another report entitled *Socialism and 'Social Credit'* (Labour Party 1935). The authors of this report consulted a number of social crediters, including Philip Mairet, then editor of the *New English Weekly*, who can be assumed to have shared the views of Reckitt and S.G. Hobson as described in Reckitt's autobiography. Reckitt describes Hobson as a socialist who favoured 'Socialist Unity' and had come to perceive that Parliament was 'incapable of seriously influencing the economic situation at all'. Labour's attack was not being conducted in the area where the enemy's real strength lay. Hobson, rejected by the Fabians, doubted the nature of a socialism which was no more than a 'Collectivist reorganization [which], however far it might be pressed, would leave the status of the worker unaffected. That could only be changed by the discovery and attainment of a new basis of industrial partnership' (Reckitt 1941: 106). The authors of the Labour Party pamphlet, however, make no reference to this aspect of social credit thought, and concentrate on dismissing the financial technicalities as propounded by the later Douglas. Although published by the Labour Party, the report is described as representing the views of 'three individual Socialist economists' (Labour Party 1935: 3). Two of these, Durbin and Gaitskell, had already established their reputations by touring the country speaking against social credit (Durbin 1985: 220) and had published a number of works to that effect. The 'report' is little more than a reformulation of these opinions.

Heightened popular interest in 'Douglas Social Credit' followed the publicity surrounding Douglas's evidence to the Macmillan Committee (1930) and the publication of *Warning Democracy* (Douglas 1931a) and *The Monopoly of Credit* (Douglas 1931b). Reacting to the groundswell of support, radical economists and Labour politicians, predisposed to defend a particular world view, shared a common interest in seeking to discredit social credit. Radicals made no serious attempt to provide an objective assessment of the Douglas/*New Age* proposals as a coherent economics of socialism. Since no alternative existed, in the form of a Labour Party economic policy which could be distinguished from liberal orthodoxy (Durbin 1985), the firm rejection by the Labour Party of the Douglas/*New Age* economics as 'incompatible with socialism' (Durbin 1985: 219) leaves unanswered (even unasked) the question of what socialism is.

Labour's economic policy

Economic theory provides causal explanations of economic phenomena. Meanwhile, political, social and ethical values, conscious or latent, define problems, determine goals and influence policy recommendations. Hence the interactions between economic theory and policy formation are complex. In August 1931, in the face of high unemployment associated with world depression and an overvalued pound, arising from the partial return to the gold standard in 1925, the Labour government remained dependent upon a body of theory designed to analyse a capitalist economy. Labour's policy was formulated by the Fabians, with the economic orthodoxy of the LSE providing the training ground of aspiring Labour economists.

Pre-1914 Fabian policies of 'work or maintenance' plus financial orthodoxy (Booth 1983) were underpinned by enduring faith in the inevitability and efficacy of nationalisation as a means to create a socialist economy in the long term. Although the Fabians rejected Marxism, their attraction to socialism can be traced to Marx indirectly, through Henry Mayers Hyndman (Kenney 1939: 114). Their faith in nationalisation arose from the conviction that all forms of private ownership of the means of production were necessarily exploitative of labour. This conclusion was strongly influenced by Henry George's *Progress and Poverty*, first published in 1880 (Kenney 1939: 114). The marginal productivity theory of distribution, which Fabians drew from Wicksteed (1894), appeared to establish that capitalists inevitably appropriated an 'unearned income' of economic rent. On the basis of this unproved supposition (the mathematical approach provided no proof that the increment was unearned) and observation of extended state intervention during World War I, Fabians embraced as certainty a belief that progress to state ownership would gradually but inevitably create a socialist society (Burkitt 1984: 100). In 1931 these economic policies failed to satisfy not only the electorate at large but also the labourist goals of the trade unions which formed the mainstay of the Labour Party, as well as the aspirations of socialist groups within and outside the Labour Party.

The two main authors of the *Socialism and 'Social Credit'* report, Evan Durbin and Hugh Gaitskell, established their reputations as Labour economists by responding to requests from Labour groups across the country for an explanation of social credit (Durbin 1985: 220). A graduate of LSE, Durbin's first professional publication, *Purchasing Power and Trade Depression* (Durbin 1933a), was a systematic critique of underconsumptionist theories. Although Douglas can be classed as an underconsumptionist only by distorting the definition of, or misinterpreting, the original Douglas/*New Age* texts, Durbin reviewed Douglas alongside the work of J.A. Hobson. In an exercise of erudite overkill, Durbin used Hayekian diagrams to establish the 'fallacy' of this 'extreme form of underconsumptionism'. In the course of his review of *Money and Prices*, included in *What*

Everybody Wants to Know about Money, edited by Cole (1933), Durbin accepts the Foster and Catchings (1925) version of Douglas's analysis of the circulation of money (although without reference to Douglas). He then, briefly, presents and refutes the theory that consumers' incomes should be high enough to cover the aggregated costs of production (Durbin: 1933b).

Gaitskell, also influenced by Hayek, classified Douglas more accurately as a 'monetary heretic' alongside Silvio Gesell, Robert Eisler and Frederick Soddy (Gaitskell 1933). Gaitskell recognised the 'inexact and non-experimental' nature of the science of economics and, anticipating King (1988), defined heresy as the obverse of orthodoxy, although it may in time become part of a new orthodoxy. Monetary heretics were therefore defined by Gaitskell as those who have never held an academic appointment in economics (Gaitskell 1933: 346). In a footnote a couple of pages later, however, Gaitskell confuses the issue somewhat by noting that Douglas's first two books were used as academic texts in 1921 (Gaitskell 1933: 348).

In his opening remarks Gaitskell described Douglas as holding the most prominent position among the many unorthodox writers on money. A sense of the feelings of frustration and resentment on the part of contemporary radical economists and socialist politicians at the popularity of social credit emerges in the course of Gaitskell's examination of Douglasism. The 'ambiguous statement' and the complexity of Douglas's writing style provide Douglas and his followers with the perfect defensive weapon against rational criticism. Supporters can furnish themselves with interpretations tailored to their intelligence and knowledge, while 'for the critic there is not one but a collection of heads to cut off' (Gaitskell 1933: 369).

Comparison of the Douglas/*New Age* texts as outlined in Part I with Gaitskell's critique indicates that radical economists are no less adept at tailoring their interpretations of texts to suit their political purposes. Gaitskell neatly summarised the orthodox critique of 'Douglas Social Credit'. If the body of theory had any substance at all, it must centre on the A + B theorem. The purpose of A + B was to establish an inherent deficiency in consumer purchasing power which required correction if the economy were to function efficiently and periods of stagnation were to be avoided. To confirm the charlatan nature of social credit it was necessary to prove that no such deficit existed. Having established this, it was only necessary to state the obvious: any attempts to remedy the (non-existent) deficit would be inflationary.

Gaitskell's first step was to extrapolate from Durbin's Hayekian diagrams published earlier that year in *Purchasing Power and Trade Depression* (Durbin 1933a; Gaitskell 1933: 351). The diagram makes the same *inter paribus* assumptions as Durbin in his original misrepresentation of 'A + B', claiming that Douglas aggregated total turnover, counting each 'B' payment twice, to arrive at a final figure of 3,000 (200+400+600+800+1,000) which had to be met by consumers, 'a sum three times as large as the costs to the final producer' (Gaitskell 1933: 351–2).

As a novel approach to economic analysis this Hayekian model no doubt presented the young economists with impressive copy. Durbin made considerable mileage by including the same material in an early New Fabian Research Bureau (NFRB) pamphlet (Durbin 1933c). Gaitskell's inclusion of the diagram is, in any other light, something of a puzzle. In the following paragraph he at once dismisses the possibility that Douglas could have made so glaring and elementary a mistake and have continued to be taken seriously by so many for so long (Gaitskell 1933: 352). More recently, however, referring to Durbin's original diagram, King (1988: 147–8) accepts Durbin's criticism of A + B as valid. Since at least one Douglas supporter not only claimed that this interpretation was correct but also had his explanation published in the *New Age* (1935c) and reprinted in pamphlet form, contemporary and subsequent confusion is entirely comprehensible. From the very earliest years the most effective detractors from the original Douglas/*New Age* texts were social credit supporters who enthusiastically embraced the 'Age of Plenty' theme, and produced propaganda in that vein (e.g. Hattersley 1922).

Appreciating that the Durbin approach was a gross misrepresentation, Gaitskell proceeded to demonstrate that there was no *necessary* deficiency of credit so long as new loans were created when old ones were repaid. In this way production can continue and fresh 'A' payments can be made. Extrapolating further from his earlier diagram, he explored the special case of depreciation and sinking funds, with reference to the Hawtrey debate (Hawtrey and Douglas 1933). He concluded that this minor factor is insufficient to account for the recurrence of trade depressions. Therefore attempts to compensate financially for the effects of capital depreciation in an increasingly mechanised productive system would be inflationary. Equally, technology might, as Douglas suggested, decrease returns to labour (wages) and increase returns to financial capital in the form of interest payments. But since wages and interest payments are *both* classed as 'A' payments a shift between the two need not create a deficit in consumer purchasing power. Finally, viewed as a mechanism for overcoming a non-existent deficit, the 'just price' system would also be inflationary, although perhaps less so than the critics had suggested (Gaitskell 1933).

There are indications, however, that Gaitskell recognised the possibility of an alternative purpose in the texts. His attempt to pressgang the just price ratio of production and consumption into service to make up the 'deficiency' of 'A' payments is followed by recognition that the ratio might refer not to new investments but to 'some vague notion of capacity or potentiality' (Gaitskell 1933: 375). However, Gaitskell failed to engage in discussion of the major theme of the Douglas/*New Age* texts. Douglas claimed that the financial system exerts an overriding but unnecessarily deterministic influence on the nature and extent of production and the mechanics of distribution, limiting choices in respect of the priority production of necessities and the selection of leisure in preference to employment. Gaitskell's only reference to the financial system is in a footnote observing that Douglas 'is aware that new investment is quite frequently financed not out of general savings but out of Bank credits'. Although Douglas 'believes' that these credits swell the volume of purchasing power, according to Gaitskell he mistakenly imagines that they disappear when the loan is repaid and that 'the deficiency therefore again appears' (Gaitskell 1933: 368, n. 1).

Gaitskell's uncritical acceptance of financial orthodoxy and scarcely veiled hostility to Douglas are all the more remarkable in view of his sympathetic discussion of the similar but far less comprehensive range of theories pursued by Silvio Gesell, Frederick Soddy and Robert Eisler later in the book (Gaitskell 1933). In particular, he recounts uncritically the incident of the Worgl 'Free Money Experiment'. A successful scheme to adapt finance on a local scale to meet local requirements for municipal and home improvements, and to overcome the effects of depression and unemployment, the experiment in a small Austrian town had attracted the attention of the American economist Irving Fisher. The 'stamp scrip' scheme based upon local interest-free currency was introduced in 'a score or more of American townships', whilst also attracting the hostile attention of the Austrian National Bank. Highly disturbed by the whole proceeding, the bank took legal action against the municipality and its democratically elected mayor (Gaitskell 1933: 399–401). At the time of writing (May 1933) the case was yet to be settled. Subsequently the National Bank won and similar schemes across Europe and the United States were abandoned (Schwarz 1952; Kennedy 1995: 24–7). Worgl and other experiments of the type were remarkably successful. For that reason they were declared illegal, being perceived as threatening to centralised decision-making and the central banks' monopoly of issuing currency.

In recent years Mehta (1983) has demonstrated the illogicality of the 'standard interpretation' used to discredit the Douglas/*New Age* texts. The text mileage produced by socialists to condemn social credit in these same narrow terms throughout the 1930s would appear to indicate a high degree of concern within Labour ranks at the extent of the popularity of social credit ideas. In the meantime, the *New Age* continued to reprint many articles attacking social credit, accompanied with explanations of the misapprehensions contained therein. Many of the explanations are models of lucidity (see e.g. Adamson 1934) in comparison with the Labour texts.

Since the publication of the Labour Party's first report on social credit, two events of some relevance had occurred: the General Strike of 1926 and the economic crisis of 1931. The two events demonstrate the chaos which can result when politicians, of whatever persuasion, confuse sound finance, as advocated by bankers, with sound economics. The problem occurs, and will continue to occur, so long as economists are of the opinion that money acts as a pure numeraire and must therefore remain outside the bounds of neoclassical economic theory. So long as finance is relegated to being a matter for mere accountants, economists will continue to advise against social and environmental sustainability on grounds of cost, confusing financial viability with economic reality.

In January 1918 a committee of bankers advised the British government in favour of an early return to the gold standard, which had been abandoned at the outbreak of war. Given the aim, it was necessary for the Bank of England to restrict the note issue and raise Bank rate in order to bring down the level of borrowing. The result was a cut-back in factory, house-building and other developments considered on non-financial criteria to be necessary after the war. The exercise, deemed necessary not only by the governor of the Bank of England and Churchill as Chancellor of the Exchequer but also by Labour's shadow chancellor, Philip Snowden, was an attempt to return Britain to its pre-war standing as the financial capital of the world.

Keynes foresaw, however, that a sharp increase in the price of British exports would result from the return to the gold standard which would cause massive unemployment as export orders fell. Furthermore, to improve their competitive position, exporters would be forced to cut wages in an attempt to reduce prices. Such reductions in wages and living standards would be resisted by the workers through their trade unions. The mining industry was, predictably, hit by this policy, and the General Strike was the foreseeable result of the interests of the bankers taking priority over other issues and concerns.

The economic crisis of 1931

The crisis of 1931 has been variously described as a 'political' or an 'economic' crisis. More accurately, like the General Strike of 1926, it was a financial crisis. As noted in Douglas (1924a), World War I saw a vast increase in the national debt. In the days of balanced budgets, which antedate the 1940s, the interest payments on the national debt could be met through an increase in taxes or through a reduction in government spending on the infrastructure, the salaries of civil servants (including the armed forces and teachers) and unemployment benefit. Both types of measure were attempted by governments of various colours during the 1920s in an attempt to balance the budget while meeting the increased interest payments. Again, the policy recommended by the Bank of England was to reduce the amount of money available to borrowers, reduce the note issue and cut government spending. The resultant fall in business activity, with the associated drop in wage rates and rise in unemployment, was entirely predictable. These drastic steps could have been avoided had Keynes's modest suggestion of deficit finance been adopted, as in the United States and Germany. Instead the Labour Party, coming to power in 1929 on a pledge to solve unemployment within three weeks, continued to follow traditional financial advice as unemployment continued to rise. Ignoring Oswald Mosley's Keynesian-style proposals, Snowden pursued the policy of 'sound finance' dictated by the governor of the Bank of England. It was in the interests of private shareholders of the Bank to increase the country's gold deposits, held by the Bank of England, by encouraging British exports, which brought in gold, and discouraging British imports, which caused gold to be exported. The Bank of England could increase its gold deposits by borrowing gold from foreign banks, and could profit by lending the gold to other foreign banks.

For example, in the 1920s the Bank of England borrowed from French and American banks at 2 per cent and lent gold to German and Austrian banks at 8 per cent. However, the loans to the German and Austrian banks were long-term, leaving the Bank of England vulnerable to recall demands from American and French banks. Hence the problems which occurred in 1931 when, in order to achieve a balanced budget, it was considered necessary to raise taxes and cut unemployment benefit. The financial crisis resulted in the American and French banks threatening to recall their loans. Rather than cut benefits and salaries, the Labour government resigned. However, Ramsay MacDonald, the Labour Prime Minister, agreed to lead a national government prepared to implement the measures deemed necessary by the Bank of England. The salaries of public servants were cut by 10 per cent, as was unemployment benefit. When the industrial unrest which followed these measures led to renewed failure of confidence in Britain on the part of foreign bankers, the gold standard was abandoned. Despite this departure from the gold standard the Bank of England continued to function and Labour's faith in the efficacy of orthodox finance remained untarnished (Bassett 1958). Four years later, the implications of this experience had failed to impress themselves upon the authors of *Socialism and 'Social Credit'*.

SOCIALISM AND 'SOCIAL CREDIT'

The report entitled *Socialism and 'Social Credit'* was produced for the Labour Party by a sub-committee consisting of E.F.M. Durbin, Hugh Gaitskell and W.R. Hiskett in 1935. It purports to deal 'fully' with 'Major Douglas' "Social Credit" proposals', reaching its conclusions 'impartially and objectively' (Labour Party 1935: 3–4). The 'introductory note' sets the tone of the report by quoting from 'the late A.R. Orage, one of the leading exponents of Major Douglas' ideas'. Orage's statement, taken from the *New Age* supplement of 22 November 1934, is quoted to indicate the 'very serious limitations' of social credit proposals from a 'Socialist standpoint', since it explicitly indicates that social credit measures would 'merely' alter the financial system, without expropriating property, imposing new taxes or

changing the management of industry. The significance of the full implications of the alterations to the financial system proposed in the Douglas/*New
Age* texts is not alluded to here or in the main body of the report.

In the preface to the report an account is given of the sub-committee's
attempts to 'explore the possibilities of partial agreement between the
Labour Party and the Social Credit Movement'. That neither Douglas nor
any member of the Social Credit Secretariat accepted the invitation to meet
on these terms was put down to lingering 'suspicion and hostility' towards
the Labour sub-committee of 1922. However, an appeal through the pages
of the *New English Weekly* resulted in Philip Mairet, the editor, and two
other social crediters, Albert Newsome and W.T. Symons, attending one
meeting. The sub-committee also drew upon the advice of the Rt Hon.
Thomas Johnston, PC, whose *The Financiers and the Nation* (1934) advocating the nationalisation of the banks included a preface by Sidney Webb.
Norman H. Smith also advised the sub-committee.

Predictably enough, in the opening section of the report it is stated that
although the Labour Party was a 'Socialist Party' Major Douglas was 'not a
Socialist'. His aim was to make capitalism function more effectively, and his
supporters, some of whom could be numbered among the 'active supporters of the Labour Party', were mistaken if they believed that financial
reform of the type proposed by Major Douglas would 'remove the evils
which are inherent in Capitalism itself' (Labour Party 1935: 6–7). The body
of the report rehearses the standard arguments against purely monetary
reform as previously set out by Durbin and Gaitskell and includes a restatement of the same 'financial policy' declared in the 1922 report (Labour
Party 1922). Again, the 'Nationalisation of the Banking System' is stated to
be Labour policy. In the absence of analysis of the relationship between
finance and politics, despite the experience of the General Strike in 1926
and the events of 1931, the plan to nationalise the banks appears to be a
policy in name only. It is justified on the basis of the identical observations
made by Douglas (1924a: 134–42) on Britain's method of financing its
participation in World War I. Indeed, the main passage in this section reads
as an edited version of Douglas's original text. Noting that the 'most striking
effects' of the 'present arrangement' are to be seen in the 'financial history
of the war', the report continues:

> The National Debt of this country increased between 1914 and 1919
> from £600,000,000 to £7,000,000,000. How was the money raised.
> Ostensibly it was borrowed from private individuals and firms. In fact
> part of it was borrowed by those individuals and firms from the banks
> and then lent to the Government, and another part borrowed directly
> from the banks. The banks did not have to borrow this money. They
> were able simply to create it. Thus although they admittedly incurred
> a liability for the payment of interest in respect of part of the new

deposits which accrued from the money so created, such interest payments were small in comparison with the earnings of the assets which they gained. They were able, in fact, through the national emergency of the war, to enormously increase their business and enrich themselves at the public expense.

(Labour Party 1935: 11)

Drawn from Sir Walter Layton's *Introduction to the Study of Prices*, a foot-note describes the exact increase in deposits at the joint stock banks as a result of the process. However, the conclusions reached were entirely different from those amplified in the Douglas/*New Age* texts. The authors of the report conclude rather lamely that, if the government wishes for some reason to increase the money supply, the banks should not be left in a position to profit at 'the public expense'. There is, they state, a strong moral case against 'the exploitation of credit creation for the purpose of making private profits' (Labour Party 1935: 11). They do not, however, examine the implications in terms of the relationship between finance and income in the form of 'wage slavery' or any of the other issues raised in the original texts. Significantly, the concept of a national dividend, the popular demand of the time, is dismissed in a paragraph as mistaken and inflationary (Labour Party 1935: 27–8). The report advocates an 'expansionist programme' of credit creation during a depression, in order to solve the problem of unemployment. They have no quarrel with Keynes's quest to maintain the viability of the capitalist system.

As late as 1935 the negative critique of social credit, a report on *Socialism and 'Social Credit'*, commissioned by the NEC under pressure from delegates the previous year, formed the sole discussion on financial policy at the annual Labour Party conference. The report concluded that Douglas was not a socialist, because he did not believe that the state should own and control the means of production (Labour Party 1935). The authors failed to explore the possibility that a financial system based upon social credit principles would lack the mechanisms whereby capitalists could exploit scarcity to claim rent, the unearned income of capital; and, conversely, that the orthodox capitalist financial system could not function within a socialist system.

Attempts to discredit social credit on both practical (i.e. orthodox financial) and theoretical (central planning was essential to socialism) grounds failed. By the mid-1930s the rising popularity of the social credit movement in the United Kingdom was proving a serious threat to the Labour Party. Hugh Dalton, future Chancellor of the Exchequer, and Kingsley Martin, editor of the *New Statesman*, were galvanised into co-operation with W.R. Hiskett and J.A. Franklin in the production of two weighty texts intended to discredit social credit once and for all. *Social Credits or Socialism*, with a preface by Hugh Dalton, appeared in 1935 (Hiskett 1935), and the more

113

hysterical *Searchlight on Social Credit*, with an introduction by Kingsley Martin, was published in 1939 (Hiskett and Franklin 1939). Neither book added anything of substance to the labourist critique of social credit as adumbrated by Durbin and Gaitskell. In Dalton's view, social credit was an 'intellectual nightmare' (Hiskett 1935: 8). Martin, a member of the Cambridge circle in which Douglas's theories were discussed immediately after World War I, regarded Ramsey's (1922) refutation as definitive, adding that 'Douglasism' was an 'intellectual error' and a 'great nuisance', popularised by the economic circumstances of the early 1930s (Hiskett and Franklin 1939: vii). The impressive list of Labour intellectuals cited by Dalton and Martin as having weighted their opinions against the 'Douglas Credit Scheme' is a telling indication of the extent of Labour concern at the challenge presented by the social credit movement of the 1930s.

CONCLUSION

On the publication of *Economic Democracy* in the *New Age* in 1919 the hegemony of economic liberalism based upon financial orthodoxy had yet to be established. The concept of orthodoxy could still be challenged by 'serious' writers, who lost neither credibility nor career promotion prospects by raising ethical issues. Until the rejection of the Douglas/*New Age* texts by the Labour Party in 1922 it was possible to subject the growing power of finance as a capitalist tool to objective scrutiny. Thereafter the labour movement joined forces with capitalism in endorsing the legitimacy of financial mechanisms which were essential to capitalist growth economics. Other attempts to present alternatives to capitalism were equally unsuccessful. Strachey's advocacy of the Birmingham Proposals with all the stylistic brilliance which Douglas's writing lacked and the backing of the Independent Labour Party Federation (and the young Oswald Mosley) failed to attract the serious consideration of the Fabians (Strachey 1925). By 1939 the labourist 'right to work', which accorded with the capitalist requirement of a class dependent upon 'wage slavery', had achieved legitimacy as radical orthodoxy. The right to an income regardless of wage status could not be accommodated within a capitalist financial system. Its appeal had to be countered by capitalists and labourists alike.

Moreover, had the Labour Party presented a coherent economic policy based on a development of the themes originally developed by Douglas and Orage, it would have been well placed to turn the economic situation to advantage and retain power throughout the 1930s. Instead, the powerful arguments for an economy based on sufficiency were rejected in favour of a continuation of the quest for debt-driven material growth.

6

SOCIALISM, LABOURISM AND SOCIAL CREDIT

The Douglas/*New Age* texts gave rise to a broadly based, often vehement debate which did not view the central precepts of the texts in an entirely negative light. Nevertheless, socialists of all types respected the language of orthodoxy, restricting debate to the strictures of neoclassical terminology. Smith draws a distinction between economic life, where the relevant decisions are those of the individual, and political life, which is concerned with collective decisions. He notes that the organisation of economic life necessitates co-operation, often between very large groups of individuals (Smith 1962: 207). That being the case, the claim that a clear distinction can be drawn between economic and political activity becomes untenable. However, economic orthodoxy has continued to profess its ability to analyse the economic actions of individuals unhindered by consideration of the political implications of means or ends.

Since the marginalist revolution of the 1870s the central actor in orthodox economics has been the 'standard breed' of 'rational economic man'. He operates as an individual, as a 'self-centred, self-interested economic maximizer' (Lutz and Lux 1988: 77–100) who engages in 'non-tuistic' exchange (Wicksteed 1933) for purely economic ends. From within this theoretical framework Keynes held the sole aim of economics to be consumption. According to the Keynesian attitude shared by others in the Cambridge circle, e.g. Meade (1993), people throughout Western civilisation live a large part of their lives in the economic sphere, where they are motivated by greed, ambition and self-interest: these *emotions* drive the capitalist system. Faster economic growth is essential because, as long as the world is poor, many must starve. Hence unethical behaviour, e.g. usury, must be tolerated so that all can be better-off. Competition to maximise utility and minimise disutility takes precedence over co-operation, and the 'free rider' represents the ultimate in rationality (Lutz and Lux 1988: 220; Lee 1989: 124–5). Orthodoxy takes the normative view that economic growth is essential for the maintenance of a stable economy.

The desire for economic growth was entirely in accord with the aspirations of the group of Fabian economists, including Cole, who, through the New Fabian Research Bureau, shaped the economic policies of the Labour Party after 1931 (Durbin 1985). Their statistical evidence of the despair and deprivation which could result from lack of employment in a capitalist society dated from the last decades of the nineteenth century (Burkitt 1984). Fabians were therefore predisposed to view Keynesian measures for the maintenance of full employment with ever-increasing favour in the 1930s. In the long term, state ownership of the means of production was the only way to remove the evil of capitalist exploitation of labour. A sound and expanding economy was the first prerequisite to generate wealth and maintain the high levels of employment necessary to finance insurance and taxation schemes to redistribute wealth in times of (temporary) hardship.

This labourist approach culminated in the third guiding principle of the Beveridge Report and determined the character of the post-World War II welfare state. According to this principle, 'social security' is to be achieved through co-operation between 'the state and the individual'. Security is a reward for 'service and contribution', not an inalienable right of citizenship. Rather, the state must offer 'incentive, opportunity and responsibility to the *individual* to take voluntary action to provide more than a basic minimum for *himself and his family*' (Beveridge 1942; emphasis added). Since the individual's ability to contribute depended on the maintenance of economic growth, arbitrary nationalisation without compensation was not an option seriously contemplated by the Labour Party (Durbin 1985).

In these circumstances 'Douglas Social Credit' could not be classed as socialist according to its labourist definition. To the Labour Party, socialism was encapsulated in the progressive nationalisation of the means of production in an economy based on wealth expansion through full employment. State provision of the 'incentive, opportunity and responsibility' (UK Parliament 1942: 6–7) for the individual man to provide for himself and his family is in comfortable accord with the duty placed on rational economic man of following his competitive instincts as presented by economic orthodoxy. Hence labourism serves to enhance the status and conditions of the worker *within* capitalism, while the success of its measures to redistribute wealth depend upon the continuation of economic growth as defined under capitalism. Further, as Cole has shown, redistribution resulting from social welfare legislation in the 1930s was from the working class in employment to the working class in need, and not from rich to poor. The social insurance and indirect taxes (including price rises to cover employers' social insurance contributions) which funded welfare payments were drawn from the working class (Cole 1944: 133–48). More specifically, in its economic sense, 'working class' denoted a male waged worker in employment. Women, the young, the elderly, those employed in the professions, the unemployed and a host of 'minority groups' were excluded as economic actors in this definition of the 'working class'. Labour politicians and their economic advisers devised economic measures for a working class to which they did not, by definition, belong.

Commonly 'socialism' is taken to imply collective ownership and control over the greater part of the land and capital of the community. It has, however, been argued that the defining criterion of a socialist economy is the minimisation of economic conflict (Smith 1962: 9). Collective owner-ship has been assumed to be the prior condition for removing economic conflict and substituting voluntary co-operation founded on freedom and equality. However, as later theorists have detected, nationalisation of the means of production may merely substitute a public managerial elite for the class of private owners (Djilas 1957). It therefore cannot be the defining criterion of a socialist economy (Smith 1962). Economic conflict is inevitable in any society 'which runs because of the spur of permanently unsatisfied economic wants' (Smith 1962: 212). A socialist economy cannot exist where the motive power of society relies on the worker as consumer being stimulated to want 'an unattainable standard of living so badly that he will work hard enough to maintain and improve his existing one' (Smith 1962: 212). State exhortation to conform can be as effective as any commer-cial advertising in maintaining conditions of economic conflict.

Elimination of the private ownership of the major part of the means of production need not, therefore, result in a socialist economy. However, '[t]here need be no economic conflict in a world in which, to use the technical terms, the marginal disutility of labour and the marginal efficiency of capital approach zero' (Smith 1962: 208). Where enforced economic necessity is no longer the primary motivation of labour, and where scarcity of equipment no longer gives rise to profits for the owners of the tools, economic conflict will cease to arise. In that event, revenue would no longer accrue to the owners of (scarce) capital, and capitalism, whether in its private or in its state form, would cease to exist (Smith 1962: 205–16).

A class based on wealth and power will emerge whenever the marginal productivity of capital (and land) is much above zero. Similarly, a positive marginal disutility of labour indicates the existence of a powerful minority elite. Class conflict may be softened in rich countries where labour produc-tivity is rising. In that event labourist demands for a fair or 'living' wage, health and social security, and protection of working conditions, may be met. Under adverse economic conditions such concessions are easily withdrawn. The welfare state constitutes no guarantee of a transition to a socialist economy.

Viewed in this light, the quest of the labour movement in the 1930s for the guaranteed right to work, a minimum wage and social insurance is more accurately described as 'labourism' than as 'socialism'. The trade union movement which backed the Labour Party and the Fabian think-tanks (e.g. the NFRB) which guided policy had a vested interest in the continued existence of a class who were *forced* to sell their labour power to survive. No section of the labour movement had anything to gain from a serious appraisal of proposals to introduce a national dividend by right of citizenship to every man, woman and child in the country, as was proposed in the Douglas/*New Age* texts. Where paid employment (or dependence on employment-related or means-tested benefits) ceased to be the *sole* source of income, the marginal disutility of labour would automatically be reduced; the power of private or state employer to impose coercive terms of employment would be substantially reduced. A weakening of the trade union and labour movements as they were constituted in the inter-war years could also be anticipated (Jordan 1984). Consciousness of this fact contributed in no small measure to the adamant refusal of radical economists to undertake a systematic analysis of the Douglas/*New Age* texts, despite their acknowledgement of the existence of radical elements within those texts.

Radical economists asserted that social credit would not 'work'. In terms of orthodox economics the assertion is no doubt correct. However, the Douglas/*New Age* texts contain the seeds of the second requirement for the existence of a socialist economy as defined by Smith above. It would reverse the trend towards increasing the marginal productivity of capital by decentralising control and ownership of the means of production and drastically reducing the profits accruing to the exploitation of scarcity. For a labourism intent upon the redistribution of the growing wealth of the economy, be it private or state-controlled, this spelled disaster. For a socialism giving priority to the meeting of need in an economy based on freedom, equality and co-operation, the Douglas/*New Age* texts provided a potential route to the elimination of exploitation which thrived on the artificial stimulation of wants and scarcity.

THE FABIANS AND LABOUR POLICY

In *The Labour Party and Social Credit* the observation is made that in view of the preponderance of Fabian influence and London School of Economics (LSE) connections the committee was highly unlikely to submit any other description or report than that which it did in fact submit. The Fabian Society had been 'notably successful in intercepting, sterilising and misdirecting intelligent enquiry into the causes of social unrest'. The Fabians translate the word 'socialism' and substitute the 'Supreme State (to which every man must bow, and by whose officials all human activities from the cradle, or before, to the grave, and after, shall be regulated) for individual freedom and initiative' (Douglas 1922a: 23). Observing the close connections between the Fabians and the LSE, the authors note that the committee assumed that the laws of orthodox finance were 'manifestations of natural law' (Douglas 1922a: 29). The LSE, founded by the Webbs, is unquestionably an orthodox institution. Its officials are quoted in support of government economic and financial policy, and its more promising graduates are assured of consideration in the Treasury, the banks and the more important financial establishments. The institution is solidly entrenched on a 'Bankers' Theory of Banking' (Douglas 1922a: 24).

Douglas was to recall discussing his proposals with the Webbs:

> After disposing, one after the other, of the objections raised to the feasibility of the scheme, I was met with an objection with which, I confess, I found myself wholly unable to deal, and I recognise that objection in the Labour Party report on the Douglas proposals. The words were, 'I don't care whether the scheme is sound or not: I don't like its object.'
>
> (Douglas 1923: 11–12)

The widespread popular appeal of this alternative to the 'labourism' of the Webbs and other leading Fabians necessitated powerful negative reactions on the part of the Labour Party to reaffirm its recently adopted constitution. The Clause IV demand for nationalisation followed logically from the policy programme laid down in *Labour and the New Social Order* (1918). In sharp contrast, acceptance of the Douglas proposals would have necessitated rejection of the economics which Sidney Webb cherished as the most enduring contribution of Fabianism. From a practical angle, it was not in the interests of a national Labour Party dependent upon funds from centrally run trade unions to question the economics upon which their funding rested. The Fabians therefore sought modifications of the existing system on grounds of greater efficiency, putting their faith in a programme of minimum wage legislation and social planning.

G.D.H. COLE

Economics

The labour movement remained united in its opposition to social credit. As a leading guild socialist G.D.H. Cole (God Damn Hell to his 'New Age' friends) (Cole 1940: 75n.) was from the outset a determining influence upon the relationship between the Labour Party and 'Douglasism'. Although he later expressed sympathy with the basic tenets of 'Douglas Social Credit', Cole edited the book in which Gaitskell's dismissal of Douglasism appeared (Cole 1933). Writing in the *New Statesman*, Cole anticipated the arguments of Durbin and Gaitskell, although his co-operation with Orage in the guild socialist movement left him sympathetically disposed towards 'an approach to economic problems [which] is preferable to . . . complacent orthodoxy' (Cole 1932: 225). The Douglas theory was, Cole concluded, 'mostly nonsense', its popularity arising from 'a confusion of thought'. His lengthy article defines economic problems in terms of orthodox analysis.

119

In Cole's view the transfer of wealth was desirable but redistribution of wealth was feasible only in so far as it did not destroy the capacity to create wealth. To Cole the vitality of the economic system rested upon induce-ments to produce; 'interest, profits and wages and salaries – are primarily incentives – to the money-owner to save, to the employer to organise production, to the worker to work' (Cole 1927: 83). If these incentives were removed 'they must be replaced by other means of producing the same, or better, results'. Social distribution of income would remove motivation. The state could not, therefore, provide income security '*and retain the present economic system*' (Cole 1927: 82; emphasis original).

Cole never appreciated the Douglas/*New Age* thesis that economic conflict (as encapsulated in the incentives listed by Cole) led to time-consuming and wasteful patterns of production and consumption. Cole failed to draw the distinction, emphasised in the Douglas/*New Age* texts, between the production of wealth and wasteful production. When he later endorsed the principle of social dividends on the basis of the 'social heritage' he remained convinced that the payment of a social dividend was incompatible with a system of private enterprise (Cole 1944: 145). He may well have been correct in his surmise that many Douglasites, including Douglas himself, remained unaware of the radical economic change which would result from the implementation of their proposals. Cole's work as adviser and educator in the labour movement remained an intellectual exercise. Like so many of his colleagues, Cole had no direct experience of industry, management or finance. Although he did not see himself cast in the role of the urban industrial worker, the working man was the backbone of his ideal society, with women, children, professional and agricultural workers tacked on as an afterthought.

Cole's agricultural guilds, for example, would share democratic control with the village council (Cole 1921: 166). He envisaged the growth of inten-sive, large-scale industrial farming, supervised by the agricultural guilds. A variety of forms of agricultural activity might supplement this main method of food production, including the cultivation of small plots of land by the agricultural worker. However, the agricultural worker's freedom to exploit the labour of his wife and children would be subject to regulation 'by the whole community in the case of children, and in that of women, by women enjoying the economic and social independence which Guild Socialism must assure them' (Cole 1920: 167).

Cole's utopia, like that of Penty in *Guilds, Trade and Agriculture* (1921) is peopled by the emancipated labourer, be he (*sic*) industrialised urban worker or landless labourer. The concept of peasant proprietors, with a personal relationship with the land, is as foreign to Cole as it is to Penty (1921: 80). Inspired by social concern though it was, Cole's guild socialism was designed to ameliorate the plight of the urban industrial worker, the standard 'unit of labour'. Divorced from the land, the worker was conceptualised as having a role to play in the industry in which he happened to be employed. Unlike Orage, Cole envisaged management and workers co-operating to increase production in an industrial system which would remain basically unchanged save for a greater degree of co-operation. Each industrial guild would be governed by committees at the level of factory and workshop, democratically elected by the workers. The hierarchical system would be headed by an executive committee in whom authority would reside. Foremen and works managers would be elected by the workers, with other officials being appointed by district and national committees (Cole 1921).

Orage's vision, on the other hand, can be compared with that of Massingham's later rejection of the concept that the wage system had emancipated the common people. In Massingham's view, the open field system, with all its faults, did enable the peasantry to 'achieve and live an extremely durable and tenacious peace between Socialism and Individualism' (Massingham 1942: 2). The village formed 'a single farm or self-sufficient complex of production in which every member of the hierarchy was at once servant and master, owner and shareholder' (Massingham 1942: 2). Massingham draws a sharp distinction between the serf and the slave, concluding that:

> the English peasant was a social being and that peasant society was in essence a cluster of free localized democracies, just as were the Guilds in the town.
>
> (Massingham 1942: 9)

This system offered a security which was the norm rather than the exception. Until the mid-nineteenth century, total dependence for subsistence upon a wage drawn from an employer was unusual. In this light, Cole's vision of workers sharing control through democratic agreement on a set of operating rules was more unpractical than the vision of S.G. Hobson, Bechhofer and Reckitt's of workers taking on the role of owner/proprietors of guilds in which the actor accords more closely with Massingham's 'servant and master, owner and shareholder'. Cole, on the other hand, shared the more common British tendency to dismiss the peasant as ignorant and backward, to be brought 'forward' to the 'emancipated state' of industrial wage-dependent worker, albeit gradually, as in the case of the collectivist reforms in bolshevik Russia (Cole 1920: 164).

Nevertheless, it is Cole's conventional view of the role of finance in the economy which renders his guild socialism impracticably utopian. Cole did not share Orage's vision of Douglas's monetary reform set within the guild socialist context. In his recommended reading at the end of *Guild Socialism Re-stated* Cole lists Orage's *Alphabet of Economics* along with the work of S.G. Hobson, Penty, Reckitt and Bechhofer, Russell, de Maeztu and Tawney. He also refers his readers to two books by members of the

121

National Guilds League, Frank Hodges and G.C. Field, and to the work of Morris, Belloc (*The Servile State*), Lenin, Postgate (*The Bolshevik Theory*), Lagardelle (*Le Socialisme ouvrier*), Kropotkin, Figgis (*The Churches in the Modern State*), MacIver and Laski. Of Douglas's work, already published since 1919 in the *New Age*, there is no mention. The Coles, who struggled to keep guild socialism alive, through the journal *Guild Socialist*, after the collapse of the building guilds, blamed the splits in the National Guilds League in part on Orage, Reckitt and others embracing the 'financial fantasies' of the 'Douglas Credit Scheme' (Cole 1940: 101).

Cole never took to Douglas. He maintained the standard misconception that Douglas's monetary reform ideas were designed merely to put capitalism on to a firm financial footing, and that even in this Douglas was mistaken. Cole edited *What Everybody Wants to Know about Money*, in which Gaitskell analysed 'Douglasism' alongside the works of three monetary reformers. Although accepting much of social credit theory Cole continued to attack Douglas as late as 1944.

In Cole's view, Douglas claimed there was an endemic deficiency in purchasing power. While this was not the case, epidemic deficiencies did occur from time to time. That did not, in Cole's view, negate 'Say's Theory' of the tendency of markets to clear in conditions of 'static equilibrium' (Cole 1944: 291). Using a detailed chart of the stages of production from primary materials to the retailer, Cole went to considerable lengths to demonstrate that, over multiple stages of production and distribution, all 'B' payments appear as 'A' payments in some past period. He failed, however, to make the key observation of the implications in terms of future production of this patently obvious fact. If today's goods and services are to be exchanged, fresh finance in respect of future production must be made available: the economy is dynamic, not static. Instead, he follows this eight-page refutation of A + B with a further appendix in which he accepts virtually every tenet of the Douglas/*New Age* texts except the dynamic nature of capitalist finance.

Cole remained concerned about 'overproduction', in the underconsumptionist sense, as the cause of economic stagnation. Unlike the Douglas/*New Age* texts, which attacked the growing trend to 'super-production', Cole had no quarrel with the maintenance of a 'high level' of output. Indeed, in Cole's view, socialists must seek to protect against 'disturbing forces' in order to keep the 'level of production and employment to the maximum' (Cole 1944: 291). Cole's 'Fifty Propositions about Money and Production' are followed by acceptance of three social credit arguments and rejection of three others. He accepts that: (1) the tendency to 'underproduction' results from inadequacies in consumer incomes; (2) banks create financial instability; and (3) in view of the social nature of production a 'social dividend' should be available to all citizens. Strictly speaking, only the third of these can rightly be described as a proposition arising from the original texts. This garbled version of the theory is followed by Cole's rejection of the 'so-called A + B theorem', despite its 'elements of truth', followed by rejection of 'consumers' credits' which are not 'cancelled against prices'. Finally, he rejects the idea that:

> the flaw in the price system can be put right by operating *solely* on the money system, without introducing a controlled system of income distribution, price-fixing and production so as to ensure a balance of production and consumption at the highest point consistent with the demand for leisure.
>
> (Cole 1944: 317; emphasis original)

Cole concludes that, although he is an unorthodox socialist, he does not believe social credit can be made to work 'without the institution of the socialistic measures which I have outlined' (Cole 1944: 317). In short, he accepts the basic 'social credit' themes but misses the vital point relating to the dynamics of the money-driven economy. The impetus to production comes from a financial system which is inherently based upon competitive, expansionist principles. In all his years of writing, in the course of which he came to be recognised as *the* guild socialist economist, Cole skirted around the apparently minor but indeed revolutionary concept which Orage had spotted as long ago as 1918: that control of the productive system lies in finance rather than in the ownership of the means of production (Orage 1926). However, as Cole observed, isolated from socialistic measures, social control of finance was an empty concept.

Political philosophy

In his self-appointed role as political adviser to the working man, Cole accepted the Marxist view of the state as an organ of class domination (Cole 1921: 121). Nevertheless, he opposed the communist concept of the dictatorship of the proletariat, retaining liberal views. Throughout his life he sought to bring the disparate strands of socialism into a working relationship (Carpenter 1973: 97). He rejected the idea of general blanket political representation, putting his faith in the 'functional idea' of the representation of individuals by individuals for specific functions only, devolved to the lowest practicable level of workplace and community. He envisaged collectives of workers existing alongside similar co-operatives of both consumers and providers of public services. In *Guild Socialism Restated* he notes with disapproval the growing 'capitalistic character' of the medical and teaching professions, and of other 'civic services' (Cole 1920: 96–7). Already the 'incursion of economic factors' had infected the services with the 'spirit of greed, grab and acquisitive struggle . . . [as] underpaid teachers and overworked general practitioners . . . are compelled to assume an acquisitive attitude in the desperate attempt to make ends meet'. Cole envisages guilds for education, drama, medicine and public health. However, the 'independent professions' of scientists and artists may, he considers, be more difficult to 'organise'.

This failure to encompass 'non-productive' workers within the guild economy demonstrates Cole's fundamentally flawed approach to the question of economic democracy. Cole views society through the rose-tinted glasses of the British leisure class. He was, according to Margaret Cole, 'a man of leisure and possessions . . . in the sense that he never had to shop or to wash up and could not be expected to begin to do so . . . [He was also] a born accumulator of good things' (Cole 1940: 80–1). An insight into the Coles' world view is offered by an incident recounted in the same work. In 1920 Ford Madox Ford stayed with the Coles while his wife was giving birth to their first child in a nursing home. Ford himself required nursing, and the Coles' housekeeper appealed to the Coles to obtain the luxury foods he required. Margaret describes their housekeeper as being 'born to be a family retainer', and recollects sending Ezra Pound up to town to fetch the required oysters (Cole 1940: 82). At that time the poet was dependent upon payments from the *New Age*, payments which Orage could ill afford to make. Pound later became a leading exponent of social credit. Cole, on the other hand, remained convinced that the workers required incentives to maintain the productive system.

J.A. HOBSON

While the Labour Party report was still in course of preparation J.A. Hobson, a member of the committee, challenged the proposals from an underconsumptionist stance. Using the 'standard interpretation' of the A + B theorem, Hobson assumed Douglas to be claiming that there is never sufficient purchasing power to purchase all the goods on the market (Hobson 1922: 70–7). In his reply Douglas (1922c) clarified his argument that the wages of the current period cannot physically buy the production of that period. Such production may not appear on the market for several months. The financial system is dynamic, and the products available today are the result of past investment. They can be distributed today only by a draft on future purchasing power. Nevertheless, Hobson restated his theory that excessive saving and investment are at the root of the problem of 'industrial collapse' (Hobson 1922: 194–9). As in all subsequent debates about the 'validity' of 'social credit', Hobson assumed that Douglas's primary concern was to blame 'our credit system' for 'the disturbances of financial machinery' which lead to industrial stagnation (Hobson 1922: 70). Increases in output and employment were assumed to be the sole goal of the economic system. The Douglas proposals were reviewed against this standard.

OTHER RADICAL REACTIONS

The 1920s

Other left-wing publications, reacting to popular interest in social credit, were initially sympathetic but ultimately repeated the standard argument that 'B' payments had previously been paid out as 'A' payments, so that attempts to stimulate demand through additional finance were merely inflationary. The publications included *Justice*, the paper of the Social Democratic Federation, *Clarion* and *Plebs Magazine*, the Marxist paper. The latter concluded, accurately enough, that social credit would reduce working-class solidarity (Finlay 1972: 195–6) which was considered vital to the survival of socialism in any form.

Writing in the *Communist Review*, Dobb (1922) asked, 'Does the world need more money?' Using a quantity theory of money approach, Dobb attacked the 'inflationist fallacy' which claimed that shortage of purchasing power is the sole obstacle to overcoming all social ills. Expansion of production, according to Dobb, rests on social savings. Following six pages of generalisation, he mentions Douglas specifically, but only to state categorically that 'the Douglas theory says that the main evil of the present is lack of purchasing power' (Dobb 1922: 36). In the following pages he proceeds to demolish his own misinterpretation of the Douglas theories and proposals, concluding that they are no more than a *petit-bourgeois* attempt to prolong the evils of capitalism and dispossess the workers of the world. He concludes 'that the working class cannot afford to be led astray by petit-bourgeois currency theories, which claim to be able to solve the present crisis, while leaving the more fundamental economic and social factors untouched'. 'Douglasism' was a 'quack remedy' (Dobb 1922).

Dobb's reaction is typical of the socialist response. Social credit was a threat to be disposed of without risking engagement in a thorough debate on the merits of a comprehensive alternative approach to economic and political orthodoxy or class-based social protest. Douglas and Orage argued that the 'official Labour Party and High Finance' had a common agenda, in sharp contrast to that of the social credit movement and opposed to the best interest of 'nine-tenths of the populations of every country, whether they be rich or poor' (Douglas 1922a: 29).

The 1930s

Reactions in the 1920s set the terms of subsequent debate. Although the Douglas/*New Age* proposals aroused some academic interest, they attracted most fire from the very quarter to which they might have been expected to appeal. Leading UK socialists across the political spectrum reacted vigorously and negatively to widespread popular enthusiasm for an alternative to finance-dominated capitalism or state-controlled socialism. Ostensibly their objection was to the 'fallacy' of the A + B theorem and the supposed inadequacy of the proposals as a solution to trade depression. However, social credit was perceived as inimical to working-class solidarity, and hence to the power base of socialist leaders, in its deflection of the central demand for the right to work, i.e. for the full-time, waged employment of adult males without 'private means' or a professional income.

Further, had the Labour Party presented a coherent economic policy based on a development of the themes originally evolved by Douglas and Orage, they would have been well placed to turn the economic situation to advantage and retain power throughout the 1930s. Instead the powerful arguments for an economy based on sufficiency were rejected in favour of a continuation of the quest for debt-driven material growth.

The range and extent of public reactions to social credit in the 1930s reflect elements in the evolving character of the social credit movement as well as Douglas's later development of particular aspects of the original themes. Although Douglas and his followers continued to publicise the earlier texts, which were frequently reprinted, they ceased to prioritise the advisability of *restraining* material output and increasing leisure time. Reactions in the 1930s reflected the decade's social credit phenomenon, which owed more to the interpretations placed on the original ideas by social crediters in the light of the events of the 1930s than to the original texts. Historical presentations of sociological and psychological interpretations of the social credit movement treat the political economy of the original texts as little more than incidental (Macpherson 1953; Irving 1959; Finlay 1972; Finkel 1989).

Leading Marxist economists continued as strident in their criticisms as their labourist colleagues. Dobb rehashed his 1922 attack in 1933 ('Social Credit and the Petit Bourgeoisie') and again in 1936 (*Social Credit Discredited*) in response to the growing waves of social credit popularity. According to Dobb, social credit had nothing to offer the working class. Having again proved that his own misrepresentation of the theories was theoretically unsound, he dismissed social credit as an attempt to preserve capitalism by, and in the interests of, the *petite bourgeoisie* (Dobb 1933, 1936).

Lewis (1935) also attributed the popularity of social credit to its appeal to the *petite bourgeoisie*. In contrast to Dobb, however, he held that most of Douglas's theories were in close accord with Marx, the main point of divergence being the question of the ownership of the means of production. Equitable payment through a national dividend was necessitated by the failure of the wage system as a method of distribution in the light of increasing mechanisation. Employment was not an end in itself, and wealth rightly belonged to the community as a whole (Lewis 1935). Lewis's stated intention was not, however, to create a synthesis between Marxist theory and 'Douglasism'. He sought to rescue 'the attentive crowds' who fill 'the largest halls in the country' to hear Douglas, and to reunite them in the socialist (collectivist) fold (Lewis 1935: 1).

In his influential work *The Nature of Capitalist Crisis* John Strachey (1935) included a chapter on Douglas. He acclaimed heterodox amateurs as a useful stimulus to thought, referring to the many strands of social credit theory, of which 'the main contemporary variant' is expounded by 'Major Douglas and his followers'. Noting that such theorists cannot provide 'satisfying answers to our questions', Strachey disappointingly failed to define the criteria which establish the authenticity of the questions being asked.

Strachey followed Durbin and Gaitskell's critique, suggesting that Douglas maintained a mere one-tenth of necessary purchasing power was available to consumers (Strachey 1925). His determination to distance himself from the 'amateur' Douglas, by pursuing the now standard line of misrepresentation of the A + B theorem to the point of farce, is curious in view of his inclusion of a footnote which is worth quoting in full. Strachey noted this 'element of truth lying at the bottom of Major Douglas' thesis':

> If it is true that the greater part of the money necessary to the purchase of the community's output of consumers' goods is only distributed via the producers' goods department, then it is clear that anything which interrupts activity in that department will at once react upon the demand for consumers' goods. It looks as if most of us were dependent under capitalism upon money paid to us for working in the producers' goods department. Hence any interruption in the production of producers' goods will create a situation in which not enough money is distributed to individual consumers to buy the available consumers' goods; will create, in a word, the very situation which Major Douglas describes.
>
> (Strachey 1925: 30, n. 1)

In the main body of the text Strachey notes that Douglas 'catches a glimpse of the idea that the object of capitalist production is the accumulation of capital, and that the distribution of purchasing power is dependent upon the perpetual enlargement of that process' (Strachey 1935: 36–7). Strachey dismisses social credit as 'quintessentially *petit bourgeois*', but recognises more in Douglas's writings than mere 'economic fallacy, as professional capitalist economists would have us suppose. It is also a well-founded, though necessarily confused, cry of protest . . . against the ever growing domination of the great monopolistic capitalist groups' (Strachey 1935: 36). Douglas is a 'keenly accurate observer' of the trends to centralisation and control, and 'excellent' on the control exercised by the monopoly of finance capital over the government machine via all major UK political parties. Strachey agrees that the internal logic of the system is towards war. Although Douglas falls 'easy prey' to 'professional capitalist economists' they are impotent to present a coherent alternative (Strachey 1935: 36).

Nevertheless, the following year Strachey felt it necessary to issue a pamphlet refuting the 'Social Credit . . . analysis of the existing economic system' (Strachey 1936: 3). Strachey remained sympathetic to the aims of social credit policies and their criticism of a system which allowed starvation to persist amidst plenty:

> All schools, and there are many, of Social Credit theorists (and this is their true merit) point insistently to the great staring paradox of the modern world. They point to the fact that we have today the technical capacity necessary to the production and distribution of at least a decent sufficiency of commodities for all of us.
>
> (Strachey 1936: 4)

Despite his sympathy with social credit, Strachey remained attached to orthodox economic theory, failing to perceive the significance of the dynamic time element in the A + B theorem. His conclusion remains, therefore, that social credit theorists are mistaken.

CONCLUSION

Throughout the inter-war years social credit was a subject of debate among leading proponents of radical thought. It was found wanting because it did not conform with existing agendas on the left. Fabians and Marxists alike championed the interests of the working man in an industrial society. The capacity of social credit to appeal to a wider cross-section of the community, including women, artists and engineers, rendered the movement suspect to established radical tradition. Furthermore, proposals which would reduce both the disutility of labour and the marginal productivity of capital, resulting in progress towards a socialist economy as later defined by Smith (1962), could not be incorporated in the radical discourses of the 1920s and 1930s. Although socialists closed ranks in asserting that Douglas social credit was not socialism, the range of debate in socialist circles gives some indication of the widespread popularity of the Douglas/*New Age* texts and the later social credit publications.

Part III

Historical accounts of the social credit movement have focused almost exclusively upon the Canadian experiment (Macpherson 1953; Irving 1959; Grayson and Grayson 1974; Finkel 1989). Even Finlay's *Social Credit: the English Origins* was designed as an explanatory text for a Canadian audience (1972: preface). Where reference is made to Douglas's economic theories, contemporary criticisms of the texts, outlined in Part II, are taken at face value. In Macpherson and Finlay, for example, it is assumed that the economic theory behind social credit constituted no more than an elementary misinterpretation of the workings of orthodox finance. The popularity of the social credit movement has therefore been ascribed to purely socio-economic factors. Furthermore, historians of social credit have been preoccupied with the eccentricities and religious allegiances of leaders of 'populist' movements in times of economic adversity. By implication, the economics of growth was to be considered the norm, regardless of its unsustainability in terms of society and the environment over the long run. Social credit has been variously pigeonholed as *petit-bourgeois*, populist, anti-socialist, right-wing, antisemitic, proto-fascist, anarchist and even communist. Social crediters' denunciation of orthodox finance and attacks upon the banking system were readily associated with Jewish conspiracy theories, and it is these aspects of the history of social credit which are most readily recalled by contemporary historians. It is not intended here to add to that debate.

The guild socialist origins of the texts which subsequently gave rise to the movement, and the reasons for the failure of contemporary socialists to appreciate their potential as a basis for a socialist economics, are more intriguing. What follows is a brief review of the main events which surrounded and followed from publication of the Douglas/*New Age* texts, with a view to placing them in their historical context.

7

THE SOCIAL CREDIT MOVEMENT TO 1930

THE ORIGINS OF SOCIAL CREDIT

The social credit movement was born out of the guild socialism of the National Guilds movement which flourished briefly after World War I. It inherited the mantel of a philosophy which appealed to people of generous mind, 'intelligence, social conscience, and genuine capacity for self-denying effort' as no other English social movement has done since (Mairet 1936: 76). The Draft Mining Scheme was a combination of guild socialism and Douglas finance. It sought to provide an alternative to debt-driven capitalism by giving workers in industry a share in credit creation through the mechanism of a producers' bank. Devised for the spring conference of the National Guilds League executive in 1920, its emergence was considered a contributory factor in the sinking of the 'guild ship . . . when the Communists finally scuttled it' (Mairet 1936: 76). The split between the 'Douglasites' and the communists within the National Guild movement was, like all internal dissension, counterproductive and led to a weakening of the movement. However, it is more realistic to see the 'guild ship', in the shape of the Building Guilds, as setting out into uncharted waters, to be sunk by the undercurrents of capitalist finance.

The National Building Guilds originated in the building unions of Manchester and London, and were influenced by a company director, Malcolm Sparkes. In January 1920 building unions in Manchester came together to form a 'Guild Committee', with S.G. Hobson as their secretary. In May a second guild committee was formed in London under Sparkes's guidance. By the end of the year the idea had spread to other parts of the country and a National Building Guild was set up, with Hobson as general secretary (Glass 1966: 54).

The aim was to provide the service of building good houses at cost price while offering workers security of pay and conditions. The National Building Guild delegated its legal authority to local guild committees of trade union representatives and representatives of workers in the guild. Foremen were responsible to the guild committees, and not directly to the

131

workers. The scheme was made possible as a result of finance being made available for local authority housing. Finance supplied by central government was administered in such a way that guilds could proceed with work with very little capital outlay, receiving payment as work proceeded on a 'cost-plus' basis (Glass 1966: 54). The theory was that the guild workers and their committees could provide the service without interference from a profit-seeking employer. Indeed, in practice the supply of willing labour enabled hundreds of houses to be built to the satisfaction of all concerned. Despite the initial enthusiasm and exploration of the scope for adapting the scheme to other industries, this attempt to operate socialism within a capitalist economy was inevitably doomed to failure.

Strictly speaking, the Building Guilds were not vertically integrated bodies capable of eliminating wage slavery and pointing the way to a post-capitalist society. In practice they proved to be an ill-judged attempt to ameliorate working and living conditions under capitalism. As Glass describes it, delegation of responsibility to local committees was 'not a success' because it resulted in 'overmanning of jobs' and the hiring of unqualified labour. As a result, the National Guild had to take more 'direct control' over contracts and manning and give 'increased disciplinary powers to the foremen' (Glass 1966: 55). In other words, the National Building Guild could not function within capitalism unless it acted like a capitalist employing body.

More specifically, the 'acceptance of unremunerative contracts was reported' (Glass 1966: 55), unremunerative, that is, in terms of capitalist finance. Further problems with finance occurred when government policy on payment changed from 'cost-plus' to 'fixed sum', which meant, in effect, that government ceased to supply the bulk of the working capital required by the guilds. The brave experiment served to demonstrate the accuracy of Orage's observation that the national guilds could not operate within a capitalist system of finance. Reckitt attributes the NGL 'problem' to failure to address economic questions in general 'and the challenge of finance capitalism in particular' (Reckitt 1941: 156). Hobson's version of the setting up of the National Building Guild appears in a chapter in the 1920 edition of *National Guilds*. In earlier editions Hobson observed the emergence of 'a great financial network [which] rules the world' where money power 'rules the rulers of kingdoms' (Hobson 1914: 173).

Although 'unsuccessful' the guild socialist movement gave rise to the crystallisation of ideas for alternatives to a capitalist 'civilisation' based upon greed, competition and self-interest. As Reckitt observed, the guild idea may in the long run reassert itself (Reckitt 1941: 157).

THE SOCIAL CREDIT MOVEMENT

Strictly speaking, there was no 'social credit movement' until late 1921. Indeed, the term 'social credit' itself did not emerge until 1920, when Orage first used it in his explanatory text to the Draft Mining Scheme. It appears in the following context:

> By 'cornering' Money, and by requiring that no Real Credit shall be employed save in so far as its employment 'makes money'; further-more, by controlling the distribution of Money among producers and consumers alike, they (a small handful of individuals) are actually able to control . . . the whole of Real Credit, which . . . is a communal creation and possession. We are not accusing the Financial Power of malignant hostility to society . . . [but] the effect is inherent in the separation of Real Credit from Financial Credit – Social Credit, that is to say, from Financial Credit privately controlled. And the chief purpose of the present Scheme is to restore to the community the full use of Financial Credit as a necessary instrument towards the full use of its Real Credit.
>
> (Douglas 1920: appendix, 165–6)

By the time the term 'social credit' emerged, Douglas and Orage had explained the results of their joint deliberations in numerous articles published in Douglas's name in the *New Age*, some of which were subse-quently included in the 1922 text of *The Control and Distribution of Production*, and in the editorial 'Notes of the week'. *Economic Democracy* had been published, and Douglas's second book, which does not contain the term 'social credit', had been prepared for publication. As late as 1922 'social credit' was certainly not in general use as a descriptive term for the Douglas/*New Age* texts. In that year they are variously referred to as 'The Douglas Proposals' (Ramsey 1922), the 'Douglas Credit Scheme' (*New Statesman* 1922), 'The Douglas Theory' (Hobson 1922), 'Douglasism' (Dobb 1922) and 'The Douglas–*New Age* Credit Scheme' by the Labour Party (Labour Party 1922). The last term resulted from correspondence between the Labour Party and Douglas and Orage, in which the Labour Party assumption that they were inquiring into the 'Douglas Credit Scheme' was corrected, most probably by Orage (Douglas 1922a: appendix). Later in 1922, however, in the response to the Labour Party report they used the title *The Labour Party and Social Credit* (Douglas 1922a), and the title of Douglas's fourth book, published in 1924, was *Social Credit*. By that time the term 'social credit movement' was already in use.

Taken as a whole, the Douglas/*New Age* texts provide a comprehensive body of theory coupled with practical proposals for the reform of finance as a prerequisite to establishing a socialist economy. To that extent the authors of the texts were successful. According to Reckitt, however, the texts emerged at an inopportune time. Douglas's articles in the *New Age* and Orage's 'brilliant' commentaries on them were widely read in guild socialist circles in 1919. Leading figures in the movement, including Rowland Kenney, Will Dyson, J.M. Paton (a shop steward from the Clyde) and Willie Gallagher, accepted the need to expand upon the slogan that 'economic power precedes political power'. They questioned the concept that ownership was the basis of economic power, noting the existence of 'some force' which determined the conditions under which ownership could operate. This 'force' was capable of determining the price level and affecting the purchasing power of wages. Reckitt quotes Chesterton, a few years later, on the question of where the communists obtained their money: 'Does anybody know,' asks Chesterton, 'where any money comes from?' (Reckitt 1941: 167–8).

As Reckitt explains, following World War I socialists were working energetically through the urban working class. The social credit analysis demanded a review of ideas about the source of power in society, requiring socialists to recast their methods of replacing those ideas through the examination of the unfamiliar and unattractive subject of finance. In the midst of the 'revolutionary fever' within the National Guilds League, and sweeping across Europe on the communist tide, the concept that revolution was superfluous if financial reform were adopted inevitably fell on stony ground. It was not the appropriate time to explain that the community needed to resume control over credit so that, instead of 'striving artificially to tie income to employment' it could 'distribute a proportion of the unearned increment of association in the form of a universal dividend' (Reckitt 1941: 169).

Moreover, neither Douglas nor Orage possessed the personal qualities, skills or motivation to engineer a political movement capable of translating their theories into policy. The social credit movement, which arose despite rather than because of any active steps taken by Douglas and Orage, prevented the texts from fading into total obscurity. However, the later adaptation and reinterpretation of the texts according to the individual and sectional interests of minority groupings outside the urban working class served also to obscure the original central socialist theme.

With hindsight, it is clear that the Douglas/*New Age* texts had little chance of being transformed into practical policies within the lifetime of the authors. Although they came from very different backgrounds, both the authors saw their role as that of advisers to opinion formers and influential public figures within existing institutions and political organisations, not as practical organisers of a new political movement. Although Orage was central in the conception of the idea of guild socialism, he did not favour the establishment of the National Guilds League, and joined it only briefly, late in its history. To simplify almost to the point of caricature, the main strategy available to Douglas and Orage was to seek to influence key figures in commerce and industry, leaders of the main political parties or the trade union movement, which was emerging as a political force. At this early stage Douglas and Orage, in their different ways, sought the support of the powerful and influential. Both, however, retained a perhaps undue optimism as to the power of the intellect to assimilate a reasoned argument.

Reckitt, who met Douglas in 1921, describes him as a man of 'original mind and . . . forceful personality'. However, his social thinking was 'unreliable'. He lacked the qualities of leadership, appearing 'autocratic, susceptible to flattery' and lacking in judgement. At that time (1921) Douglas was predicting that war between Britain and the United States would break out precisely in 1923. He continued to predict that social breakdown would make the adoption of his ideas inevitable. Along with his followers, he imagined that he would be required by those in power to advise on ways out of their predicament (Reckitt 1941: 171–2).

In reality, the reform of the capitalist financial system along socialist lines proposed in the texts was unlikely ever to prove an attractive proposition to the leaders of commerce and industry, or to their political counterparts in the Conservative and Liberal parties. Although social credit for capitalists was never a serious possibility, socialists were still seeking a power base from which to influence political events. Theoretically, such power could be sought through revolution or reform. However, British working-class reverence for, and emulation of, the economically successful offered little prospect of revolutionary Marxism. The outlook for proponents of policies which would pave the way to what has come to be termed 'welfare state capitalism' was more promising.

The dictum that 'economic power precedes political power' required that reformist socialists should seek to foster the one form of economic power available to force the hand of capitalism towards reform, that of organised labour in the shape of the trade union movement. In this light, the quest of Fabian socialists to comprehend orthodox economic theory by establishing the London School of Economics as a training ground for Labour economists and politicians was entirely logical. The outcome was equally predictable. For the majority of citizens who, by virtue of their youth, old age, sickness or disability, unemployment, gender or artistic vocation failed to register as significant components of the formal industrialised economy, access to the economy could be achieved only through dependence upon a wage earner or a hand-out from the capitalist-funded state.

In terms of orthodox theory, accepted by British capitalists and socialists alike, the needs of the 'non-workers' could be met only on condition that the capitalist economy was functioning effectively. Hence the 'unempayed', those without an income, were deemed 'unemployed' and in need of 'work' to supply an income. Although the 'unemployed' required an income more certainly than they desired to work for a capitalist employer, all major political parties of the inter-war years were in complete accord that the reverse was the case. At issue was merely the justice of redistributive measures and the extent to which they could be tolerated by a healthy economy.

In the immediate aftermath of World War I Fabian aspirations were not limited to the amelioration of the worst effects of capitalism. There was confidence that state intervention in the economy during the war, facilitated by the Northcote–Trevelyan reforms of the 1870s which gave rise to the modern civil service, indicated a steady and inevitable progression towards permanent state control of the major industries (Burkitt 1984). A central tenet of the labour movement at this time was that socialism could only, and must inevitably, follow from state ownership of the means of production. Policy proposals which did not appear to question the rights of ownership of property were thus, by definition, dismissed as 'not socialist'. Proposals which questioned the right to work, as distinct from the right to an income, were as incomprehensible to labourists as they were to capitalists.

Social credit held no appeal for the influential opinion formers who derived their political power from their relation to major forces in the economy. In this light, the vigour of the social credit movement in the inter-war years is remarkable. It appealed to the powerless majority. The Douglas/*New Age* themes were kept alive, albeit often in garbled form, by individuals whose prior claims to fame – and there were many proponents of note – lay outside the field of political economy. The themes were expounded by leading figures in the world of art and religion, and spread through a host of alternative socio-political movements to become a major threat to emerging 'welfare state capitalism' before World War II rescued capitalism from its plight.

THE SOCIAL CREDIT MOVEMENT 1918–22

Between 1918 and 1922 Orage and Douglas co-operated to formulate the body of ideas contained in the Douglas/*New Age* texts, explaining and publicising their conclusions through the *New Age*, seeking the support of influential groups and individuals on the left. As early as April 1920 Orage recognised the futility of the task. In 'Notes of the week' he observed that 'the scheme associated with the name of Major Douglas and *The New Age*' had been 'altogether neglected, not so much as cursorily examined by any of our Labour officials, Party leaders or professional social pioneers'. By way of contrast, he refers to Douglas's successful visit to America (where Ezra Pound published an early review of *Economic Democracy* (Pound 1920)). He forecast it would be another half-century before the scheme would be 'safely lodged in an English Labour leader's brain' (*New Age* 1920b).

In seeking to influence the Labour Party, and in particular the Fabians, Orage started at a disadvantage. As editor of the first influential socialist weekly he had been outspoken in his opposition to Fabian policies which favoured a bureaucratic state and a trade union movement dependent upon the centralisation of economic and political power. His attacks on the 'wage system' and conversion of the *New Age* into 'the forum of guild politics' had led to the establishment of the *New Statesman* as the major socialist weekly (Mairet 1936: 68–71). Indeed, the 'Fabian authorities . . . had always been somewhat nervous of Orage' and had 'guilefully' broken up his earlier power base in the Fabian Arts Group (Mairet 1936: 68). The National Guilds League, with which Orage was closely associated alongside Cole, Penty and S.G. Hobson, favoured the decentralisation of workers' control. Its popularity among rank-and-file trade unionists has in the past been attributed to the brief upsurge in the economic power of labour arising from wartime conditions.

In developing the 'New Economics' Orage sought to establish a viable economic framework for the National Guilds. Douglas's address to the National Guilds League in September 1919 was a vital component of this strategy, and the text was reproduced in *The Control and Distribution of Production* (Douglas 1922b: 53–4). The speech was well received and Douglas was complimented for the 'brilliant and entertaining character of the address' (Finlay 1972: 120). For a brief period there was a prospect of deflecting rank-and-file trade unionists, the power base of the Labour leadership, towards a version of guild socialism based on the 'New Economics'. However, even within the ill-fated movement of the National Guilds, opposition to the concept of transferring economic power from producers to consumers carried the day. In this connection G.D.H. Cole played a powerful role, insisting that the control of finance could be pursued only when the socialist goal of control over production had been achieved. Throughout his life Cole supported the main body of themes and proposals encompassed in the Douglas/*New Age* texts. Hence his opposition at this point must be ascribed to his negative assessment of the political expediency of rejecting financial orthodoxy. There may also have been an element of personal distrust of Douglas's motives. Like Penty, Cole was of the opinion that Douglas was 'in no sense a Guildsman' (Cole, quoted in Finlay 1972: 121).

The demise of the National Guilds League, a section of which continued to favour the Douglas/*New Age* themes, and the rejection of the 'Scheme' by the Labour Party in 1922 (Labour Party 1922) confirmed Orage in his opinion that the Labour leadership was unreceptive to the proposals. Before the end of the year he resigned his editorship of the *New Age* and, after seeking spiritual refreshment at the Gurdjieff–Ouspensky retreat at Fontainebleau, moved to America, where he continued to advocate the proposals.

Although Douglas and Orage spent the rest of their lives publicising and seeking support for the themes contained in their texts, from 1922 they ceased to have a proactive role. Their involvement in the social credit movement, which achieved fame throughout the English-speaking world and beyond, was reactive to the course of events, and the socialist aspects of social credit were developed no further. Although he never repudiated any sections of the texts, Douglas increasingly emphasised the purely technical aspects which had been his original contribution.

'Social credit', as the Douglas/*New Age* texts came to be known, was never acceptable to mainstream, orthodox economists or politicians. Their assertions that social credit represented a false analysis of the existing economy, that the proposals would be inflationary or would not 'work' have been analysed in Part II. The inference is that the social credit proposals would, indeed, make a system dependent upon privilege and private greed unworkable. They contain the potential to enable human needs to be met efficiently, allowing citizens to attend to other aspects of their lives without being preoccupied by their role in the formal economy. While these ideas did not appeal to professionals who had a stake in the existing system, from an early date they elicited a positive response from individuals of all political allegiances who had not opted for careers within the mainstream of orthodox political economy.

In 1921 the first of many simplifications of the original Douglas/*New Age* texts started to appear. Although the first such texts were issued by Cecil Palmer, who published the first two Douglas books, their writing and publication were not encouraged by Douglas and Orage. Indeed, *Dividends for All: Being an Explanation of the Douglas Scheme* (Young 1921) attempted an explanation of the A + B theorem in which A and B payments are reversed. Perhaps more disastrously, the pamphlet states categorically that prices based on cost + profit must 'always' be too high for all goods produced to be consumed on the home market (Young 1921). Yet this inaccurate simplification was never repudiated by Douglas or Orage. Its appealing title, offering 'dividends for all', coupled with the issue of the Draft Mining Scheme in short pamphlet form, may have been helpful in popularising 'social credit' concepts among a wider audience, albeit in garbled form. Cecil Palmer also issued 'A book designed to be a topical introduction to the ideas, economic and social, of Major Douglas' by Hilderic Cousens (1921). In *A New Policy for Labour: an Essay on the Relevance of Credit Control* Cousens refers the reader to the original Douglas/*New Age* texts. As the title implies, his intention was to support the case for Labour to adopt social credit policies on the control of finance.

A third publication, issued by the recently formed Credit Power Press in 1922 with the title *The Community's Credit: a Consideration of the Principles and Proposals of the Social Credit Movement* (Hattersley 1922), arose from a series of papers discussed by the Swinton (Yorks.) group of the social credit movement during the latter part of 1921 and the spring of 1922. The papers were based on *Economic Democracy* and *Credit-Power and Democracy*, the authorship of the latter book being attributed in part to Orage, 'late editor of *The New Age*'. Unlike Cousens, Hattersley asserts that Douglas presents a 'permanent solution to the present economic difficulties' – in other words, that his purpose is to put the economy right (Hattersley 1922: i).

Two of the three main strands of the social credit movement began to emerge in these three books by Young, Cousens and Hattersley. The Swinton group referred to by Hattersley were one of an estimated number of thirty-four study circles which were formed across Britain in 1921–2 to study and publicise social credit (Finlay 1972: 121–2). Although these groups appear to have centred on the remnants of guild socialism (Finlay 1972: 122), they subsequently formed the caucus of the later network which held ambivalent attitudes towards socialism. Cousens, on the other hand, became a member of the Chandos group of intellectuals who met from the mid-1920s to discuss social credit from an Oragean perspective. Douglas initiated neither of these developments.

Douglas and the social credit movement

As the author of the original texts, however, Douglas remained the focal point of groups and individuals who sought to publicise them. He responded to invitations to speak at formal gatherings up and down the country and abroad, giving lengthy evidence to the Canadian Inquiry on Banking and Commerce in 1923 (House of Commons, Canada 1923). He continued to see his role as purely 'advisory', and refused to take on the mantle of leader or to endorse formally the nationwide network of groups which waxed and waned throughout the 1920s. Interest in the Douglas/*New Age* texts continued to grow throughout the late 1920s as Douglas was invited to speak to gatherings which included the Institute of Mechanical Engineers (1927), the London Socialist Forum (1930) and the World Engineering Conference in Tokyo (1929) (Douglas 1931a).

Douglas's working knowledge of political theory or the realities of practical politics was extended very little after 1922. However, he retained the view that economic democracy, i.e. economic security for all citizens, must precede effective political democracy and was unlikely to be achieved within a society which could at best offer enhanced equality of *opportunity* to claim economic rights within the contemporary unethical financial system (see Douglas 1924a: 168–77). A fundamental distrust of parliamentary democracy underlay Douglas's reactions to subsequent events, and explains his reluctance to support and encourage party-political social credit activity. Although Douglas continued to incorporate the social aspects of the original texts in his later writing and speeches, he ceased to develop their implications further. As Reckitt described it, 'after Orage's withdrawal to France at the end of 1922, social credit became less and less social and more and more concentrated on the technical aspects of finance' (Reckitt 1941: 189). This, and Douglas's suspicion of parliamentary democracy (for the reasons given above) did little to make social credit appear congenial to public-spirited socialists.

Orage's hasty departure from the editorship of the *New Age*, which followed the negative reaction of the Labour Party to the proposals, left the paper temporarily to an editor who was out of sympathy with social credit. This was remedied in June 1923 when Arthur Brenton, editor of *Credit Power*, the small house journal of the emerging social credit movement, took over the editorship. Although the *New Age* was never again more than a pale echo of the journal once edited by Orage, it continued to provide Douglas and the broad range of 'social credit' followers with an avenue of publicity until the late 1930s. Publications on social credit in this period included A. Brenton's *The Veil of Finance* (1926) and H.M.M. (Murray), *An Outline of Social Credit* (1929).

The Chandos group

The Chandos group, the second main strand of the social credit movement, first met in May 1926 at the invitation of Dimitrije Mitrinovic, a contributor to the *New Age* under Orage. The group was formed to explore the possibility of publicising social credit ideas, and the original members were joined at their regular meetings by academics, clerics and business people. G.D.H. Cole, Lewis Mumford and T.S. Eliot were often in attendance (Mairet 1936: 110).

Named after the restaurant at which it invariably met fortnightly, the group was influential in the many spheres in which the members and their associates conducted their daily lives. The seven who first dined together on the evening of the termination of the General Strike were joined by three or four others and continued to meet throughout the 1930s. According to Reckitt, one of the original members, the core of the group were W.T. Symons, Philip Mairet and V.A. Demant, with Egerton Swan, Alan Porter and Albert Newsome attending up to the publication of their first joint attempt to explain their stand, *Coal: a Challenge to the National Conscience*. They were joined by B.T Boothroyd, Hilderic Cousens, R.S.J. Rand and Geoffrey Davis. The latter had a background of distributism and was a member of the Sociological Society. The members of the group were, to a varying extent, contributors to the *New Age* under Orage and/or active social credit supporters. There was a strong Christian influence within the group. T.S Eliot, 'that gracious personality of crystalline intelligence', attended from time to time (Reckitt 1941: 190–5).

The group acted as a focus of its members' interest in social credit, and steered through a couple of minor publications on the social credit theme. Already in the late 1920s, however, 'it had become evident that "social credit" aroused considerable prejudice' and neither publication mentioned the term, regarding it as counterproductive (Reckitt 1941: 189–95; Finlay 1972: 168–72). As Reckitt noted, the monetary reform ideas in social credit would not appear attractive to public figures unless or until they were commonly discussed and accepted by the public at large. In effect, that is what happened. Within a few years of the publication of the original texts the ideas were being studied throughout the British Isles, in the United States, Canada, Australia, New Zealand and Scandinavia (Douglas 1937: xiii). Following the economic crisis of 1931, finance became news and the work of a host of monetary reformers was subjected to public scrutiny. At this point, the early promotional material enabled the social credit movement to flourish on a worldwide scale (Reckitt 1941: 172–3).

8

THE SOCIAL CREDIT MOVEMENT AFTER 1930

The relegation of social credit to a footnote in the history of economic thought is accurate only to the extent that 'economic thought' is defined as the principles accepted by mainstream orthodoxy, i.e. of capitalism. Social credit has a separate history as a school of economic thought of the common people, encapsulating resistance to the economics of exploitation. The main events associated with the history of the social credit movement in Canada during the 1930s have been extensively documented (see Douglas 1937; McCarthy 1947; Mallory 1954; Irving 1959; Macpherson 1962; Finlay 1972; Sinclair 1972; Finkel 1989). This chapter focuses upon the social credit movement in the United Kingdom.

Social credit was swept along by the flow of external events during the 1930s. Despite the groundswell of interest in social credit ideas, and the worldwide existence of regular study groups, the movement failed to throw up a cohesive series of leaders capable of translating the Douglas/*New Age* texts into effective policies. Such leadership as did emerge remained outside the mainstream body of career economists and politicians. The popularity of social credit has been ascribed to the desperate quest for solutions to the economic problems of the depression years. Its 'failure' has been attributed to two factors: first, the 'success' of Keynesianism and welfare state capitalism which followed World War II; second, the accusation that social credit had discredited itself by its association with the *petit-bourgeois* small farming interests in Canada and with fascist proponents (e.g. Ezra Pound) of antisemitic conspiracy theories of international finance in the United Kingdom. The evidence is that the political economy of social credit gave rise to a lively, widespread and informed debate throughout the 1930s. The volume of publications and periodicals available during the 1930s sets social credit apart from the work of other heterodox monetary reformers. The following review of the social credit literature of the 1930s reveals the extent to which the themes of the original texts were debated.

SOCIAL CREDIT PUBLICATIONS

By 1930, when the Macmillan Committee on Finance and Industry (Macmillan 1931) heard evidence from Douglas (see Part II), Arthur Brenton, as editor of the *New Age*, had already settled to a well-established policy of reporting on all shades of opinion favourable to social credit ideas and publicising the activities of all factions within the movement regardless of in-fighting or disagreements. The sole limitation related to material which was hostile to social credit. Although such articles were published in full from time to time, as a matter of policy they were accompanied by articles carrying social credit counter-arguments.

Although differences of approach on tactics occurred, there was general consensus on the importance of study and the necessity to publicise social credit ideas. Through this process, adherents sought to educate the wider public into the theories contained within the original Douglas/*New Age* texts and expounded in subsequent texts (*New Age* 1935a). Brenton, as editor, lacked the charismatic flair of Orage. Nevertheless, he presented an accurate account of social credit political economy. The 'credo' carried in the *New Age* in 1934/5 stressed monetary reform:

> Supporters of the Social Credit Movement contend that under present conditions the purchasing power in the hands of the community is chronically insufficient to buy the whole product of industry. This is because the money required to finance capital production, and created by the banks for that purpose, is regarded as borrowed from them, and, therefore, in order that it may be repaid, is charged into the price of consumers' goods. It is a fallacy to treat new money thus created by the banks as a repayable loan, without crediting the community, on the strength of whose resources the money was created, with the value of the resulting new capital resources. This has given rise to a defective system of national loan accountancy, resulting in a reduction of the community to a condition of perpetual scarcity, and bringing them face to face with the alternatives of widespread unemployment of men and machines, as at present, or of international complications arising from the struggle for foreign markets.
>
> (*New Age* 1934a/b)

A second paragraph of the credo recommends the Douglas texts as providing a remedy for defective consumer demand, and stresses the need for price regulation. Despite growing interest Douglas consistently refused, until 1934, to be drawn into taking on the formal role of leader. However, he became the central point of reference for the burgeoning interest in social credit ideas across the United Kingdom and overseas. Douglas's evidence to the Macmillan Committee, followed by the publication in 1931 of *The Monopoly of Credit* and *Warning Democracy* (a compilation of

143

speeches made between 1920 and 1931), brought social credit ideas to a far wider audience during the 1930s.

In its 30 August 1934 supplement the *New Age* provided a 'Social-Credit Press Directory'. The journals were listed as follows:

Great Britain

Attack! 44 Little Britain, London. Green Shirt Organ. Not published regularly.
The New Age 70 High Holborn, London. 7*d* weekly.
The New English Weekly 38 Cursitor Street, London. 6*d.*
Prosperity St. Peter's Vicarage, Paynes Lane, Coventry. 2*d* monthly.
Social Credit 9 Regent Square, London. 2*d* weekly.

Overseas

The New Economics 20 Queen Street, Melbourne, Australia. 3*d* fortnightly.
The New Era Bligh Street, Sydney, Australia. 2*d* fortnightly.
New Democracy 55 Fifth Avenue, New York. 10 cents fortnightly.
Farming First PO Box 782, Station F, Toronto, Ontario, Canada (no price).
The Social Credit Bulletin PO Box 5919, Johannesburg, South Africa.

Listings of this type appeared regularly, indicating a general degree of co-operation between different groups studying the Douglas social credit literature. Each of these publishing houses advertised books and pamphlets on social credit. In November 1935, for example, the *New Age* listed the following in its 'Credit Research Library':

ARTHUR BRENTON
Social Credit in Summary. 1*d.*
The Key to World Politics. 1*d.*
The Veil of Finance. 6*d.*
Through Consumption to Prosperity. 2*d.*

C.G.M.
The Nation's Credit. 4*d.*

C.H. DOUGLAS
Social Credit. 3*s* 6*d.*
The Douglas Manual. 5*s.*
The Breakdown of the Employment System. 1*d.*
Canada's Bankers. (Evidence at Ottawa.) 2*s* 6*d.*
The Monopoly of Credit. 3*s* 6*d.*
These Present Discontents: The Labour Party and Social Credit. 1*s.*
The Use of Money. 6*d.*

144

The World after Washington. 6d.
Social Credit Principles. 1d.

E.M. DUNN
The New Economics. 4d.
Social Credit Chart. 1d.

C.F.J. GALLOWAY
Poverty amidst Plenty. 6d.

M. GORDON CUMMING
Introduction to Social Credit. 6d.

H.M.M.
An Outline of Social Credit. 6d.

C. MARSHALL HATTERSLEY
The Community's Credit. 1s.
This Age of Plenty. 3s 6d. and 6d.
Men, Machines and Money. 3d.

A.W. JOSEPH
The A + B Theorem. 6d.

R.S.J. RANDS
The Abolition of Poverty. A Brief Explanation of the Proposals of Major C.H. Douglas. 4d.

A.E. POWELL
The Deadlock in Finance. 3s 6d.
The Flow Theory of Economics. 5s.

EARL OF TANKERVILLE
Short Papers on Money. 6d.

W. ALLEN YOUNG
Ordeal by Banking. 2s.

The themes of the Douglas/*New Age* texts were restated by Douglas (1932, 1935a, 1936a, 1936b, 1937, 1939) and by many advocates of social credit, including Murray (1929; this pamphlet was repeatedly reissued during the 1930s), Symons (1931), O'Duffy (1932), Colbourne (1933, 1934), Holter (1934), Corke (1934), Rands (1934, 1970), Tavistock (1934), Tankerville (1934), Muir (1934), Pound (1935), Jameson (1935), Joseph (1935a), Hargrave (1945) and Monahan (1947, 1957). The covers of the Pound and Jameson pamphlets published in 1935 advertise the following 'Pamphlets on the New Economics', some of which are now unobtainable: Douglas, *The Use of Money* and *The Nature of Democracy*; the Marquis of Tavistock, *Short Papers on Money*; the Very Rev. Hewlett Johnson, DD (Dean of Canterbury), *Social Credit and the War on Poverty*; William Ward, *The National Dividend: a Symposium by Sixteen Public Men*; 'Poems by Alfred Venison', *Social Credit Themes by the Poet of Titchfield Street*; Herbert Read, *Essential Communism*; Bonamy Dobrée, *An Open Letter to a Professional Man*; Edwin Muir, *Social Credit and the Labour Party*; A.L. Gibson, *What is this Social Credit?* Monetary reform had a high profile, both in public debate and in frequency of occurrence in the literature. Nevertheless, the guild socialist Draft Mining Scheme continued to be reprinted, for example in Dunn (1934), apparently remaining the subject of discussion in some circles.

Local social credit periodicals in the United Kingdom include the *Keighley Green Shirt Review*, the *Challenger* (North of England, Keighley offices) and *Social Credit News*, published by the London Social Credit Club. The flow of periodicals and publications indicates wide interest in the study of monetary reform. Given the limited extent of contemporary television coverage, it can be assumed that these weighty tracts were not only purchased but also widely read throughout the 1930s.

The above listings are by no means exhaustive. Social credit libraries include scores of further books and pamphlets from authors in many different walks of life. Church people are particularly well represented. For example, in their series 'Pamphlets on the New Economics' the publisher Stanley Nott published *Social Credit and the War on Poverty*, by the Very Rev. Hewlett Johnson, Dean of Canterbury. Advocating a national dividend, the dean dismisses, in no uncertain terms, a financial system 'which flings God's gift, as it were, back in His face' (Johnson 1935: 29).

Further evidence indicates the spread of social credit publications and groups on a worldwide basis. Norway saw the publication of *Douglas Planen* by R. Millar and H.J. Murstad. The movement spread to France (*Green Shirt Review*, January–February 1934). A listing of social credit literature available in French included (*Social Credit*, 1 November 1935: 94):

1 *Principes de Crédit social* by Count W.G. Serra (FF 3). A French translation of H.M.M.'s *Outline of Social Credit*.
2 *Le Crédit social* by Count W.G. Serra contains translations of Douglas's articles and explanations of the A + B theorem and just price. 'The work is perhaps most suited to advanced students of Social Credit' (FF 1).
3 *Esquisse de crédit social* by Constant de Wit (BF 1). Based upon a lecture delivered by the author to the Institut d'Économie Européenne, Brussels, this work provides a concise summary of the social credit analysis and proposals.

4 *Sécurité économique de l'individu* by Constant de Wit (BF 5). A survey of world politics and finance 1918–29 from a social credit perspective.

5 *Résumé de l'économie nouvelle* by J. Dhooghe. A thirteen-page pamphlet printed in 1935 for distribution among Antwerp businessmen.

A network of study groups and political campaigning gave rise to both academic and official discussions and publications which circulated in many countries, e.g. Copland (1932), McConnell (1932), Waites (1932) and Binns (1947). Popular critiques and explanatory texts in Australia and New Zealand included Holmes (1932), Armitage (1932), Da Costa (1933), Emery (1934), Barclay-Smith (1940) and Allen (1942). (Information supplied by John Pullen, personal communication, April 1993.)

Historical interest in social credit has centred on the political success in Canada. To date, little documentation of the movement in Australia and New Zealand exists. Davis (1978) recorded the powerful influence of social credit within the Tasmanian labour movement in the 1930s and 1940s. A review of the history of social credit in Australia was being undertaken by J. Pullen and G. Smith (1991). The policy of working for social credit *within* existing political parties was also explored in New Zealand until 1953. At that point social crediters realised that, having been assisted into office by espousing social credit on their platforms, Labour would neglect to honour their promise to implement social credit policies. In 1953 the Social Credit Political League was formed (Milne 1966).

A similar dearth of historical material exists about the social credit movement in the United States. During his stay in America (1924–31) Orage publicised the Douglas theories. One of the leading converts, the literary critic and publishers' consultant Gorham Munson, founded the New Economics Group of New York in 1932 to promote social credit throughout the United States. The social credit journal *New Democracy* (1933–6), edited by Munson, provided a clearing house for American social crediters (Generoso 1981). Articles on social credit by Douglas, Munson, Pound and others appeared in American journals, most notably the *Rotarian* and the *Commonweal*, throughout the 1930s. Wesleyan University, Middletown, Conn., holds 'the most nearly complete collection of social credit materials', and other substantial collections are at the New York Public Library and the Library of Congress. Collections also exist at Harvard, Columbia, Yale, UCLA, Duke University and the University of California, Berkeley (Generoso 1981: 29).

SOCIAL CREDIT THEMES IN THE 1930s

Some indication of the subjects under discussion can be gleaned from the publications and periodicals which circulated in the United Kingdom during the 1930s.

National dividend and the just price

Social credit publications and periodicals at local and national level carried detailed explanations of the proposals for a national dividend, regulated through a national credit office and dependent upon the scientific adjustment of the just price to avoid inflation. For example, in an article covering the just price, *Attack!* observes:

> The price factor is only the technical method employed to make the number of tickets issued equal to the number of goods on the market. The declaration of a national dividend without the operation of this factor would mean that in a short time there would be more tickets in circulation than goods on the market and prices therefore would always be trying to catch up to the tickets. This is what is technically known as inflation and the price factor is the only method of preventing it.
>
> (*Attack!* 16 September 1933: 3)

Although the quality of economic analysis inevitably varies throughout the extensive social credit publications of the period, in many instances it cannot be faulted. In 1935 the *Challenger*, a North of England broadsheet, carried an article entitled 'A private income for life'. It referred, not to social credit, but to the introduction of advertising by insurance companies for a private income without working. The article observed that since insurance companies are 'one of the pillars of the financial system' opponents of social credit can hardly claim that it is immoral to offer 'summat for nowt'. However, it would be misleading for readers to imagine that the insurance company was going to hand over its 'ill gotten gains' and pay out an income which was not dependent upon work. On the contrary, premiums must be paid according to age:

> In short, the scheme, on examination, turns out to be a matter of gambling on your expectations of life and has been drawn up to provide the company with cash which it will invest so as to secure control over industrial assets.
>
> (*Challenger* No. 14, January–February 1935: 7)

The article goes on to define workers as the 'creditors' of society. Having increased output during the industrial revolution, they are now entitled to control industry through controlling the supply of money. Accusations that 'Douglas Social Credit' was a hairbrained scheme of monetary reform, the upshot of which could be rampant inflation, owe much to dulled imagination.

Banking and finance

The periodicals explore the spectacle of international finance producing experts to advise national banks and their governments on how to balance their budgets in order to run a sound financial system. Where a country has plenty of goods, workers and even gold, as in the case of Australia, this 'advice' clearly determines the nature of economic activity itself. In a democratic country like England, Cabinet decisions relating to finance are taken behind closed doors on the advice of the Bank of England. If the ruling oligarchy considers that a particular industry is unlikely to acquire a sufficient share of the world's purchasing power

> to enable it to buy back its bank loans and interest, credit is withheld and the industry must decline. Any industry that fails to get back its costs quickly becomes the Cinderella of the country's activities, such as agriculture has become.
>
> (*Green Shirt Review* No. 6, January–February 1934: 1–2)

The same article connects the decline of British agriculture with this system of finance. It quotes the banker Ernest Cassel's warning that the inability of a country to grow its own food could be as disastrous as a 'German submarine' for the future. It concludes that small capitalists are being 'crushed out or absorbed by large concerns with the help of the banks', and quotes Lenin's observation on the emergence of 'finance capitalism' which has no frontiers and no 'patriotism: its chief supporters are unknown and unknowable'. Indeed, 'one country is being played off against another' as the financiers 'demand that money shall be free to find its own level'. The banking system has, in the words of Lenin, become 'an alliance of a small number of monopolisers'.

In the same issue of the *Green Shirt Review* (No. 6 Jan.–Feb. 1934: 3–4) the relationship between banks and industry is explored further. 'How banks make money' provides a neat, Galbraithian (Galbraith 1975) history of banking and observes that vast sums of money have been made available to facilitate advances in industrial production over the previous fifty years. The power of banks to create fresh loans, or to refuse to do so, determines the economic choices of nations, governments and individuals.

Inevitably, the identification of the power of banking and finance over industrial policy formation led to conspiracy-theory accusations. As 'outsiders' to the mainstream political economy social crediters observed that the major players held the same world view. In November 1935 the *New Age* noted the connection between 'High Finance and High Society' by quoting a passage from the *Evening Standard* of 7 November:

> The new chairman of the B.B.C. Board of Control became related by marriage to the Royal Family by yesterday's wedding. Mr R.C. Norman, who was appointed to this position at the B.B.C. only last month, is married to the youngest sister of the Earl of Bradford, and he is therefore the uncle of the newly-wed Duchess of Gloucester,

whose mother is another sister of the Earl of Bradford. He is also brother of Montagu Norman, Director of the Bank of England.

(*Evening Standard*, 7 November 1935)

In the same year *Attack!* asked the question 'Who has control? The Treasury or the Bank?' as it quoted from the evidence of the deputy governor of the Bank of England to the Macmillan Committee:

> The Bank of England is in daily touch with the Treasury, sometimes many times a day. . . . We have no secrets from them. We keep them fully acquainted as to the general trend of affairs in the City and the outlook as we see it. We, on our part, never venture to interfere in any question which is considered a political question unless we are asked to express an opinion as to what the financial effect of any political operation may be. The Treasury, on the other hand, are good enough to reciprocate. That is to say, that while we keep them fully informed as to the general trend of affairs in the City, and as to any occurrences affecting the position of finance and credit, they do not seek to dictate any alternative lines of financial policy if we, in our judgement, consider a particular line of policy essential for the protection of the country's main reserves.

(Quoted in *Attack!* No. 29, 1935)

Social crediters favoured economic nationalism as offering the greatest potential for democratic control of finance. They viewed proposals for world unity supported by a world money and international banking as the height of folly. Such proposals were advocated by H.G. Wells in his radio broadcast of 9 January 1934 entitled 'Whither Britain?' As the editor of the *Green Shirt Review* (January–February 1934) commented, 'there is quite enough international banking already'. The 'ordinary' citizen of England, Germany, France or America had no reason to distrust their counterparts in other countries. If, however, they could be persuaded that their quality of life depended upon the home country's ability to export goods in excess of imports, 'then war is inevitable'. The connection between international economic competition and war as a theme recurs throughout the social credit literature.

The A + B theorem

Frequently, articles on the A + B theorem display comprehensive understanding of the role of finance in a dynamic economy. For example, the third and final instalment of a series of articles on A + B, published also in pamphlet form, opens with the following paragraph:

> The interpretations of the A + B theorem discussed above [i.e. in the previous issue of the *New Age*] is the one where A means the

payments made to individuals at all stages of production, semi-finished goods as well as finished goods, and B means the payments made to institutions in all stages of production. That A is less than A + B is a direct arithmetical inequality. It has been shown that A + B *is* added to costs in a form that will emerge later in the prices of final consumable goods. An actual deficiency of purchasing power may be masked by the issue in advance of the marketing of the goods of A payments for new production. If for any reason the new production is stopped or slowed up the deficiency of purchasing power must be revealed.

(Joseph 1935a: 22)

The necessity to produce goods in the form of armaments, cars, no matter what, so that basic necessities could be circulated to the population, was a constant theme in social credit literature and publications. Joseph demonstrates an understanding of the dynamic relationship between money and the past, present and future production and distribution of goods. 'A' payments today may be made in respect of present or semi-finished goods, the production of which was financed in a past period and the circulation of which is dependent upon money available in the present period. Although there is no necessary deficiency, there is no necessary congruity between money and goods available. At the same time, production must continue if goods available at present are to circulate.

Joseph's article, illustrated with variants on the diagrams used by Gaitskell and Durbin, forms part of a debate with Gaitskell in the columns of the *New Age*. It provides an example of the purely 'technical' nature of the social credit debate in the 1930s. Joseph was technically correct that the diffusion of ownership of the means of production through social credit measures was more practical than the communist plan to smash the capitalist system through violent revolution (Joseph 1935c: 15). However, the political obstacles to, and practical implications of, the establishment of a national credit office and the scientific adjustment of prices remained on the periphery of the debate in the 1930s.

The 'poverty amidst plenty' debate

The social credit press of 1934–5 carried a series of articles on the implications of the coexistence of unemployment and food destruction. It was observed that between 1933 and 1935, while unemployment ran high, food was being destroyed across the civilised world. Examples included:

1 In 1933 the Danish government was using special incinerators to burn cattle at the rate of 5,000 per week.
2 In 1933 22 million bags of coffee were destroyed.

3 In the United States Roosevelt's scheme allocated $33 million to 'pig–sow slaughter', $350 million to 'corn–hog production control' and $102 million to wheat acreage reduction.

4 In 1934 5,000 lambs were driven into the sea in New Zealand.

5 Thousands of tons of fruit were being left to rot in British orchards; thousands of sacks of potatoes were destroyed every year. Farmers were pouring milk away and 2 million tons of sugar were 'withheld from the market'. Sprats and herrings were being thrown back into the sea, and corn production was to be reduced.

6 The economic position in Cuba was 'improved' with the destruction of the glut of sugar in 1932.

7 Beer was being poured away in Ireland to help the economic situation.

8 Ten million gallons of wine was poured away in Portugal.

Attack! No. 29 (1933), which carried the report, included a picture of a grain ship unloading its cargo into the sea. An article in the *Green Shirt Review* of 1934 (No. 6) questions the reasoning powers of mature adults. An intelligent child might question the evidence of experts in economic science when their advice is tailored to the requirements of vested interests. The child will continue to question 'insane methods of working', failing to understand why fish should be thrown into the sea when people would be only too glad too eat them. When told:

> that there is no money to buy them because so many people are not working, he wonders why the fish should not be given to those who need them, but this is – to his elders – an utterly absurd idea. 'Imagine giving things away!' Why, if that were to be done nobody would want to work. The child ponders on this problem for a while but cannot see why people should starve simply because they cannot get work.
> (*Green Shirt Review* No. 6, 1934: 6)

The article imagines the child trying to reconcile the supposed overproduction with the facts of ill clad and starving thousands. Perhaps, the child wonders, the machinery is at fault? Scrap the machinery and put people back to work with their hands. Would that help? The adults disagree. Technical improvements make work lighter for all. So perhaps the answer is to give money to everyone for not working? The adults are 'scandalised', but the child is right. Instead of praying for abundance, as in pre-industrial society, civilised people are praying that 'nature and science become more niggardly'. The article concludes that the national dividend backed by the 'scientific price' is a more rational approach.

The different factions of the social credit movement were united in their condemnation of a financial system which dictated the destruction of food stocks while families starved. Rowland Kenney, the first editor of the *Daily Herald*, noted the same destruction of food as listed in *Attack!* in 1933, noting that in the autumn of 1931 a London financial journal was 'jubilant' at the destruction of the wheat crop through bad weather, labelling the financial prospects 'distinctly encouraging'. While people went hungry, 'representatives' of Canada, Australia, Argentina and the United States met to discuss the disposal of 'surplus' wheat stocks (Kenney 1939: 288). As Kenney, former editor of the *Daily Herald*, noted:

> In June 1936 an Australian newspaper congratulated its readers because drought had ruined much of the wheat crop of the world. In the autumn of 1931, a London financial journal was equally jubilant because bad weather was ruining wheat crops, so prospects were, it said, 'distinctly encouraging'.
>
> (Kenney 1939: 288)

In the mid-1930s schemes for reviving economic prosperity in Britain included the 'reduction of arable land by a quarter of a million acres', cutting the production of wheat, potatoes, sugar beet and roots, and driving 33,000 agricultural workers from the land (Kenney 1939: 288).

The *New Age* of 1934 published a verbatim report of an address by Douglas to a public meeting in Aberdeen on 28 April 1932. Douglas argued that the higher up the 'ladder of control' he went, the more likely people were to agree with the technical aspects of his analysis of the monetary system. However, attempts to convert those in positions of power could not be conducted rationally because of the underlying 'unreasonable objection, and that is that they do not wish to be deprived of the power to lay out the lives of other people for them'. Douglas argued that he had no blueprint of what society ought to be like: each individual has a different world view, and he had no desire to impose his utopia on anyone else. He was convinced, however, that the material conditions already existed for the needs of all to be met comfortably.

> All we say is that the economic system at the present time will supply everybody with an easy living; and it is our business to put it at their disposal; but that is exactly what the powers who are ruling the financial system are absolutely determined shall not be the case. They are not in the least concerned that you could eventually get very good bed, board and clothes; that is perfectly possible and reasonable, as they say; but they are determined that you shall have them on terms which shall be *their* terms, not *your* terms. Our point of view is that, on the contrary you must have them on your own terms.
>
> (Douglas 1934b: 271–2, emphasis original)

As is evident from this article, Douglas had no desire for personal power or aggrandisement. Equally, he had no blueprint for the organisation of necessary work in the 'good society', putting his faith entirely in the panacea of monetary reform. Nevertheless, his observations are acute. He observed:

Whatever may be true or untrue about the present situation, it is
certainly not true that the productive organisation as it exists, and as
it is administered at the present time, cannot produce the goods. In
fact, it is very often said that the present crisis is a crisis of overproduction; I have never heard it called a crisis of underproduction
(I have heard it called a crisis of underconsumption, but that is a
different thing), and yet the financiers, or rather the Bank of England,
are saying that the crying need of this country is reorganisation of the
productive system. Can there be anything more ridiculous than to
suggest that a crisis which is on the one hand described as a crisis
of unemployment, and is on the other hand described as a crisis of
overproduction, should be cured or could be cured by making industry more efficient, assuming that were to be done?

(Douglas 1934b: 272)

If that were to be done, more goods would be produced by fewer people,
intensifying the overproduction while simultaneously intensifying unemployment. This is, however, the inevitable result of an overcentralised industrial
system operating under the control of the banking system. Decentralisation
of administration in both industry and banking is the only way out of the
impasse. This is an unlikely outcome in a political system where the vast
majority of the voters are 'twenty-five years behind the times'. He arrived at
the conclusion that individual action was the only way forward.

No idea was ever invented by a committee. The public will never do
anything; you, individually, have got to do it. I am certain that the solution of the world's difficulties at the present time will only be carried
out against the will of those people who control large organisations.

(Douglas 1934b: 272)

The subsequent history of the social credit movement demonstrated the
inadequacy of this anarchistic attempt to redesign society on the basis of
monetary reform alone. Although the different strands of the movement,
Douglas and the 'Secretariat', Hargrave and his 'Green Shirts' and the *New
Age* disagreed on tactics, they shared an underlying perception that social
reform which ignored the determining qualities of finance would fail in the
long run. Equally, they shared a belief in the necessity to use meetings and
publications to engage in educational activities. (See e.g. 'Movement notes',
New Age, 14 November 1935: 13–14.)

Throughout the period, pamphlets, books and articles were frequently
reprinted, and therefore can be assumed to have been the subject of
informed debate. Although the guild socialist background appears to have
waned in the 1930s, there is evidence that the Draft Mining Scheme was
reissued in pamphlet form. In the decades following World War II many
pamphlets from this period were repeatedly reprinted, as were some of

Douglas's later pamphlets (e.g. Douglas 1942a, 1942b, 1943, 1945). In the 1980s Eric de Maré attempted a restatement of some of the social credit themes (De Maré 1983).

DOUGLAS: WORLD TOURS

Throughout the 1920s and early 1930s Douglas continued to tour the United Kingdom and other countries in response to invitations to speak, reaching Tokyo (where he addressed the World Engineering Congress in 1929), Norway (speaking to the King of Norway and the Oslo Merchants' Club in February 1935) (Douglas 1935a) and the United States. His largest audiences appear to have been in the dominions. However, the very popularity of social credit ideas put a strain on Douglas which he was unable to handle. Two significant events were his world tour of 1933–4 and the election to power of a social credit government in the province of Alberta, Canada.

On his 1934 world tour Douglas visited Australia, New Zealand, Canada and the United States. The highlight of his visit to Australia was his address in the Sydney Stadium on 25 January 1934, attended by an audience of 12,000. Five thousand were turned away, and an estimated audience of a million across Australia heard the radio broadcast, factories being shut down to provide sufficient power for the event (Douglas 1989; Finlay 1972: 135). In New Zealand he gave evidence to the New Zealand Monetary Committee (Pullen and Smith 1991; New Zealand 1934). According to Audrey Fforde (personal interview, April 1993) and Finlay, he received an equally enthusiastic reception in western Canada and the United States, addressing meetings and speaking with politicians and leading monetary reformers. A coast-to-coast broadcast in America was estimated to have reached an audience of 90 million (Finlay 1972: 135). Although the original texts had been studied throughout the dominions in the early 1920s, these tours rekindled interest in social credit, and a sustained flow of social credit publications supplied study groups in those countries. Disillusionment with the Bank of England was particularly strong in the dominions. In Canada, Australia and New Zealand active social crediters were numbered in 'tens of thousands' (Reckitt 1941: 172–3).

The Social Credit Secretariat

Douglas's world tours had the unfortunate effect of galvanising him into attempting to play the role of leader of the social credit movement, a role to which he was quite unsuited. On his return to England Douglas took control of the Social Credit Secretariat, which had recently been revived as an educational body to promote co-ordination, consultation and research. Douglas converted it into a 'dictatorial directorate demanding rigid conformity in pursuit of an ill-conceived and quite impractical' electoral campaign (Reckitt 1941: 173). Douglas's authoritarian manner resulted in open disagreements between the secretariat and Arthur Brenton, editor of the *New Age*, which eventually led to the demise of the paper. Douglas's high-handed manner also led to splits, schisms and regroupings within the secretariat itself. The 'electoral pledge campaign' was an unhappy attempt to sidestep the issue of seeking direct democratic representation by social crediters. Pledges of support for social credit were sought from candidates of all political parties during local and parliamentary elections, a policy which all social crediters with a modicum of political foresight saw was doomed to failure (Finlay 1972: 135–41).

Throughout the United Kingdom sixty groups were affiliated to the secretariat by the end of 1934. Despite misgivings, groups embarked upon the ill-fated 'electoral campaign'. The plan was to undertake a canvass of the electorate, seeking pledges from voters to withdraw support from any sitting MP who would not pledge to place the demand for a national dividend high on the agenda. The movement lacked the resources to undertake so vast a canvass of voters. Moreover, the concept was flawed. Voters could not be expected to forsake their traditional party loyalties for an unfamiliar single-issue campaign. Even those making pledges were unlikely to remember on polling day. As events proved, even where a social credit candidate stood, and gained a respectable number of votes, they were far fewer in number than the pledges which had been recorded over the previous year. Those social credit groups which had declared the campaign a mistake, including John Hargrave and his 'Green Shirts', were summarily expelled from the secretariat (Reckitt 1941: 173–4). That did not prevent them from campaigning for 'social credit' under their own banner, nor did it preclude social crediters from combining across sectional interests at local level.

HARGRAVE AND THE GREEN SHIRTS

The third main strand of the United Kingdom social credit movement emerged simultaneously with the others, increasing awareness of the Douglas/*New Age* texts whilst giving rise to further confusion as to their political significance. John Hargrave, founder of an alternative Scouting movement in the late 1920s (with appeal to all ages), adopted Douglas's theories on behalf of his nationwide organisation. Douglas neither officially endorsed nor repudiated the activities of Hargrave and his Kibbo Kift. The *New Age* carried articles and letters by Hargrave and his supporters, and publicised their events. The street parades of green-shirted supporters demanded 'Douglas social credit – now'. National and locally produced publications and broadsheets, including *Attack!* and the *Green Shirt Review*, were widely circulated and gave rise to the propagation of regular study groups. Branches were formed in most towns and villages of any size, with cities like Bradford supporting at least three separate groups. When Hargrave's 'Social Credit Party' fielded three candidates in the 1935 general election, the electoral campaign was viewed with barely concealed hostility by the main-line Social Credit Secretariat. However, activists associated with the differing strands of the movement co-operated in these highly public events.

In appealing to the 'rank and file' unemployed Hargrave spread awareness to, and established the relevance of, social credit principles to a wider audience. He had a flair for publicity, not only in the handling of high-profile marches and demonstrations, but also in producing pamphlets and publications. His epic social credit novel *Summer Time Ends* was reviewed by James Agate, a leading reviewer on the *Daily Express*. Acclaiming it as 'a great work', Agate placed it 'in the James Joyce class' (quoted in the *New Age*, 14 November 1935).

Evidence from the *New Age* in 1934–5, and from national and local Green Shirt publications, including, for example, the weekly *Keighley Green Shirt Review*, 1933–5, indicates extensive discussion of monetary reform as a means to income security via a national dividend. The election manifesto canvassed for votes for a national dividend of '£300 a year for every family, over and above wages and salaries and in place of "doles"'. Poverty amidst plenty was an absurdity to which 'Douglas social credit' had the solution. The simultaneous existence of a glut of goods and services alongside poverty and near starvation were due to the 'Bedlamite money system imposed on us by the bankers'. Three of the four pages of the document carried an outline of the plan to set up a 'national credit office' to administer the new money system. As a result, economic security would replace poverty and war. By spending their national dividends the unemployed would help 'set the wheels of industry turning at full speed' and would cease to be dependent upon taxation or charity. Freedom and self-respect would be restored as all became 'happy citizens of a Sane, Debt-Free Community'.

Hargrave's Green Shirts issued this manifesto of 'The Social Credit Party of Great Britain' in the name of John Hargrave as national leader and carrying the address of the national headquarters. It was widely available not only in the three constituencies in which 'social credit' or 'national dividend' candidates stood. It also appeared carrying the imprint of local headquarters in other towns throughout the country, and would appear to have been used in support of the secretariat's election pledge campaign. The proposal of a national dividend payable to the family rather than the individual is curiously at variance even with Hargrave's own booklet, which advocates the right of individuals to an income regardless of family circumstances (Hargrave 1945: 52–3). The suggestion that money reform could secure a vast increase in industrial output is equally contrary to much social credit literature. Hargrave's pamphlet stressed the need for agriculture to cease to be subject to the insecurity of debt financing, and for food to be grown locally for local markets (Hargrave 1945: 46–7). In its emphasis on the importance of income security for all, however, the manifesto was in line with the original Douglas/*New Age* texts.

Like Douglas, Hargrave understood that the pursuit of political power in the absence of an economic power base was a fruitless exercise. 'Social Credit cannot be "put through" by political methods . . . [it] is not an electioneering proposition' (Hargrave 1934: 272). It was, however, possible to use the machinery of political democracy as an educational aid in the dissemination of social credit ideas to the general public.

ORAGE AND THE CHANDOS GROUP

The Chandos group, the focal point of intellectual socialist and religious interest in social credit since 1926, formed the basis of support for Orage's new venture on his return from the United States in 1932. Having acquired financial patronage from his American contacts, Orage sought to resume journalistic support for social credit in the United Kingdom. Since Arthur Brenton refused to be ousted from the *New Age*, the Chandos group formed a vital reservoir of willing contributors to his new social credit publication, the *New English Weekly*. The journal circulated widely in the United Kingdom and also in the United States.

By the 1930s the basic tenets of international finance and capitalism held complete sway over orthodox economic thought across the political spectrum. Alternatives, in the form, for example, of economic nationalism and land redistribution, were exploited by Hitler and Mussolini for their own ends. Hence the *New English Weekly*'s support for autarky, and attacks upon international finance, led to superficial and inaccurate accusations that the weekly was an attractive vehicle for the expression of proto-fascist attitudes (Finlay 1972: 173–8), enhancing the legitimacy of capitalist economic orthodoxy.

Over the intervening years since 1922 Orage had lost little of his influence on intellectual left-wing thought. His contributions on economics and politics to the *New English Weekly* between April 1932 and November 1934 were selected and edited by M. Butchart, assisted by M. Colbourne, H. Cousens, Will Dyson (the cartoonist), T.S. Eliot, P. Mairet, I. Newsome, M. Reckitt and W.T. Symons (Butchart 1936). They offer evidence of continuity with the buoyant optimism of the earlier *New Age* years, coupled with stridency of attack upon the growing powers of international banking and finance over the daily lives of ordinary people.

Contributors to the *New English Weekly* over the two years of Orage's editorship included Penty, Bechhofer, Belloc and Cole. At Orage's suggestion, Mairet compiled *The Douglas Manual*, an attempt to provide a completely representative, authoritative statement of the principles of the

New Economics formulated by Douglas in the form of extracts from Douglas's own writings (Mairet 1934: foreword). Orage died in 1934 on the evening of his BBC speech on social credit, broadcast in the 'Poverty in Plenty' series. The text of this speech was combined with a lecture on *The Fear of Leisure* and published by Stanley Nott in the New Economics series of pamphlets (Orage 1935). On Orage's death Mairet became editor of the *New English Weekly*.

The Chandos group maintained guild socialist concepts of the decommodification of labour, the utility of work and social equity based on a sustainable sufficiency of production. The growing focus of the social credit movement upon the technicalities of monetary reform was viewed with unease by the Chandos group and their guild socialist associates, most notably Reckitt and Kenney (Reckitt 1941; Kenney 1939). Nevertheless, in a dozen or so pages of his autobiography Kenney drew upon the original Douglas/*New Age* texts to explain the ways of 'sound finance' (Kenney 1939: 289–303). Bank loans, which form the greater part of the money supply, are not a loan of existing money saved up by somebody else. Nine-tenths of money is bank-created, a ledger entry. The loan does not preclude any savers from reclaiming the money they have saved and paid into the bank. What the loan does do is enable *those businesses approved by the banks* to invest in capital equipment, produce goods for profit and repay the loan with interest. The issue of money in this way by the banks bears no relation to the supply of goods or the price put upon them. The business of finance is to 'make money'. To the financier 'money is a commodity; he trades in it; its proper function, of helping to facilitate the production, distribution and exchange of commodities, only incidentally concerns him' (Kenney 1939: 296).

Kenney refers to the phrase 'Guns before butter' and its suggestion that 'only a certain amount of money can be made available, and that, if it is spent on guns, butter cannot be had'. Evidence in Great Britain suggests, on the contrary, that butter became available to 'hundreds of thousands' of people only when rearmament commenced. In order to make the guns, the government went to the banks, which had ample stocks of their raw materials, ink and paper, and were only too ready to oblige. 'They lent the nation – the mass of the people whose brains and brawn provide the basis of the nation's credit – bits of paper . . . and there we were!' (Kenney 1939: 297). Kenney quotes from a report in the *New English Weekly* in respect of the first half of 1938, when well over half of total capital expenditure in Britain was by the government for rearmament. A 'great steel trust' was formed under the direction of Montagu Norman, governor of the Bank of England, capable of dictating methods and prices to the rest of the industry. In this way millions of pounds could be created out of nothing, specifically for the manufacture of guns. However, the manufacture of those guns:

did not deprive one person of one quarter-ounce of butter; on the contrary, it brought bread and butter, boots and clothes, fuel and house room, health and life to millions of people.

(Kenney 1939: 297)

Kenney concludes that under a 'sane financial system', those goods could have been made and distributed without rearmament. The policy of the banks is 'No guns, no butter – and no bread either'. If the whole of Europe were to decide not to rearm on a given day, there would be an 'appalling economic–financial catastrophe' such that in sheer despair some nation would precipitate war in order that the insane financial system could 'restart the machine of money printing for war production' (Kenney 1939: 298). It is impossible, Kenney observes, to discuss this rationally with business people who are concerned at the evils of the present system. They merely argue that no one has come up with a 'practical' cure. On investigation, it emerges that a 'practical' cure is one which will not interfere with the working of the present system.

An informed approach to the dissemination of the social implications of social credit was essential, in Reckitt's view, to create the conditions for a well-grounded reform of capitalist finance. In his autobiography he includes an entire chapter on 'Christian sociology' and the work of the high Anglican Father Widdrington, who worked to promote social credit ideas in the Coventry area. In Widdrington's view, shared by many social crediters:

> Either the Church must accept the challenge of the social problem or it must abdicate. It has been too long the Church Quiescent here on earth, content to serve as the scavenger of the capitalist system. If it refuses the challenge it may survive as a pietistic sect . . . administering religion as an anaesthetic to help men endure the hateful operation of life, an ambulance picking up the wounded . . . it will have abandoned its mission and become apostate.
>
> (Reckitt 1941: 251)

Links between members of the Chandos group and Christian socialists like Widdrington, who sought an end to wage slavery, remained strong throughout the 1930s.

WOMEN, ARTISTS, THE UNEMPLOYED AND THE SMALL FARMER

Social credit's most powerful appeal was to the vast sections of society whose income insecurity precluded their active participation as mainstream actors in the political economy. Industrial capitalism and organised labour had clearly defined economic roles. Women, the unemployed, small farmers and 'artists' had essential supporting roles, but these roles were less easy to specify within the terms of the formal economy. The 'artist' could include all whose work springs from internal motivation, not only the fine artist but also the writer, the musician, the craftsperson, the inventor and the engineer, without whose work civilisation would not exist. These were the mainstay of support for the social credit movement.

Feminist aspects of social credit

The futility of securing political freedom without economic freedom is stressed throughout the literature. Recognition is also given to the significance of a national dividend payable to the individual rather than the family unit as a means of securing women's civil rights (see e.g. *Attack!* 16 September 1935: 4). The active role of women in the worldwide social credit movement has received scant attention in historical accounts, and remains a fruitful area for future research. To date the involvement of many thousands of women in the study and promulgation of social credit lies hidden by male command of public platforms, publications and historical analyses. Nevertheless, traces of women's presence can be detected.

A series of articles on women and social credit gave rise to a spirited debate in the correspondence pages of the *New Age* on the relevance of social credit ideas to women. R. Laugier argued that 'Man has made a mess [of managing the economy]. Woman revolted once to become the equal of man; let her revolt again and be his superior' (Laugier 1934). Men's responsibility for 'the mess' was not at issue. The debate centred on the extent to which men had usurped women's role as providers and protectors. 'Woman, when she does not imitate man, is a realist' (*New Age* 1934b).

The question of the value of labour was presented in novel form, fully capable of amplification. In assessing the value of work, whether paid or unpaid, how is an hour's work to be valued? What yardstick may be most appropriate to an evaluative comparison between the hourly value of the work undertaken by:

(1) a Professor at the LSE,
(2) the Editor of *The New Age*,
(3) the late Mrs Norman for her feat in bearing and rearing her son, our Montagu [Governor of the Bank of England]?

(*New Age*, 27 December 1934)

The rhetorical question encapsulates the vitality of the debate on social credit issues among women in the 1930s. The economics of work, and women's role in the economy, have, like the broader political movement, repeatedly risen to prominence, only to give way to 'more important' mainstream considerations. The social credit movement of the 1930s provides a further example of a failed attempt by women to step 'out of the margin' (Hutchinson 1995). For example, women of the Green Shirts

Movement, led by Carol Dixon, national organiser of the Women's Section, marched in uniform to present an official letter in support of 'a Sane Economic System as propounded by Major C.H. Douglas' to the Prime Minister at 10 Downing Street (*New Age*, 14 June 1934). Similar reports of women activists in the social credit movement are commonplace in the social credit press.

The quest of the 1990s women's movement to free both women and men from the wage slavery of capitalism is echoed not only in the pages of the *New Age* but also in Hargrave's presentation of the case for social credit. Since paraphrasing may appear to distort the original meaning, the relevant passages are quoted in full:

> *Q.* How will Social Credit affect the position of women in general?
> By giving every woman a birthright income – i.e., the National Dividend based on the productive capacity of the community – it will ensure economic independence *and* freedom, for it will release her from being:
> 1 Tied to the home when she wishes to lead her own life.
> 2 Treated as a drudge, or as an inferior – i.e. the 'chattel' status.
> 3 Driven to marry for the sake of economic security.
> 4 Bound to some man who ill-treats her, or is in some other way unsuitable as a person to live with.
> 5 Driven into work-wage slavery in competition with men in order to keep alive.
> *Q.* Will women get 'equal pay for equal work'?
> Yes, they will. (1) Because a Social Credit Government will naturally stand for fair play for all citizens without distinction; (2) because employers will no longer need 'cheap labour'; and (3) because each individual woman will be able to say – 'If I do this job as well as a man could do it, I shall want the same pay as a man.' And if the employer says, 'No,' she will be able to say: 'Very well, I refuse the job. After all, I can live on my National Dividend.' This places every woman in a very powerful position. (It will apply equally, of course, to badly-paid male workers.)
>
> (Hargrave 1945: 52–3)

Following from women's growing interest in 'the new economics' of Douglas across Britain and Canada, and 'more noticeably in Australia and New Zealand', American women were encouraged to banish the notion that economics is a 'man's subject'. Man's lust for power could be countered if women applied the simple test to all economic proposals: 'Is it good *social* housekeeping?' (Munson 1934; emphasis added). Women's emancipation into 'salaried slavery', observed a writer in the *New Age* in 1934, had done nothing to ameliorate women's status or conditions (11 October).

Tantalisingly obscure advertisements for meetings, alongside readers' letters and minor articles, offer evidence of women's enthusiasm for, and participation in, the social credit movement in the United Kingdom. Its major publications, the *New Age* and *Social Credit*, provide glimpses of women's participation in the movement, not only in support of their men, but also in their own right. 'Women actively interested in Social problems and the abolition of poverty should read the Women's Section of *Prosperity*', says a notice in the 11 October 1934 issue of the *New Age*. Women's sections were formed in central London, Shoreditch, Battersea, Deptford, Stockton-on-Tees and Rochdale, with nuclei of members in Coventry, Sheffield, Leeds, Edmonton (Alta.), Preston and Blackburn (*Social Credit* and *New Age* 1934–5).

The Canadian *Calgary Herald* of 1934 provides more specific indications of women's active involvement. The 'conversion' to social credit of a number of women 'leaders' in the province caused 'invitations for lectures on the new economics to pour [in] from women's groups in every corner of the city [Edmonton]' (Irving 1959: 68). 'On January 17 a mass meeting of 700 women . . . voted unanimously to wire a resolution to the United Farm Women of Alberta, then in convention in Edmonton, to give its support to an investigation by the Alberta government of the Douglas System' (quoted by Irving 1959, from the *Calgary Herald*). On this occasion the principal speaker, Mrs W.E. Callbeck, 'claimed that since manual labour is being replaced by mechanisation, work can no longer be the medium by which purchasing power may be distributed' (Irving 1959: 69). At the same meeting 'Mrs W.W. Rogers outlined her work as women's organiser.' Aberhart, the charismatic leader of the movement in Alberta, claimed a minimal mention. He was allowed to speak briefly at a busy meeting which did not require any instruction from higher up the hierarchy. Irving notes an announcement 'typical of scores of others' inviting 'women who are interested in economics' to a discussion of 'the Douglas System of social credit'. 'Members of the economics groups of the University Women's Club, the Business and Professional Women's club, and the women school teachers of this city are especially invited to attend.' A series of classes was organised, and women speakers promoted social credit at evening meetings in outlying towns and villages (Irving 1959: 70, 244–8).

Women writers on social credit included Elizabeth Sage Holter, Helen Corke, Gladys Bing, Jean Campbell Willett and the novelist Storm Jameson. Holter's *ABC of Social Credit* (1934) was 'one of the most succinct introductions to the subject. The first book on social credit written by an American had a clear common sense approach to economics and describes the social credit analysis for American readers' (Generoso 1981: 40). Corke provided a competent and concise history of the evolution of the relationship between banking and industrialisation from a social credit viewpoint. She supported the view that scarcity was an invention of the financial system in the technological age. Corke defined the 'dismal science' as 'the study of the processes concerned in the production and distribution of goods and services' (Corke 1934: 3). Within the contemporary education system, history and geography supplied information on production in a general education. Lessons on distribution, however, were confined to the consideration of transport 'and rarely touch upon the working of the financial machinery on which distribution, no less than production, depends' (Corke 1934: 3). As a leading figure in social credit, Corke planned a history of the movement. Her collection of material, alongside that of Mairet, formed the basis of McCarthy's study (McCarthy 1947). Jameson's powerful pamphlet on the value of 'leisure' as self-governed time is summarised in the next section of this chapter.

Women social crediters dismiss the mystique of economics, approaching the subject with refreshing directness. In her pamphlet *What is Social Credit?* Bing observes:

> sound economics *are* sound ethics. Which means that if you have to make your competitor bankrupt in order to remain solvent yourself – then the economic system which forces you to these wicked actions is a bad system and must be changed.
>
> (Bing 1935: 5)

Bing advocates social credit as an alternative system. The key is to plan production according to consumption, enabling the consumer to exercise effective demand. Money should be issued to consumers. It is 'ethically wrong', and therefore bad economics, for money to be created as debt in respect of goods and raw materials which already exist. The 'credit of the people' should instead be issued by the Bank of England direct to the individuals who comprise the nation. The economics of social credit is designed to develop a 'better life, morally and spiritually'. Central to it is the idea of 'quality' to replace the 'price-cutting nastiness that prevails today'. Appreciation of quality extends beyond commodities, to ideas, the arts and human relations. Bing concludes:

> If you have read this booklet and wish for your children this great, free world of wealth and culture, do not blame the boss, the capitalist, the loafing worker, the exploiter, the blacks, the Jews, the Government – blame the chap or girl you see in the mirror when you shave or wash in the mornings.
>
> (Bing 1935: 7)

In her more substantial booklet *Women and Poverty* Willett provides an even more striking example of the vibrancy of the women's movement in social credit. The booklet dispels the notion that women social crediters were right-wing and reactionary, providing graphic descriptions of poverty in urban slums. The plight of families in general, and the problems of women in poverty, are set within the context of 'poverty amidst plenty'. While women struggle to provide their children with the basic necessities of life, 'surplus' food is destroyed. Willett delineates the pressures on women to accept low pay and poor conditions of work. She attributes toleration of crime and degradation to 'unemployment', leisure without an income, which is the inevitable product of an outdated financial system. As machines displace labour, and so remove incomes from the poor, a national dividend should be provided for all. In that way the 'Real Capital Wealth' of one of the richest countries of the world can be equitably distributed (Willett 1935: 15).

> Today the machines and labour-saving devices are taking the place of the slaves of old, and we, too, should be free to devote our time and energies to pursuits in which we are genuinely interested.
>
> (Willett 1935: 17)

Willett's concern extends to women in the non-traditional role of 'bachelor woman', referring to the 'surplus' women robbed of a partner by World War I. Forced into an unequal struggle for financial independence, such women are unable to make proper provision for their old age.

Women make a valuable contribution to the real wealth of the country through marriage and child-rearing. Nevertheless,

> while other branches of work for the country, which can be valued in terms of money, are subsidised, the work of rearing families which constitute the nation is left to find money where it can, either by earnings, by voluntary contributions through organisations, or through charity.
>
> (Willett 1935: 19)

In the meantime, high wages are paid to those who make guns and weapons of destruction.

Willett advocates economic independence for women as a means of creating emotionally stable marriages. A national dividend

> would go far towards removing two of the most insidious foes of understanding between men and women – masculine arrogance and feminine coquetry. Where either party is entirely dependent upon the other, true values may become distorted, unworthy artifices for gaining things desired may be resorted to, and honesty and understanding give place to reservations and strain.
>
> (Willett 1935: 21)

Throughout the booklet Willett expresses concern at the psychological stress caused by the unhealthy financial system. Much poor parenting is due to families having to live in poor economic circumstances. Equally, the abusing father and violent husband could be better dealt with by a woman who is financially independent. Willett explores the illogicalities of a financial system in which poverty exists alongside 'overproduction'. Women work for low pay in poor conditions, with disastrous consequences for their mental and physical health. Poverty can also lead to prostitution.

> The real cure is to remove the financial necessity for women to sell themselves . . . With a National Dividend to support her, a woman could reasonably be blamed for selling herself for money; and with the easing of financial strain both men and women would be freed from the urge to take love, so-called, as a reaction and recreation from mundane and sordid conditions, and value it as truly as their own weighed choice and inclination for what is beautiful.
>
> (Willett 1935: 31)

Education also suffers when it merely serves 'the temples of "Sound Finance"'. 'Everything becomes subservient to the need of finding a living; education for leisure, and to produce liberal minds, is either ignored as not paying or voted out as too idealistic' (Willett 1935: 32). In words which could have been written six decades later, Willett documents the ills of an education system governed by financial considerations: oversize classes, inadequate equipment, old and unhealthy buildings, physical and mental stress on teaching staff and nervous strain reflected in the children themselves. Formalism and routine replace the 'freshness which is all-important in the teaching profession' (Willett 1935: 33). Many are forced into teaching for financial reasons, unable to secure financial support for the university research they are capable of producing. Under a social credit system all children should be able to stay at school to pursue a 'more liberal, less exam-ridden education – an education for the leisure in which they must one day share – and face after-school life with the assurance that they will not be confronted with the mad rush for employment for employment's sake' (Willett 1935: 34). Additionally, Willett urges women to resist the pressure to train their sons for war, which has ceased to be a matter of religion or politics but has now become 'a financially controlled affair' (Willett 1935: 36).

Willett concludes that poverty and misery are not inevitable.

> It is against the iniquity of the existence of poverty in the midst of abundance that women should direct the power given them by their votes. Let us vote for the one thing needful, the abolition of poverty; let us insist upon it in no uncertain terms.
>
> (Willett 1935: 38)

As machines replace labour a national dividend can usher in an age of 'prosperity and anxiety-free leisure'. All that will be lost is 'an archaic and false monetary system' (Willett 1935: 39).

The literary dimension

For poets, playwrights, craftspeople, actors and novelists the concept of economic democracy through social credit possessed immediate appeal. Lack of financial security has been an incessant impediment to artistic endeavour. Names associated with the social credit movement include Ezra Pound, T.S. Eliot, Herbert Read, Storm Jameson, William Carlos Williams, James Laughlin (American publisher), Charlie Chaplin, Eimar O'Duffy, Aldous Huxley, Sybil Thorndike and Bonamy Dobrée (Munson 1933; Mairet 1936; McCarthy 1947; Martin 1967; Finlay 1972; Generoso 1981; *New Age* 1933–6). Involvement included the authorship of articles and pamphlets, and organisational activities. In contrast with the silence surrounding the thousands of ordinary women and men social crediters, the social psychological attributes of these public figures have been analysed in extensive detail (Finlay 1972).

For a comprehensive analysis of Pound's economics see Davis (1968). Pound's support for social credit subsequently lent credence to the belief that it was a movement of the far right. However, Davis argues that it was not until the final stages of World War II, and the opening up of the concentration camps in Germany, that the full horrors of Nazism, the modern form of fascism, became apparent, not only to fascist sympathisers but also to the armed forces who opposed Nazism. Hence Pound's support for fascism in Italy can more accurately be attributed to reaction against the rampant commercialism of the US economy than to malicious intent to slaughter innocent civilians in the name of a master race. Following his early review of *Economic Democracy* Pound wrote two social credit pamphlets (Pound 1922, 1935). His *ABC of Economics* (1933) was based on social credit, and he contributed material and poems to social credit publications. For example, in *Attack!* (the Green Shirt publication) No. 29 (1935) his poem 'Work???' is followed by the footnote 'Work is not a commodity.' A number of the *Cantos* revolve around the same theme. According to Davis, it was 'essential to emphasize for American readers the major difference between the Marxian and Douglas analyses, if only to ward off dismissal of all parts of the Social Credit philosophy because of its connections with the bogy of Communism' (Davis 1968: 73). Pound's fascist sympathies continue to be used in evidence against social credit.

Storm Jameson's pamphlet *The Soul of Man in the Age of Leisure* explored the development of 'the machine-enslaved mind'. The majority have little choice but to obey the

> forces [financial] which control all our lives from birth to death. . . .
> The army of us who serve the machines, either by minding them or
> by giving orders to the minders, or by purveying ideas, religions, a
> literature, apt to amuse without unsettling, have really only one
> choice offered us at birth – obey, conform, or starve.
>
> (Jameson 1935: 10–11)

The 'only important business a human being has on earth is to create. If he is cheated of it . . . he goes bad' (Jameson 1935: 21). The pamphlet is an eloquent and prophetic plea for 'a stable and healthy society . . . in which the creative instinct will have the fullest play' (Jameson 1935: 23).

Social credit provided the central theme of the Cuanduine trilogy of Eimar O'Duffy. The latter also published a social credit text, *Life and Money*, described as 'a critical examination of the principles and practice of orthodox economics with a practical scheme to end the muddle it has made of our civilization' (O'Duffy 1932) which went to several editions. He questioned the assumption underlying the growth of competition. Why should the 'manifold devices for the saving of labour' coupled with the multiplication of the fruits of nature and 'increasing social aggregation . . . have so utterly incongruous a result?' (O'Duffy 1932: 19).

O'Duffy's mythical science-fiction fantasy in three volumes is a comic indictment of politics and economics in the contemporary world. *King Goshawk and the Birds* (1926) portrays the philosophy of the capitalist financial system followed through to its logical conclusions: a monopoly has been established over song-birds and wild flowers. In the second book, *The Spacious Adventures of the Man in the Street*, a world where a sane credit system secures sufficiency and leisure for all is viewed through the unsympathetic eyes of a speculative opportunist. Finally, in *Asses in Clover*, the god-hero travels through the kingdom of Assinaria. There professors of the dismal science discuss how far the standard of living must be lowered in order to raise it, and the impossibility of providing an income for all in a land of plenty when there is no demand for labour. Despite their comic form, the books carry a sombre message. A social credit Utopia on the moon is destroyed by capitalist financial pressures. On earth, those who can afford to pay to see song-birds and wild flowers are content to do so. Those suffering abject poverty are too preoccupied with their plight to care about the world they have lost. The trilogy has an uncannily prophetic ring. On his death in 1935 O'Duffy was described by Douglas as an economist of 'no mean order . . . combining the typical Irishman's hatred of pomposity with a delicate sense of proportion. . . . His books will, for many years, provide a touchstone of reality' (Douglas 1935b: 70).

Further works of fiction on the social credit theme appeared at this time, including *Alchemy in Artuega* by E. Glasbrook Richards, serialised in the *New English Weekly* (Munson 1933).

Small farmers and the unemployed

In the dominions, social credit had powerful appeal in the non-industrialised sectors of rural agriculture and amongst the urban unemployed (Finkel 1989). Where a Marxist or Fabian-style radical critique of capitalism based upon the exploitation of the industrial worker meant little, the role of the banker and financier in securing 'the crop that never fails' held immediate relevance. The attraction of social credit themes to small farmers was responsible for the growth of the movement across Canada, the United States, Australia and New Zealand during the 1920s, the 1930s and the post-war years.

Even in the United Kingdom the impact of financial pressures upon farming practices was a further recurring theme in social credit literature. The failure of capitalist finance to account for the 'true cost of living' was noted in a series of articles in the *New Age* in 1934, and Rudolph Steiner methods of care of the soil were advocated. Financial credit was forcing farmers to make unsustainable demands upon the soil on pain of being driven from the land when unable to meet the demands of taxes, tithes and loan repayments. Connections were drawn between human health and the health of the soil, demonstrating early recognition of the dangers of seeking a quick financial return at the expense of the long-term fertility of the soil (*New Age*, 11 October 1934: 286).

SOCIAL CREDIT AND THE 1935 GENERAL ELECTION

The merit of fighting elections on behalf of a 'Social Credit Party' was the subject of intense debate within the movement. Social crediters were united in the view that political democracy without economic democracy was an empty vessel. Debate centred upon whether the securing of political power could in practice deliver economic power to the people. This debate was most vigorous in Alberta, the subject of the next chapter. Even where political power was not a viable proposition, as in the United Kingdom, there was an argument for using elections as a promotional exercise. This could be done either by fielding candidates, as did the Green Shirts, or by seeking pledges from sitting members of existing political parties, as was attempted by the secretariat. The counter-argument was that a poor showing in an election could serve to discredit social crediters in the eyes of the general public they were seeking to convert.

In this light, historians' preoccupation with splits and divisions in the social credit movement is misleading. W. Townend's candidature in Leeds South in 1935 was endorsed by Lord Tavistock, Maude Royden, Sybil Thorndike and the monetary reformer Professor Frederick Soddy (*New Age*, 21 November 1935). Soddy's support for social credit (his name frequently appears in social credit publications) reveals an underlying unity of purpose across a wider movement for an alternative to socially and spiritually damaging economic orthodoxy. The electoral threat posed to Labour by the Social Credit Party was considered great enough, in terms of the marginal loss of votes, to warrant lengthy refutation. A Labour leaflet 'played up to the established prejudices of class-conscious Labour'. It stated that advocates of social credit did not believe in public ownership and control of the means of production, or in the elimination of class distinctions or in securing equality of opportunity for all, but that they *did* believe in capitalism as the best possible system. The leaflet made play in this context with a quotation from Major Douglas, 'Almost the only thing which is not open to destructive criticism about the Banks is their dividends' (*New Age* 1935b: 19).

In the event, the three 'social credit' candidates came reasonably close to saving their deposits. H.C. Bell in Birmingham (Erdington) needed 5,940 votes and won 2,050; Reginald Kenney in Bradford (North) needed 4,986 votes and obtained 4,684; W. Townend in Leeds (South) needed 4,134 and obtained 3,642 votes. These figures were fairly respectable, since none of the candidates had been in place, and in a position to campaign, for much over a month. In typically Green Shirt fashion Townend sought publicity through the manner in which he paid his deposit. In order to pay the £150 required he arrived with supporters carrying £50 bags of silver. The mayor started to count the silver. When he arrived at 40s Townend had to stop him, pointing out that silver was not legal tender above that sum. He proceeded to pay in Bank of England notes, making the point that it was not legal to use the coin of the realm. The law 'placed the credit of a private institution higher than that of the King and the People' (*New Age*, 14 November 1935). The same issue of the *New Age* carries a 'late report' from the Leeds South campaign:

> Townend's Mass Meeting Palace Cinema last night attended by enthusiastic audience 1,200. Overflow meeting 500 listened loudspeaker in pouring rain 2¹/₂ hours outside. – Tull, Election Agent, Social Credit Party.

Nevertheless, it remained a subject of debate as to whether the venture as a whole was counterproductive (*New Age*, 21 November 1935). Equally ill fated was the electoral campaign organised by the secretariat. Pledges secured were not worth the paper they were written on, and merely served to discredit the movement further.

CONCLUSION

Throughout the 1930s the movement concentrated on the technicalities of monetary reform. As this process continued guild socialists like Reckitt withdrew their support. They recognised that reform of the monetary system, were it to be achieved, would merely alter the system of distribution. On its own, monetary reform could offer no insights into the handling of the inevitable changes in the system of production which would follow reform. Orage had observed that the guild system would reform production but leave the productive system out of synchronisation with the system of finance. By the late 1930s social crediters had failed to reunite the two basic strands of the Douglas/*New Age* texts. Although the war effectively precluded development of the debate, the worldwide social credit movement served to publicise an alternative to capitalist and labourist orthodoxy.

Eimar O'Duffy's delightful fictional portrayals of the case for social credit were widely circulated in the United Kingdom and the United States in the inter-war years. They remain collectors' items and appear on the utopian reading lists of sociology departments (Sargent 1988). Social credit study groups throughout the dominions, the United States and the United Kingdom scrutinised the 'new economics', drawing upon the wealth of explanatory texts which flowed into publication. Later publications included *Elements of Social Credit*, an 'introductory Course of Lectures published with the authority of the Social Credit Secretariat', endorsed by Douglas (Social Credit Secretariat 1946). However, the 'Douglasites' stood accused by liberals and radicals alike of failing to master the rules of orthodox economics and therefore of propounding heretical, if well-meaning, nonsense. They were consigned to a footnote in texts on the history of economic thought (e.g. Preston 1991) and mass adherence to such heresies was explained away in sociological terms as an irrational reaction to adverse economic circumstances (Irving 1959; Macpherson 1962; Grayson and Grayson 1974).

Superficially, this view is supported by the flow of events in the decades following World War II. From 1938 armaments production and the general stimulation of the economy in wartime rescued capitalism from depression. Post-1945 welfare state capitalism offered workers the illusion of security in return for their co-operation in the production of wealth. Economic orthodoxy was so dominant that dissent could no longer be heard, save that couched in the terms, and based upon the premises, of liberal orthodoxy. The strains of proto-fascist sentiment within post-1945 Canadian, Australian and United Kingdom social credit movements followed frustration at the general failure to recognise the power of orthodox finance. It has served to legitimise the refusal of political reformers to examine the Douglas/*New Age* texts in the search for radical alternative approaches to economics.

9

THE ALBERTA EXPERIMENT

In August 1935 the first social credit government was elected to office in the Canadian province of Alberta. Out of sixty-three seats in the provincial legislature, fifty-six were taken by members of a party less than a year old. None of the candidates had previously been elected to office, and few had any experience in politics. Douglas, already appointed economic adviser to the Alberta administration, was invited by the incoming social credit Premier, William Aberhart, to travel to the province and advise on the introduction of social credit legislation. Despite lengthy correspondence between Douglas and Aberhart, Douglas resigned as adviser and the visit was never paid. Successive 'social credit' governments were voted into power in the province, the apparent break with orthodox politics being reviewed from the discourse of orthodoxy as a symptom of adverse socio-economic conditions.

A discourse is 'a domain of language-use that is unified by common assumptions' (Abercrombie *et al.* 1984: 71). In the mainstream press the documentation of the social credit phenomenon in Alberta has been limited to the discourses of neoclassical economic orthodoxy and the sociological analysis of minority politics (Mallory 1954; Irving 1959; Macpherson 1962; Finlay 1972; Sinclair 1972; Finkel 1989). In terms of orthodox discourse a desperate electorate turned to the monetary crank Douglas and the religious fundamentalist Aberhart. Unable to agree among themselves, the would-be reformers had to be restrained from bringing the state to the verge of bankruptcy. A deluded electorate persisted in voting-in successive social credit governments committed to a series of illegal reforms. Following World War II, economic prosperity rendered institutional change 'unnecessary'. The post-war social credit government was able 'to provide "good government" and avoid any act likely to antagonise business interests. . . . [This has] secured the reputation of the Social Credit party as a sane, conservative political force in the community' (Mallory 1954: vii). By way of contrast with earlier texts, this chapter presents the events in Alberta from the standpoint of the social credit press.

ALBERTA AND WILLIAM ABERHART

The Canadian province of Alberta covers 255,000 square miles, three times the area of Great Britain. Its population of 500,000, many from Ukrainian and German farming stock, was well versed in self-sufficiency and could theoretically be amply sustained on the fertile land. The problem was financial. In the depression years the lack of markets for grain led to debts and mortgage repossessions. Payment to financial institutions of 'the crop that never fails' drove small farmers from the land and on to poor relief, necessitating increased taxation.

When he entered politics at the age of 54 Aberhart was principal of Crescent Heights High, a large state school in Calgary. Throughout the province he was better known as dean of the Prophetic Bible Institution. The spectacle of students leaving school well equipped to make a contribution to society, but descending into despair and suicide at the absence of any opportunity to do so, drove him into politics. His political success was due to 'his vivid presentation of the general lunacy responsible for the grinding poverty so common in a Province of abounding riches, superimposed upon his peculiar theological reputation' (Douglas 1937: 22–3). In the immediate aftermath of accession to power, Aberhart and Douglas failed to comprehend each other. Nevertheless, they shared a generosity of spirit and a dedication to working for the common good regardless of personal career considerations. On the occasion of Aberhart's death in 1943, while still in office, Douglas acknowledged him in these terms:

> It was not easy for a man of 57, the greater part of whose life has been spent in teaching, to learn. It was here that one of Aberhart's outstanding qualities shone so clearly. He was, beyond all question, a man of complete integrity, more concerned to fulfil his pledges than to force his own ideas, once he was convinced that they were wrong or inexpedient. In the short space of five years, while drastically remodelling and purifying the day-to-day administration of the Province, he uncovered his enemies' hand by a series of Bills . . .
>
> (Douglas 1937: vii)

THE BACKGROUND

The 'technical' proposals for monetary reform arising out of the A + B theorem had been the subject of study across Canada since Douglas's first visit to the country in 1923. On that occasion he gave evidence to the Parliamentary Committee on Banking and Commerce, alongside Irving Fisher, Sir Frederick Williams-Taylor of the Bank of Montreal and Henry Ford. The committee, appointed to revise the Bank Charter Act, invited Douglas at the behest of prominent members of the United Farmers' party who had read social credit publications. Despite hostile questioning,

Douglas presented a comprehensive account of his theories (House of Commons, Canada 1923). The experience brought home to Douglas the extent of the difficulties he faced in communicating his theories to those potentially capable of translating them into practice (Douglas 1937: 16).

Over the following decade social credit literature continued to circulate throughout Canada, aided by the support of the editor of the Ottawa *Citizen*. A caucus of members of the federal legislature were converted to the social credit philosophy. Key members of the ruling United Farmers' Association (UFA) were well versed in social credit. They failed, however, to achieve its adoption as official party policy. The depression following the 1929 financial crisis presented an opportunity for consideration of alternatives to orthodoxy.

In Canada the depression hit western farming states particularly hard. Dependent upon a money system designed to suit the requirements of the rich, industrialised eastern states, farming communities were hard hit by falling prices and debt. As banks foreclosed on mortgages and many farmers became destitute the United Farmers' government failed to produce a remedy.

THE SOCIAL CREDIT PARTY

Introduced to social credit through one of the various interpretations circulating at the time, Aberhart set about publicising the new economic doctrine through his Sunday religious broadcasts and speeches at meetings across the province (Douglas 1937: xv). As subsequent events proved, Aberhart's comprehension of the 'technicalities' of social credit was limited. However, local study groups initiated by social credit members of the UFA provided a basis of recruitment for his campaign. At first, Aberhart attempted to persuade the UFA government and other established parties to adopt social credit. When that failed, he informed supporters of his plan to enter social credit candidates at the forthcoming general election. From the outset Douglas social crediters in Canada and the United Kingdom noted that Aberhart's economic proposals were based upon only partial comprehension of social credit political economy (Douglas 1937; Hattersley 1937).

DOUGLAS AND THE UFA GOVERNMENT

Aberhart's spectacular success in gaining support for his Social Credit Party led the UFA to invite Douglas to visit Alberta on his return to the United Kingdom from New Zealand. Although the UFA sought to emphasise the divergences between Douglas and Aberhart, the visit added further impetus to the social credit campaign. Some months later Douglas was appointed economic adviser to the Alberta administration. In correspondence Douglas stressed his political neutrality, reasoning with Aberhart that his

174

appointment was as a public servant. Nevertheless, relations between Aberhart and Douglas remained strained. Douglas presented an 'interim report' to the UFA government on the feasibility of introducing social credit to the province. When the UFA government was defeated, losing all its seats and ceasing to exist as a political party, Douglas remained economic adviser to the incoming administration.

THE SOCIAL CREDIT MOVEMENT

The new administration was elected on a programme described by Douglas as 'defective both in theory and practicability' (Douglas 1937: 22). Aberhart understood only in the most general terms that the provision of effective monetary demand was the route out of the province's difficulties. A major factor in his electoral success was his promise to pay a dividend of £5 ($25) a month to each adult citizen. In 1937 Douglas commented:

> While the arguments brought forward by Mr Aberhart as a basis for this proposal will not bear examination, I have no doubt whatever that by suitable methods the essential promise could, and can, be validated.
>
> (Douglas 1937: 23)

The new administration defied all predictions by remaining in office and being re-elected for successive terms. Aberhart's first consideration was to maintain the machinery of state by correcting the financial maladministration of the outgoing administration. To that end he approached Ottawa for a loan and, on the recommendation of the governor of the Bank of Canada, he appointed Robert Magor as economic adviser to the government. Magor had been a key figure in solving Newfoundland's debt problem through a 1930s version of 'structural adjustment', in which financial interests override political decision-making. Douglas viewed Magor's appointment with suspicion. Having warned Aberhart that Magor's advice would lead the province away from social credit, bringing the movement into disrepute, Douglas resigned as adviser. Magor's appointment led to the dismissal of government employees, a 2 per cent sales tax, a 60 per cent rise in income tax, increased taxes on petrol and cars and a reduction in interest rates on the provincial debt (Douglas 1937: 72). No steps were taken to introduce social credit monetary reform or a national dividend. In Douglas's view:

> No government was ever elected with a clearer mandate or with less excuse for delay, and whether shock tactics, peculiarly advisable in view of the imminent Dominion elections, or an immediate advance upon a limited objective, would have been better is immaterial. The sheer weight of popular enthusiasm would at this time have justified bold action.
>
> (Douglas 1937: 60)

Initially, efforts were made to win a social credit majority in the federal legislature. Alberta secured seventeen seats. Other western states, including Saskatchewan and Manitoba, returned social credit members, but not in sufficient numbers (Hattersley 1937: 248; Douglas 1937: 1). Social crediters in the United Kingdom, the United States, Australia and New Zealand were concerned that the apparent failure of a premature attempt to introduce social credit could be cited as evidence that social credit was unworkable.

In Aberhart's view, failure to comply with federal legislative requirements, which included honouring the province's external debt, would result in dismissal of the social credit government. As the correspondence between the two reveals (see Douglas 1937: appendix III), Douglas failed to comprehend Aberhart's situation.

As Hattersley observed in 1937, four factors stood out as militating against Aberhart's chances of introducing social credit measures. First, in matters of finance Alberta was subject to the federal government under the British North America Act of 1867 (the constitution of Canada). Second, as a largely agricultural province Alberta lacked the industrial base necessary for a self-sufficient economy. Third, Alberta's substantial external debt afforded her creditors the opportunity to obstruct any financial arrangements which might affect their interests. Fourth, Alberta lacked the resources to combat the ravages of drought which had turned some areas of the province into dustbowls (Hattersley 1937: 247).

The measures adopted on Magor's advice brought general disfavour and split the government. Cabinet supporters of Aberhart prioritised the continued provision of government services, especially welfare relief. The 'insurgents' resisted the introduction of measures diametrically opposed to social credit, and refused to vote the money supply measures necessary for the government to continue. As a result of the *impasse* Douglas was again invited to Alberta. In Douglas's view the Alberta government had discredited itself and social credit (Douglas 1937: xx). Two nominees, G.F. Powell and L.D. Byrne, were despatched to the province to report on the situation in preparation for Douglas to resume his position as economic adviser.

According to Byrne, Cabinet supporters and insurgents were swiftly reunited on a programme to introduce social credit. The plan which Byrne and Powell outlined was designed to secure control of the 'real credit' of the province, i.e. 'its ability to produce wanted goods and services which would lift its people out of the conditions of poverty which prevailed'.

> This real credit was, in turn, controlled by the monetary system – which was constitutionally the responsibility of the Federal Government because of its jurisdiction over banks and banking. Therefore any action to bring the real credit of the Province – involving fundamental property and civil rights – under the exclusive constitutional jurisdiction of the Provinces required of the banks to conform to the policy laid down by

the Provincial Government. As the policy being pursued by the banks under the Bank of Canada was diametrically opposed to Social Credit policy and was inherent in the system, therefore such action was bound to bring the Alberta Government into conflict with the banks, financial institutions, and through them the Federal Government.

(Byrne, introduction to 1984 edition of Douglas 1937: xxii)

The first step was to pass legislation requiring the banks to implement the measures specified by the government. The 'Credit of Alberta Regulation Act' was the subject of extensive media coverage. Financial institutions in Canada, England and the United States voiced their objections. Although the federal Minister of Justice expressed doubts as to the constitutional right of his government to disallow provincial legislation, the Act was declared unconstitutional.

At this point Byrne was appointed economic adviser to the Alberta government, a post which he held until Aberhart's death in 1943. Although Aberhart was initially cool towards Byrne, they became firm friends, working towards the goal of introducing social credit. They supported the war effort, and were planning post-war reconstruction when Aberhart died. Ernest Manning, the new Premier, though ostensibly committed to social credit, pursued policies indistinguishable from those of the mainstream parties. Nominally Alberta had a social credit government until 1971 (Douglas 1937: xxix).

DOUGLAS AND THE ALBERTA EXPERIMENT

The episode confirmed Douglas in his opinion that capitalism could not be defeated at the polls. With his close colleagues, including Byrne, he recognised that Aberhart had embraced social credit without understanding its critique of capitalist finance. Byrne noted: 'What he [Aberhart] did not understand was that Social Credit is not a plan or scheme of monetary reform, but the "policy of a philosophy" of which the financial proposals are but one means to an end' (Douglas 1937: xviii).

The core of Douglas's analysis was presented in the 'Interim Report on the Possibilities of the Application of Social Credit Principles to the Province of Alberta', published as an appendix to *The Alberta Experiment*:

> While it is clear that under a barter system there is always sufficient effective demand although it may be inequitably distributed, under a money or cheque system both inequitable and ineffective demand are certain unless production and demand are consciously and systematically related.

(Douglas 1937: 105)

In the first years of his administration Aberhart failed to distinguish between seemingly radical schemes for 'labourist' solutions to depression and social credit. He therefore introduced reforms modelled on Roosevelt's 'new deal' and local currency systems of the 'prosperity scrip' type. In a passage anticipating the ecological economics of the 1990s, Douglas noted that both these concepts diverged sharply from social credit.

> The essential point to notice is that President Roosevelt and his advisers did not criticise the objective of industrial civilisation in the smallest degree. This assumes that you cannot have too much industrial effort so long as it does not produce unemployment, and that it is a sound and safe policy to set the whole of an immense population permanently to the task of remaking the physical face of the earth in sublime disregard of the consequences which have already ensued from this policy and the dangers which threaten its extension.
>
> (Douglas 1937: 77–8)

In the 1930s Douglas's warnings of the environmental dangers of escalating industrial production did little to render his work comprehensible to the mainstream. Equally, his rejection of apparently similar schemes designed to support conventional economics appeared arrogant. Acknowledging the soundness of Gesell's theoretical work, Douglas criticised the Alberta Prosperity Certificates introduced by Aberhart as involving 'the same obsession with "production" as an end in itself' (Douglas 1937: 83). Similar to a dollar bill, the certificates required weekly endorsement of a 2c stamp, in effect a 104 per cent annual capital levy. The 'disappearing money' was designed to discourage savings and encourage the purchase of commodities. Introduced in 1936, the certificates met with initial hostility (*New Age*, 13 August 1936), until bankers came to recognise the scheme as 'the most stupendous taxation upon money resources that has ever been proposed . . . [It] increases the power of those who have the monopoly of creating money to an extent which for all practical purposes renders it absolute' (Douglas 1937: 85).

DICTATORSHIP OF FINANCE

Douglas died in 1952, labelled a spectacular monetary crank who retreated into conspiracy theories when his work was rejected by orthodoxy. It is true that Douglas noted the existence of international financiers reared to a common world view and sharing the same interests. (See Finlay 1972: 101–6 for an analysis of this aspect of Douglas.) Following from the Alberta 'experiment' he more clearly recognised that financial interests were not subject to political restraints.

> If the Social Credit Government of Alberta had done nothing – and it has done many things – to justify its existence, the demonstration afforded by its enemies of one fundamental factor in the world situation would still have made it a landmark in human history.

That factor, completely demonstrated by the actions of the Canadian Federal Government in disallowing every Act of the Provincial Legislature directed to the inauguration of Social Credit, is that the Secret Government is determined to keep the world in turmoil until its own rule is supreme, so that one uniformed mob may be mobilised against another, should either become dangerous. I do not think that anyone who will take the trouble to consider the actions of the Canadian Federal Government, can fail to apprehend exactly why centralisation, federal Union, and other 'Bigger and Better' Governments are the most deadly menace with which humanity is faced today.

(Douglas 1942a, quoted in Douglas 1937: x–xi)

Language of this type did not dispose orthodox students to an examination of Douglas's theories. Equally, unseemly arrogance appealed only to a narrow caucus of supporters. For example: 'since logical reasoning is both painful to, and almost impossible for, the typical British mind, and is therefore greatly distrusted' the British prefer to be guided by instinct rather than reason (Douglas 1937).

Nevertheless, Douglas's observations on politics remain astute. In a chapter entitled 'A digression on democracy' he referred to James Fraser's *The Golden Bough*. In his study of 'primitive' peoples Fraser observed that the king (or chief) was the servant of his people, not their master, as in European culture.

Failure to render satisfactory service was visited by the final form of dismissal, death. In our modern complex form of government, we still maintain that ancient convention, although our power to dismiss our masters has left us. Officials of the Inland Revenue still subscribe themselves as 'Your obedient servant' when writing to you on various coloured papers on matters to which you have probably given no orders.

(Douglas 1937: 53)

Douglas explored the relationship between the 'expert' and the people in a democracy:

To say that a country shall not be ruled by doctors, lawyers, or soldiers as such, is a different matter from saying that non-experts shall be allowed to practise medicine, the law, or . . . [to fight]. The place of the expert is in functional activity, and not in the formulation of general policy. He should be on tap, not on top. He is, in the widest sense of the word, a producer; and the nature of things places a producer always in the position of a taker of orders in regard to objective, while being a giver of orders in regard to method.

(Douglas 1937: 52–3)

For the financial expert to become the servant it was necessary to remove the mystique and examine the workings of capitalist finance. This, Douglas realised, could not be done without rejecting familiar precepts of orthodoxy.

CONCLUSION

Social credit periodicals supplement the above documentation of the debate on the technicalities and practicalities of monetary reform for social justice raised by events in Alberta (see e.g. the *New Age* and *Social Credit* from 1935). Additionally, reports in the social credit press refer to the debate in the mainstream press. For example, as reported in the *New Age*:

> The *Morning Post* of Saturday and the *Observer* of Sunday both made Alberta the subject of their leading articles. The *New Chronicle, Daily Express*, and *Star* contain editorial comments. The *Morning Post*'s article is a breezy one of which the tenor is summed up in the sentence: 'We're glad it's in Alberta and not here', the 'it' being the Aberhart credits to consumers.
>
> (*New Age*, 29 August 1935: 144)

The *New Age* journalist commented that most papers professed ignorance of social credit, and appeared to be waiting to take a lead from the *Times*. In its turn, the *Times* would await the return of Montagu Norman from Canada, where he happened to be on holiday.

Aberhart's election to office in 1935 was welcomed by social crediters as a publicity stunt likely to boost sales of social credit literature through interest raised by reports in the mainstream press (*New Age*, 29 August 1935). The chances of reforming the financial system in Alberta in the short term were considered remote. However, Byrne's collaboration with Aberhart after 1937 laid the foundations for exploration of the relationship between financial institutions and the operation of the political economy. The experiment remained incomplete following Aberhart's death in 1943. Nevertheless, Douglas and his colleagues held the view that the experiment illustrated the necessity for further investigation. The war and its aftermath obscured the issues, and the Douglas phenomenon was considered a temporary aberration. Although social credit literature continued to be made available by dedicated social crediters, the movement lacked adherents capable of developing the paradigm-shifting 'technicalities' arising from the A + B theorem. Ironically, lesser monetary reformers like Gesell and Soddy have received more attention in the post-war period than the enigmatic Major Douglas, despite their failure to give rise to a worldwide movement and an accompanying body of literature.

CONCLUSION

This book has provided a summary of the body of texts here called 'The Douglas/*New Age* texts', placing them in historical context. We contend that the body of economic theory outlined here merits further exploration in view of the social and ecological crises of the end of the century. Mass unemployment, Third World poverty and worldwide environmental degradation were predicted by the Douglas/*New Age* texts. The alternative economic theory they represented in the years immediately following World War I, subsequently developed to some degree in the 1920s and 1930s, has not been outdated by the passage of time.

Indeed, as Freeman has shown in relation to Marx's labour theory of value (Freeman 1995), over the decades of the twentieth century neoclassical orthodoxy has persistently diverged from economic reality. Economic theory is based upon the outdated institution of the near-barter conditions of single-stage production in a local market economy. Neoclassical theory assumes markets which clear at each stage of production, money to be a pure numeraire, technology which does not change and a rate of profit always and everywhere equal. As Douglas demonstrated, in conditions of multiple-stage industrial production these conditions do not apply. A body of economic theory based upon the assumption that they do apply universally has not become more relevant through repetition over the decades. Rather, the debt-driven nature of finance in multiple-stage production requires exploration if capitalist exploitation of society and the environment is to give way to an economy based upon sufficiency and co-operation.

Now, as in the inter-war years, production, distribution and exchange are debt-driven. In this situation, neither high wages nor cheap consumer products can be taken as indicative of a stable economic framework. Production in itself is not wealth, merely a means to human ends. What is required is mechanisms to determine demand coupled with the means to meet it without the necessity for artificial stimulation of demand. So long as there is a sufficiency of resources to meet a realistic level of needs, wants are not, as the neoclassical economist assumes, infinite and insatiable.

181

When money is reduced to its proper function as a medium of exchange, supply and demand will be free to follow textbook theory to determine price. Choices will cease to be restrained by the question 'Where is the money to come from?' In a future era 'it may be found that the chief crime of the capitalist was that he was such a very bad capitalist; in that he neither recognised his assets, nor met his liabilities' (Douglas 1918: 432). Throughout the decades of the twentieth century capitalism has continued to degrade social and environmental assets and has failed to acknowledge its mounting debts. The Douglas/*New Age* economics rejects capitalism based upon these false premises, offering instead a route to a socialist economy in which economic conflict is minimised.

THE A + B THEOREM AND FINANCE

In everyday parlance the economy serves to combine land, labour and capital in the productive process. The money generated can be spent on consumer goods or saved. Savings, consumption forgone, can be invested in capital goods, generating increased production in the future and deserving of reward for delayed consumption.

Using the A + B theorem, Douglas argued that the productive process acts to distribute income in the form of wages, salaries and dividends. Production does not make money: rather, the financial system is dynamic. Money is made in order to initiate production, coming into existence as loan 'credit' which must be repaid at a future date.

The money system regulates economic activity. It can be viewed as the tool of powerful financial interests or as a natural scientific occurrence, available for study. Douglas argued that the financial system was 'man-made'. It could therefore be managed so as to meet need while removing the pressures to superfluous production and consumption.

As things stood, most people relied upon a wage or salary for an income. Increasingly efficient technology in multiple-stage production produced a stark choice. More goods, whether useful or wasteful, had to be turned out in increasing numbers in order to distribute the product of the economy. Alternatively, people would be rendered superfluous, thrown out of 'work' and denied an income. Already, the world economy was capable of producing enough for everybody. However, the system was incapable of handling the concept of sufficiency. Douglas argued the case for the end of wage slavery based upon debt-driven production. He advocated strict regulation of the introduction of money to, and withdrawal of money from, the system such that a sufficiency of production could be regulated through consumer choice. His twofold system of producers' and consumers' credits could regulate the economy more effectively than a system based upon pure private speculation.

GUILD SOCIALISM VERSUS CAPITALIST FINANCE

In the discourse of the progressive model of capitalist 'development' guild socialism and social credit were labelled utopian misapprehensions of the nature of Western political economy and its agent, 'rational economic man'. However, as these chapters indicate, guild socialism and its sister body of economic theory social credit evolved from traditional belief systems founded upon co-operation for the common good within social institutions capable of respecting human society and the natural world. The Douglas/*New Age* texts share William Morris's vision of a society that could be 'resource-conserving, employing without exploiting human skills, blending tradition with innovation, and underpinned by a joyful faith in people and their creativity' (Seabrook 1996: 28).

The Douglas/*New Age* texts reflect a forgotten discussion which antedates 'Clause IV', Sidneywebbicalism and labourism in the United Kingdom. Although located in the early decades of the twentieth century the discussion anticipated the rise and fall of welfare capitalism, with its improvement in the conditions of wage slavery paralleled by its failure to seek its abolition. For the greening society of post-modern post-industrialism the Douglas/*New Age* themes encapsulated in the articles provide the basis of a Morrisian alternative to wage slavery and consumerism. The decommodification of labour has the potential to free the economy from the necessity to pay off yesterday's debt through tomorrow's increased production.

The Douglas/*New Age* texts anticipate Galbraith's *Money* (1975), George and Sabelli's *Faith and Credit* (1994), Handy's *The Empty Raincoat* (1994) and 'Paradox of Growth' (1996), Daly and Cobb's *For the Common Good* (1990), Gorz's *Critique of Economic Reason* (1989), Chomsky's 'How Free is the Free Market?' (1995), Parker (1989) and Jordan (1984, 1989) on basic income, and Henderson's *Building a Win–Win World* (1996).

From their inception within guild socialism, the Douglas/*New Age* texts raised questions which remain relevant at the turn of the twentieth century. They provide an early exploration of the potential for a co-operative, local, 'steady-state' economy in which industrial production, the arts, sciences, politics, learning and the caring professions are freed from the artificial restrictions of capitalist finance. In the early decades of the twentieth century an economic system premised upon conservation and reduced consumption appealed to the economically marginalised. Social credit drew its support from artists, craftspeople, the unemployed, small farmers, small businesses and women. Social credit was attractive to those who recognised the value of intrinsically satisfying work as a basis for participation in the community. In this new economy socially and ecologically destructive activities would be neither valued nor justifiable on grounds of economic necessity. Following over half a century of neglect, these texts possess the potential to provide the basis for a new economics of co-operation.

BIBLIOGRAPHY

Abercrombie, N., Hill, S. and Turner, B.S. (1984) *The Penguin Dictionary of Sociology*, London and New York: Penguin (1988 edn).

Adamson, J. (1934) 'Gaitskell on A + B', *New Age*, 27 December: 96–8 (reprinted from the *New Age*, 28 December 1933).

Allen, S.F. (1942) *Money: The Question of the Age* (7th edn, first published 1938), Sydney: Leisure Age Publishing (pamphlet).

Anderson, V. (1991) *Alternative Indication*, London: Routledge.

Armitage, C.C. (1932) *The Causes of War and Depression and the Cure*, Sydney: Leisure Age Publishing (pamphlet).

Bannock, G., Baxter, R.E. and Rees, R. (1986) *The Penguin Dictionary of Economics*, Harmondsworth: Penguin.

Barclay-Smith, C. (1940) *Victory without Debt*, Sydney: Leisure Age Publishing.

Bardsley, W.L. (1939) 'The Social Credit Movement, 1918–39', *Social Crediter* 3.15: 1–2, 23 December.

Bassett, R. (1958) *Nineteen Thirty-one*, London and New York: Macmillan.

Belloc, H. (n.d.) *The Alternative: an article written during Mr Belloc's parliamentary days for 'St George's Review'* (pamphlet).

Belloc, H. (1912) *The Servile State*, London: Constable (1927 edn).

Benton, A. (1926) *The Veil of Finance* (6th edn), reprinted 1974, Dublin: Blackrock Publishers.

Beveridge Report (1942) *Social Insurance and Allied Services*, UK Plmt Cmd 6404.

Biddulph, G. (1932) '*The Monopoly of Credit* by C.H. Douglas' (review), *Economic Journal* XLII: 268–70.

Bing, G. (*c.* 1935) *What is Social Credit?* Nottingham: Social Credit Political League.

Binns, K.J. (1947) S*ocial Credit in Alberta: a Report prepared for the Government of Tasmania*, Hobart: Government Printer.

Booth, A. (1983) 'The Labour Party and Economics between the Wars', *Bulletin of the Society for the Study of Labour History* 47: 36–42.

Braudel, F. (1979) *Civilization and Capitalism* 2, *The Wheels of Commerce*, London: Book Club Associates, 1983.

Brenton, A. (1926) *The Veil of Finance*, Dublin: Revisionist Press (1974 edn).

Burkitt, B. (1984) *Radical Political Economy*, London: Harvester.

Butchart, M. (ed.) (1936) *The Political and Economic Writings of A.R. Orage*, London: Stanley Nott.

Carpenter, L.P. (1973) *G.D.H. Cole: an Intellectual Biography*, London: Cambridge University Press.

Chesterton, G.K. (1936) 'Introduction' in P. Mairet, *A.R. Orage: a Memoir*, London: Dent.

Chomsky, N. (1995) 'How Free is the Free Market?' *Resurgence* 173: 6–9.

Clark, D.L. (1980) 'Funny Money Old and New', Melbourne Political Economy Conference, 16–17 August.

Colbourne, M. (1933) *The Meaning of Social Credit* (revised edn of *Economic Nationalism*), London and Canada: Social Credit Board.

Colbourne, M. (1934) *The Sanity of Social Credit*, London: Stanley Nott.

Cole, G.D.H. (1913) *The World of Labour*, London: Macmillan (1928 edn).

Cole, G.D.H. (1920) *Guild Socialism Re-stated*, London: Leonard Parsons.

Cole, G.D.H. (1921) *Social Theory*, London: Methuen.

Cole, G.D.H. (1927) *The Economic System: an Elementary Outline*, London, New York and Toronto: Longman (1931 edn).

Cole, G.d.H. (1932) 'The Douglas Theory', *New Statesman and Nation* III, 20 February: 223–5.

Cole, G.D.H. (ed.) (1933) *What Everybody Wants to Know about Money*, London: Gollancz.

Cole, G.D.H. (1944) *Money: its Present and Future*, London: Cassell.

Cole, G.D.H. and Postgate, R. (1938) *The Common People, 1746–1938*, London: Methuen.

Cole, M. (1940) *Growing up into Revolution*, London: Longman.

Cole, M. (1979) 'The Labour Movement between the Wars', in D.E. Martin and D. Rubinstein (eds) *Ideology and the Labour Movement*, London: Croom Helm.

Copland, D.B. (1932) *Facts and Fallacies of Douglas Credit, with a Note on Australian Credit Policy*, Melbourne: Melbourne University Press.

Corke, H. (1934) *A Short Course in Economic History*, London: Stanley Nott.

Cousens, H. (1921) *A New Policy for Labour: an Essay on the Relevance of Credit Control*, London: Cecil Palmer.

Crowther, G. (1946) *An Outline of Money*, London and New York: Nelson.

Da Costa, C.B. (1933) *Need we Repudiate? A Series of Lectures on the Douglas Credit Proposals* (2nd edn), Brisbane: Douglas Social Credit Association.

Daly, H. (ed.) (1973) *Towards a Steady-state Economy*, San Francisco: Freeman.

Daly, H.E. and Cobb, J.B. (1990) *For the Common Good: Redirecting the Economy towards Community, the Environment and a Sustainable Future*, London: Green Print.

Davis, E. (1968) *Vision Fugitive: Ezra Pound and Economics*, Kansas: University of Kansas Press.

Davis, R.P. (1978) 'Social Credit and the Tasmanian Labor Movement', *Tasmanian Historical Research Association: Papers and Proceedings* 25 (4): 114–32.

De Maré, E. (1983) *A Matter of Life and Debt*, Bullsbrook, W.A.: Veritas (1986 edn).

Dinnerstein, D. (1987) *The Rocking of the Cradle and the Ruling of the World*, London: Women's Press.

Djilas, M. (1957) *The New Class: an Analysis of the Communist System*, London: Thames & Hudson.

Dobb, M.H. (1922) 'Does the World need more Money?' *Communist Review*: 29–41.

Dobb, M.H. (1933) 'Social Credit and the Petit Bourgeoisie', *Labour Monthly*: 552.

Dobb, M.H. (1936) *Social Credit Discredited*, London: Martin Lawrence (pamphlet).

Dominion Law Reports (1938) 'Reference *re* Alberta Bills' 4: 433–43.

Douglas, C.H. (1918) 'The Delusion of Super-production', *English Review*: 428–32.

Douglas, C.H. (1919a) *English Review*, 49–58, 100–7: 'The Pyramid of Power'. 166–9: 'What is Capitalism?' 368–70: 'Exchange and Exports'.

Douglas, C.H. (1919b) *Economic Democracy*, Sudbury: Bloomfield (1974 reprint).

Douglas, C.H. (1920) *Credit-Power and Democracy*, London: Cecil Palmer.

Douglas, C.H. (1922a) *These Present Discontents and the Labour Party and Social Credit*, London: Cecil Palmer.

Douglas, C.H. (1922b) *The Control and Distribution of Production*, London: Stanley Nott (1934 edn).

Douglas, C.H. (1922c) 'The Douglas Theory: a Reply to Mr J.A. Hobson', *Socialist Review* March: 139–45.

Douglas, C.H. (1923) *The Breakdown of the Employment System*, Manchester: Manchester Economic Research Association (pamphlet).

Douglas, C.H. (1924a) *Social Credit*, Vancouver: Institute of Economic Democracy (1979 reprint).

Douglas, C.H. (1924b) *Social Credit Principles: Address at Swanwick* (pamphlet), reprinted from the *New Age* pamphlet (reprinted in Douglas 1931a: 37–43).

Douglas, C.H. (1931a) *Warning Democracy*, London: C.M. Grieve.

Douglas, C.H. (1931b) *The Monopoly of Credit*, London: Chapman & Hall.

Douglas, C.H. (1932) *The New and the Old Economics*, London: Stanley Nott (pamphlet).

Douglas, C.H. (1934a) 'Social Credit History: Address to Canadian Club, 1923', *New Economics* 9, 22 November.

Douglas, C.H. (1934b) 'Major Douglas at Aberdeen', the *New Age*, 11 October: 271–2.

Douglas, C.H. (1935a) *Money and the Price System*, London: Stanley Nott (pamphlet).

Douglas, C.H. (1935b) 'Major Douglas contributes a Preface to a new book by the late Eimar O'Duffy', *Social Credit* 3.9, 11 October: 70.

Douglas, C.H. (1936a) *The Approach to Reality*, London: KRP Publications (pamphlet).

Douglas, C.H. (1936b) *Dictatorship by Taxation: Speech delivered in the Ulster Hall*, Belfast, 24 November, London: Institute of Economic Democracy (reprinted pamphlet).

Douglas, C.H. (1937) *The Alberta Experiment: an Interim Survey*, Bullsbrook, W.A.: Veritas (1984 edn).

Douglas, C.H. (1939) 'The Devil is God turned upside down', talk to Social Crediters, December 1938, *Social Crediter*, 14 January.

Douglas, C.H. (1942a) *The Big Idea*, Liverpool: KRP.

Douglas, C.H. (1942b) *Land for the (Chosen) People Racket*, Liverpool: KRP.

Douglas, C.H. (1943) *Programme for the Third World War*, Liverpool: KRP.

Douglas, C.H. (1945) *The Brief for the Prosecution*, Liverpool: KRP.

Douglas, C.H. (1989) *Two Important Speeches in January and February 1934* (reprinted) Keith Catmur (pamphlet).

Douglas, C.H. and Robertson, D. (1933) 'The Douglas Credit Scheme', *Listener* 9: 1005–6, 1039–40.

Duesenberry, J.S. (1949) *Income, Saving and the Theory of Consumer Behaviour*, Cambridge, Mass.: Harvard University Press.

Dunn, E.M. (1934) *The New Economics: Social Credit Principles and Proposals*, Letchworth: Wardman (pamphlet).

Durbin, E.F.M. (1933a) *Purchasing Power and Trade Depression*, London: Chapman & Hall.

Durbin, E.F.M. (1933b) 'Money and Prices' in G.D.H. Cole (ed.) *What Everybody wants to Know about Money*, London: Gollancz.

Durbin, E.F.M. (1933c) *Social Credit Policy*, London: New Fabian Research Bureau and Gollancz.

Durbin, E. (1985) *New Jerusalems: the Labour Party and the Economics of Democratic Socialism*, London: Routledge.

Durning, A.T. (1992) *How Much is Enough?* London: Earthscan.

Ecologist (1994) 'Eggs, Eugenics and Economics' (editorial) 24.2, March/April: 42–3.

Ecologist (1996) 'Globalisation: Changing Landscapes of Corporate Control' 26.4 (whole issue).

Ekins, P. (ed.) (1986) *The Living Economy: a New Economics in the Making*, London: Routledge.

Emery, G.E. (1934) *Sound Finance*, Melbourne: Stanley Addison.

Encyclopaedia Britannica (1979) *Macropaedia* 12. Chicago: Encyclopaedia Britannica.

Fairhill, D. (1993) 'Top Government Arms Salesman', *The Guardian*, 6 September.

Figgis, J.N. (1913) *Churches in the Modern State*, London.

Finkel, A. (1989) *The Social Credit Movement in Alberta*, Toronto: University of Toronto Press.

Finlay, J. (1972) *Social Credit: the English Origins*, Montreal and London: McGill Queen's University Press.

Finn, E. (ed.) *The Deficit made me do it*, Ottawa: Canadian Centre for Policy Alternatives.

Foster, W.F. and Catchings, W. (1923) *Money*, London: Houghton Mifflin.

Foster, W.F. and Catchings, W. (1925) *Profits*, London: Houghton Mifflin.

Freeman, A. (1995) 'Marx without Equilibrium', *Capital and Class* 56: 49–89.

Freeman, A. and Carchedi, G. (eds) (1966) *Marx and Non-equilibrium Economics*, Cheltenham: Edward Elgar.

Gaitskell, H.T.N. (1933) 'Four Monetary Heretics' in G.D.H. Cole (ed.) *What Everyone wants to Know about Money*, London: Gollancz.

Galbraith, J.K. (1975) *Money: Whence it Came and Where it Went*, Harmondsworth: Penguin.

Generoso, J. (1981) 'Social Credit, 1918–45: an Essay and Select Bibliography' (with special reference to America). Mimeo.

George, S. and Sabelli, F. (1994) *Faith and Credit: the World Bank's Secular Empire*, Harmondsworth: Penguin.

Gesell, S. (1958) *The Natural Economic Order*, trans. from the German. London: Peter Owen.

Glass, S.T. (1966) *The Responsible Society: the Ideas of Guild Socialism*, London: Longman.

Gorz, A. (1989) *Critique of Economic Reason*, London: Verso.

Grayson, J.P. and Grayson, L.M. (1974) 'The Social Base of Interwar Political Unrest in Urban Alberta', *Canadian Journal of Political Science* 7: 289–313.

Hancock, G. (1991) *Lords of Poverty*, London: Mandarin.

Handy, C. (1994) *The Empty Raincoat*, London: Hutchinson.

Handy, C. (1996) 'The Paradox of Growth', *Resurgence* 176: 6–7.

Hargrave, J. (1934) 'Look before you leap', *New Age*, 11 October: 272–3.

Hargrave, J. (1945) *Social Credit Clearly Explained*, London: SCP Publishing House.

Hattersley, C.M. (1922) *The Community's Credit: a Consideration of the Principles and Proposals of the Social Credit Movement*, London: Credit Power Press.

Hattersley, C.M. (1937) *Wealth, Want and War*, Mexborough: Social Credit Coordinating Centre (1953 edn).

Hawtrey, R.G. (1937) *Capital and Employment*, London: Longman.

Hawtrey, R.G. and Douglas, C.H. (1933) 'A Report of Debate, Birmingham', *New Age*, 6 April: 268–79.

Henderson, H. (1996) *Building a Win–Win World: Life beyond Global Economic Warfare*, San Francisco: Berrett-Koehler.

Hewlet, J. (1934) *Social Credit and the War on Poverty*, London: Stanley Nott.

Hiskett, W.R. (1935) *Social Credits or Socialism*, London: Gollancz.

Hiskett, W.R. and Franklin, J.A. (1939) *Searchlight on Social Credit*, London: King.

H.M.M. (1929) *An Outline of Social Credit*, London: New Age Press.

HMSO (1994) 'Pergau Dam questions 42–4', *Hansard* 21 March: 18–19.

Hobson, J.A. (1900) *Money Problems*, London: Stamford.

Hobson, J.A. (1902) *Imperialism: a Study*, Michigan: Michigan University Press (1965 reprint).

Hobson, J.A. (1922) 'The Douglas Theory' and 'A Rejoinder to Major Douglas', *Socialist Review*: 70–7, 194–9.

Hobson, S.G. (1914) *National Guilds: an Inquiry into the Wage System and the Way Out*, London: Bell (1919 edn).

Hobson, S.G. (1920) *National Guilds and the State*, London: Bell.

Hogan, R. (1972) *Eimar O'Duffy*, Lewisburg: Bucknell University Press.

Holmes, E.L. (1932) *Australia's Real Wealth and How to Use it: Being a Practical Introduction to the Douglas Social Credit Proposals*, Sydney: Leisure Age Publishing.

Holter, E.S. (1934) *ABC of Social Credit*, London: Stanley Nott.

House of Commons, Canada (1923) *Select Standing Committee on Commerce and Banking*, Appendix 2.

Hutchinson, F. (1995) 'A Heretical View of Economic Growth and Income Distribution' in E. Kuiper and J. Sap (eds) *Out of the Margin: Feminist Perspectives on Economics*, London: Routledge.

Illich, I. (1971) *Deschooling Society*, New York: Harper & Row.

Irving, J.A. (1959) *The Social Credit Movement in Alberta*, Toronto: University of Toronto Press.

Jameson, S. (1935) *The Soul of Man in the Age of Leisure*, London: Stanley Nott.

Johnson, H. (1935) *Social Credit and the War on Poverty*, London: Stanley Nott.

Johnston, T. (1934) *The Financiers and the Nation*, Glasgow: Ossian (1994 reprint).

Jordan, B. (1984) 'The Social Wage: a Right for All', *New Society* 26 April: 143–4.

Jordan, B. (1989) *The Common Good: Citizenship, Morality and Self-interest*, Oxford: Blackwell.

Joseph, A.W. (1935a) *Banking and Industry*, London: Stanley Nott (pamphlet).

Joseph, A.W. (1935b) 'The A + B Theorem' III, *New Age*, 21 November: 22–3.

Joseph, A.W. (1935c) 'The A + B Theorem' II, *New Age*, 14 November: 15–16.

Kennedy, M. (1995) *Interest and Inflation-free Money*, Philadelphia: New Society Publishers.

Kenner, H. (1972) *The Pound Era*, London: Faber & Faber.

Kenney, R. (1939) *Westering*, London: Dent.

Keynes, J.M. (1936) *The Collected Writings of John Maynard Keynes* II. *General Theory of Employment, Interest and Money*, London: Macmillan (1973 edn).

King, J.E. (1988) *Economic Exiles*, London: Macmillan.

Kitson, A. (1894) *A Scientific Solution to the Money Question*, London: Boston.

Kitson, A. (1920) *Money Problems*, London: Stamford.

Kropotkin, P.A. (1906) *The Conquest of Bread*, London: Chapman & Hall.

Labour and the New Social Order (1918) London: Harvester Microfiche (set of Labour Party pamphlets).

Labour Party (1922) *Labour and Social Credit: a Report on the Proposals of Major Douglas and the 'New Age'*, London: the Labour Party.

Labour Party (1935) *Socialism and 'Social Credit'*, London: the Labour Party.

Lang, T. and Hines, C. (1993) *The New Protectionism*, London: Earthscan.

Laugier, R. (1934) 'The Point of the Pen', *New Age*, 11 October: 273–4.

Lee, K. (1989) *Social Philosophy and Ecological Scarcity*, London: Routledge.

Lewis, J. (1935) *Douglas Fallacies: a Critique of Social Credit*, London: Chapman & Hall.

Lutz, M.A. and Lux, K. (1988) *Humanistic Economics: the New Challenge*, New York: Bootstrap Press.

McBriar, A.M. (1962) *Fabian Socialism and English Politics*, London: Cambridge University Press.

McCarthy, E.E. (1947) 'History of the Social Credit Movement'. Unpublished M.A. thesis, Leeds University.

McClelland, D.C. (1961) *The Achieving Society*, London: Free Press/Collier Macmillan.

McConnell, W.K. (1932) *The Douglas Credit Scheme: a Simple Explanation and Criticisms*, Sydney: Leisure Age Publishers.

Macmillan Committee (1931) *Great Britain Committee on Finance and Industry, Minutes of Evidence* (Macmillan Report) I, London: HMSO.

Macpherson, C.B. (1953) *Democracy in Alberta: Social Credit and the Party System*, Toronto: University of Toronto Press (1962 edn). (In the original 1953 edition the subtitle read: *The theory and practice of a quasi-party system.*)

Mairet, P. (1934) *The Douglas Manual*, London: Stanley Nott.

Mairet, P. (1936) *A.R. Orage: a Memoir*, London: University Books.

Mallory, J.R. (1954) *Social Credit and the Federal Power in Canada*, Toronto: University of Toronto Press.

Martin, W. (1967) *The New Age under Orage: Chapters in English Cultural History*, Manchester: Manchester University Press.

Marx, K. (1941) *The Poverty of Philosophy*, London: Lawrence & Wishart.

Maslow, A.H. (1970) *Motivation and Personality*, New York: Harper & Row.

Massingham, H.J. (1942) *The English Countryman: a Study of the English Tradition*, London: Batsford.

Meade, J.E. (1938) *Consumers' Credits and Unemployment*, London: Oxford University Press.

Meade, J.E. (1989) *Agathotopia: the Economics of Partnership*, Scotland: David Hume Institute.

Meade, J.E. (1993) *Liberty, Equality and Efficiency: Apologia pro Agathotopia mea*, London: Macmillan.

Mehta, G. (1983) 'The Douglas Theory: a New Interpretation', *Indian Journal of Economics* 64: 121–9.

Mellor, M. (1992) *Breaking the Boundaries: Towards a Feminist, Green Socialism*, London: Virago.

Milne, R.S. (1966) *Political Parties in New Zealand*, London: Oxford University Press.

Monahan, B.W. (1947) *An Introduction to Social Credit*, Sydney: Bloxham & Chambers (1967 edn).

Monahan, B.W. (1957) *Why I am a Social Crediter*, Sydney: Tidal Publications (1971 edn).

Morris, W. (1944) *Selected Works*, Bloomsbury, N.Y.: Nonesuch Press.

Morton, A.L. (ed.) (1979) *Political Writings of William Morris*, London: Lawrence & Wishart.

Muir, E. (1934) *Social Credit and the Labour Party*, London: Stanley Nott.

Munson, G. (1933) 'The Douglasites', *Commonweal*, 13 October: 151–3.

Munson, G. (1934) 'Social Credit – the Economics of Tomorrow?' *Independent Woman*, June: 165, 182–3.

Murray, H.M. (1929) *An Outline of Social Credit*, London: New Age Press (pamphlet).

New Age (1919) 6 June: 97–9.

New Age (1920a) 'Notes of the Week' (probably Orage), 11 March: 298–9.

New Age (1920b) 'Notes of the Week', 8 April: 362.

New Age (1922a) 'Who's Who', 20 July: 152.

New Age (1922b) 'Who's Who,' 27 July: 164.

New Age (1934a) Correspondence, 6 November: 67.

New Age (1934b) Correspondence, 27 December: 103.

New Age (1935a) 'Movement Notes', 7 November: 5.

New Age (1935b) 'The "A + B Theorem"' (A.W. Joseph) 14 November: 15–16, 21 November: 18–20, 22–4.

New Age (1935c) 'The "A + B Theorem"' I (7 November), II (14 November), III (21 November).

New Statesman (1922) 'The "Douglas Credit Scheme"' (anon.), 18 February: 552–4.

New Zealand (1934) *Report of Monetary Committee*: 69–84 on the Douglas Scheme.

O'Duffy, E. (1926) *King Goshawk and the Birds*, London: Macmillan.

O'Duffy, E. (1928) *The Spacious Adventures of the Man in the Street*, London: Macmillan.

O'Duffy, E. (1932) *Life and Money*, London and New York: Putnam.

O'Duffy, E. (1933) *Asses in Clover*, London: Putnam.

O'Duffy, E. (1934) *Consumer Credit*, London: Prosperity League (pamphlet).

Orage, A.R. (ed.) (1914) *National Guilds: an Enquiry into the Wage System and a Way Out*, London: Bell.

Orage, A.R. (1917) *An Alphabet of Economics*, London: Unwin.

Orage, A.R. (1926) 'An Editor's Progress', *Commonweal*, Part 1 (10 February: 376–9), Part 2 (17 February: 402–4), Part 3 (24 February: 434–5), Part 4 (3 March: 456–7).

Orage, A.R. (1935) *The BBC Speech and the Fear of Leisure*, London: Stanley Nott (pamphlet).

Parker, H. (1989) *Instead of the Dole: an Enquiry into the Integration of the Tax and Benefits Systems*, London: Routledge.

Penty, A.J. (1921) *Guilds, Trade and Agriculture*, London: Allen & Unwin.

Pigou, A.C. (1929) *The Economics of Welfare*, London: Macmillan.

Pimlott, B. (ed.) (1984) *Fabian Essays in Socialist Thought*, London: Heinemann.

Pound, E. (1920) 'Economic Democracy' (review), *The Little Review* 6 (11): 39–42.

Pound, E. (1922) *Social Credit: the Poetic Angle* (pamphlet, not traced).

Pound, E. (1933) *ABC of Economics*, London: Faber & Faber.

Pound, E. (1935) *Social Credit: an Impact*, London: Stanley Nott (pamphlet).

Preston, R.H. (1991) *Religion and the Ambiguities of Capitalism*, London: SCM Press.

Pullen, J.M. and Smith, G.O. (1991) 'Major Douglas and the Banks', unpublished conference paper, History of Economic Thought, Monash University.

Ramsey, F.P. (1922) 'The Douglas Proposals', *Cambridge Magazine* II: 74–6.

Rands, R.S.J. (1934) *The Abolition of Poverty: a Brief Explanation of the Proposals of Major C.H. Douglas*, London: Ancient House Press.

Rands, R.S.J. (1970) *The Problem of Money*, London: Edquip Supply Co. (pamphlet).

Reckitt, M.B. (1936) 'Foreword' in M. Buchart (ed.) *A.R. Orage: Political and Economic Writings*, London: Stanley Nott.

Reckitt, M.B. (1941) *As it Happened: an Autobiography*, London: Dent.

Reckitt, M.B. and Bechhofer, C.E. (1918) *The Meaning of National Guilds*, London: Cecil Palmer (1920 edn).

Richmond, K.G. (1972) 'The Australian League of Rights: an Empirical Study'. Unpublished M.A. thesis, University of New England.

Richmond, W.H. (1978) 'John A. Hobson: Economic Heretic', *American Journal of Economics and Sociology* 37 (3): 283–94.

Robbins, L. (1932) 'Consumption and the Trade Cycle', *Economica* 12: 413–20.

Sagar, S. (*c*. 1940) *Distributism: a Reprint of Six Articles Published in the 'Weekly Review'*, London: Distributist Press.

Sargent, L.T. (1988) *British and American Utopian Literature, 1516–1985*, New York and London: Garland.

Schor, J. (1988) *The Overworked American: the Unexpected Decline of Leisure*, New York: Basic Books/Harper.

Schwarz, F. (1952) *Das Experiment von Worgl*, Berlin: Genossenschaft Verlag.

Scottish Labour Party (1920) *Annual Report*, Glasgow: Scottish Labour Party.

Seabrook, J. (1996) 'Revolutionary Craftsman', *Red Pepper*, September: 28.

Shaw, G.B. (ed.) (1889) *Fabian Essays in Socialism*, London: Fabian Society.

Sinclair, P.R. (1972) 'Populism in Alberta and Saskatchewan: a Comparative Analysis of Social Credit and the Cooperative Commonwealth Federation'. Unpublished Ph.D. thesis, University of Edinburgh.

Smith, A. (1776) *The Wealth of Nations*.

Smith, H. (1962) *The Economics of Socialism Reconsidered*, London: Oxford University Press.

Smith, H.N. (1944) *The Politics of Plenty*, London: Allen & Unwin.

Social Credit Secretariat (1946) *Elements of Social Credit*, Liverpool: KRP Publications.

Steele, T. (1990) *Alfred Orage and the Leeds Arts Club, 1893–1923*, London: Scolar Press.

Strachey, J. (1925) *Revolution by Reason*, London: Leonard Parsons.

Strachey, J. (1935) *The Nature of Capitalist Crisis*, London: Gollancz.

Strachey, J. (1936) *Social Credit: an Economic Analysis*, London: Gollancz/Workers' Bookshop (pamphlet).

Symons, W.T. (1931) *The Coming of Community*, London: C.W. Daniel.

Tankerville, Earl of (1934) *Poverty amidst Plenty*, London: Stanley Nott.

Tavistock, Marquis of (1934) *Short Papers on Money*, London: Stanley Nott.

UK Parliament (1942) *Social Insurance and Allied Services*, Cmd 6404 (Beveridge Report), London: HMSO.

Van Trier, W. (1991) 'State Bonus', Antwerp: Universitaire Faculteiten St Ignatius (mimeo).

Veblen, T. (1899) *Theory of the Leisure Class*, London: Allen & Unwin (1912).

Waites, T. (1932) Government Statistician of New South Wales, *Report on the Douglas Social Credit System*, Sydney: Government Printer.

Wicksteed, P.H. (1894) *The Common Sense of Political Economy*, London: Routledge (revised edn 1933).

Willett, J.C. (*c.* 1935) *Women and Poverty*, London: Social Credit Press.

Young, W.A. (1921) *Dividends for All: Being an Explanation of the Douglas Scheme*, London: Cecil Palmer (pamphlet).

INDEX

A + B theorem 24–5, 43–8, 122; and
finance 182; implications 48–54;
misrepresentations 84, 107–8, 138;
social credit movement 150–1
Aberhart, William 163, 172–8,
180
administration: decentralisation 73, 154;
price-fixing and 54
Agate, James 157
agricultural guilds 120
agriculture 71, 168–9
Alberta experiment 163, 169, 172–80;
social credit movement 175–7;
Social Credit Party 174; UFA
government 174–5
Alberta Prosperity Certificates 178
armament production 66, 159–60
artists 167–8
Attack! 148, 150, 152
Australia 147, 155
Austrian National Bank 109

Bank of England 41, 56, 110, 150, 161;
economic crisis (1931) 110–11
Banking Act (1844) 26, 39
banks/banking system 48, 88; control
of credit 39–40, 101; creation of
money 37–8, 57, 159; national debt
56; nationalisation 41, 112–13;
producers' banks 72, 73–5, 102–3;
real and financial credit 40–2; social
credit movement 148–50
basic necessities 64–5
Bechhofer, C.E. 14, 22, 24, 72
Bell, H.C. 170
Belloc, Hilaire 16–17
Beveridge Report (1942) 28, 116;
see also welfare state

Bing, Gladys 164
Birmingham Proposals 114
Brenton, Arthur 140, 143, 144, 156
Building Guilds 131–2
Byrne, L.D. 176–7, 177, 180

Calgary Herald 163
Calthrop, Sir Guy 11
Canada 155; Inquiry on Banking
and Commerce (1923) 37, 85,
139, 173–4; *see also* Alberta
experiment
capital: real and financial 42
capitalism: guild socialism vs capitalist
finance 183; philosophy of 21–2
Cassel, Ernest 149
Catchings, W. 46–7, 85
centralisation of power 61–2, 127
Challenger 148
Chandos group 80, 140–1, 158–60
Christian socialism 160
Clarion 125
class politics 62
clearing house 51–2; Draft Mining
Scheme 72, 73–4, 75
Cole, G.D.H. 2–3, 97, 119–24, 140;
economics 119–23; Fabian Society
17, 23; guild socialism 8, 18–19,
22–4; National Guilds League 9, 22,
137; political philosophy 123–4;
welfare payments 116
Cole, Margaret 94, 124
collective ownership 13–14, 31, 117,
135–6
committees 23, 121
commodification of labour 19, 21
concentration of ownership 25–6
consumer: producer and 20–1

192